STAR WARS
LANDO

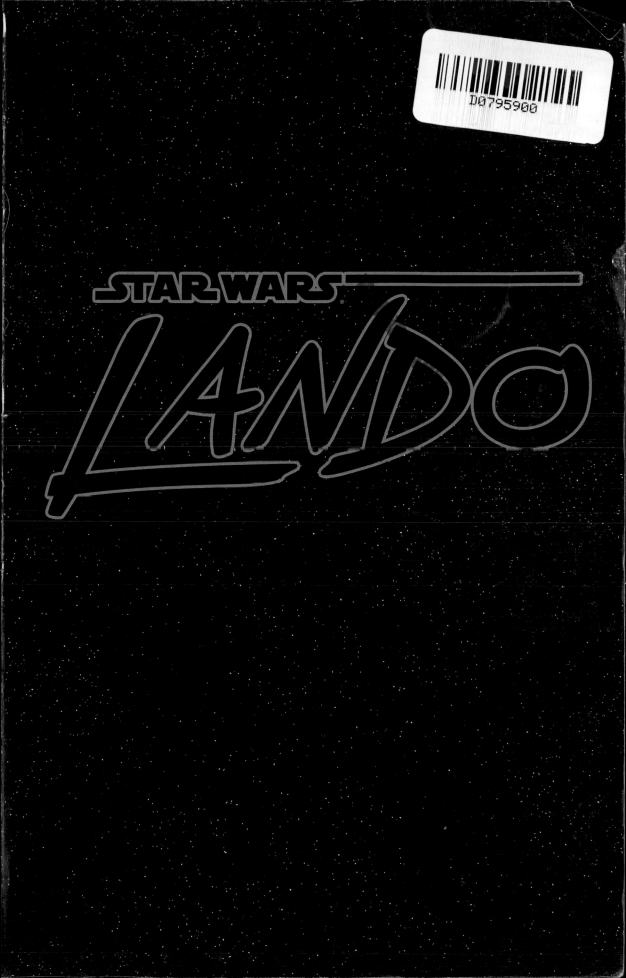

LANDO

Writer	**CHARLES SOULE**
Artist	**ALEX MALEEV**
Color Artist	**PAUL MOUNTS**
Letterer	**VC's JOE CARAMAGNA**
Cover Art	**ALEX MALEEV** WITH **EDGAR DELGADO (#1)**
Assistant Editor	**HEATHER ANTOS**
Editor	**JORDAN D. WHITE**
Executive Editor	**C.B. CEBULSKI**
Editor in Chief	**AXEL ALONSO**
Chief Creative Officer	**JOE QUESADA**
Publisher	**DAN BUCKLEY**

For Lucasfilm:

Creative Director	**MICHAEL SIGLAIN**
Senior Editor	**FRANK PARISI**
Lucasfilm Story Group	**RAYNE ROBERTS, PABLO HIDALGO, LELAND CHEE**

Collection Editor	JENNIFER GRÜNWALD
Assistant Editor	SARAH BRUNSTAD
Associate Managing Editor	ALEX STARBUCK
Editor, Special Projects	MARK D. BEAZLEY
Senior Editor, Special Projects	JEFF YOUNGQUIST
SVP Print, Sales & Marketing	DAVID GABRIEL
Book Designer	ADAM DEL RE

DISNEY · LUCASFILM

STAR WARS: LANDO. Contains material originally published in magazine form as STAR WARS: LANDO #1-5. First printing 2016. ISBN# 978-0-7851-9319-7. Published by MARVEL WORLDWIDE, INC., a subsidiary of MARVEL ENTERTAINMENT, LLC. OFFICE OF PUBLICATION: 135 West 50th Street, New York, NY 10020. STAR WARS and related text and illustrations are trademarks and/or copyrights, in the United States and other countries, of Lucasfilm Ltd. and/or its affiliates. © & TM Lucasfilm Ltd. No similarity between any of the names, characters, persons, and/or institutions in this magazine with those of any living or dead person or institution is intended, and any such similarity which may exist is purely coincidental. Marvel and its logos are TM Marvel Characters, Inc. Printed in Canada. ALAN FINE, President, Marvel Entertainment; DAN BUCKLEY, President, TV, Publishing and Brand Management; JOE QUESADA, Chief Creative Officer; TOM BREVOORT, SVP of Publishing; DAVID BOGART, SVP of Operations & Procurement, Publishing; C.B. CEBULSKI, VP of International Development & Brand Management; DAVID GABRIEL, SVP Print, Sales & Marketing; JIM O'KEEFE, VP of Operations & Logistics; DAN CARR, Executive Director of Publishing Technology; SUSAN CRESPI, Editorial Operations Manager; ALEX MORALES, Publishing Operations Manager; STAN LEE, Chairman Emeritus. For information regarding advertising in Marvel Comics or on Marvel.com, please contact Jonathan Rheingold, VP of Custom Solutions & Ad Sales, at jrheingold@marvel.com. For Marvel subscription inquiries, please call 800-217-9158. Manufactured between 11/13/2015 and 12/21/2015 by SOLISCO PRINTERS, SCOTT, QC, CANADA.

10 9 8 7 6 5 4 3 2 1

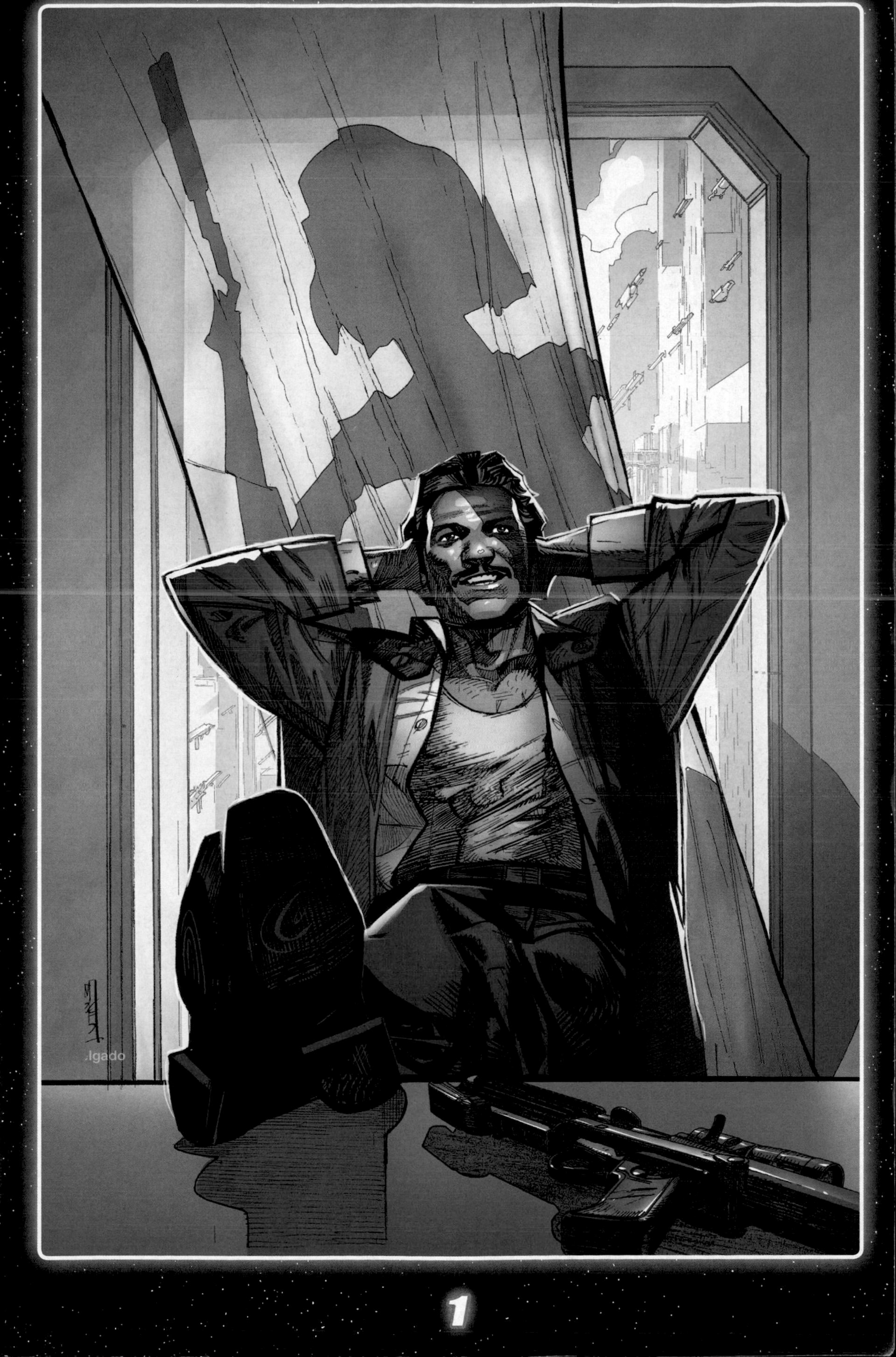

1

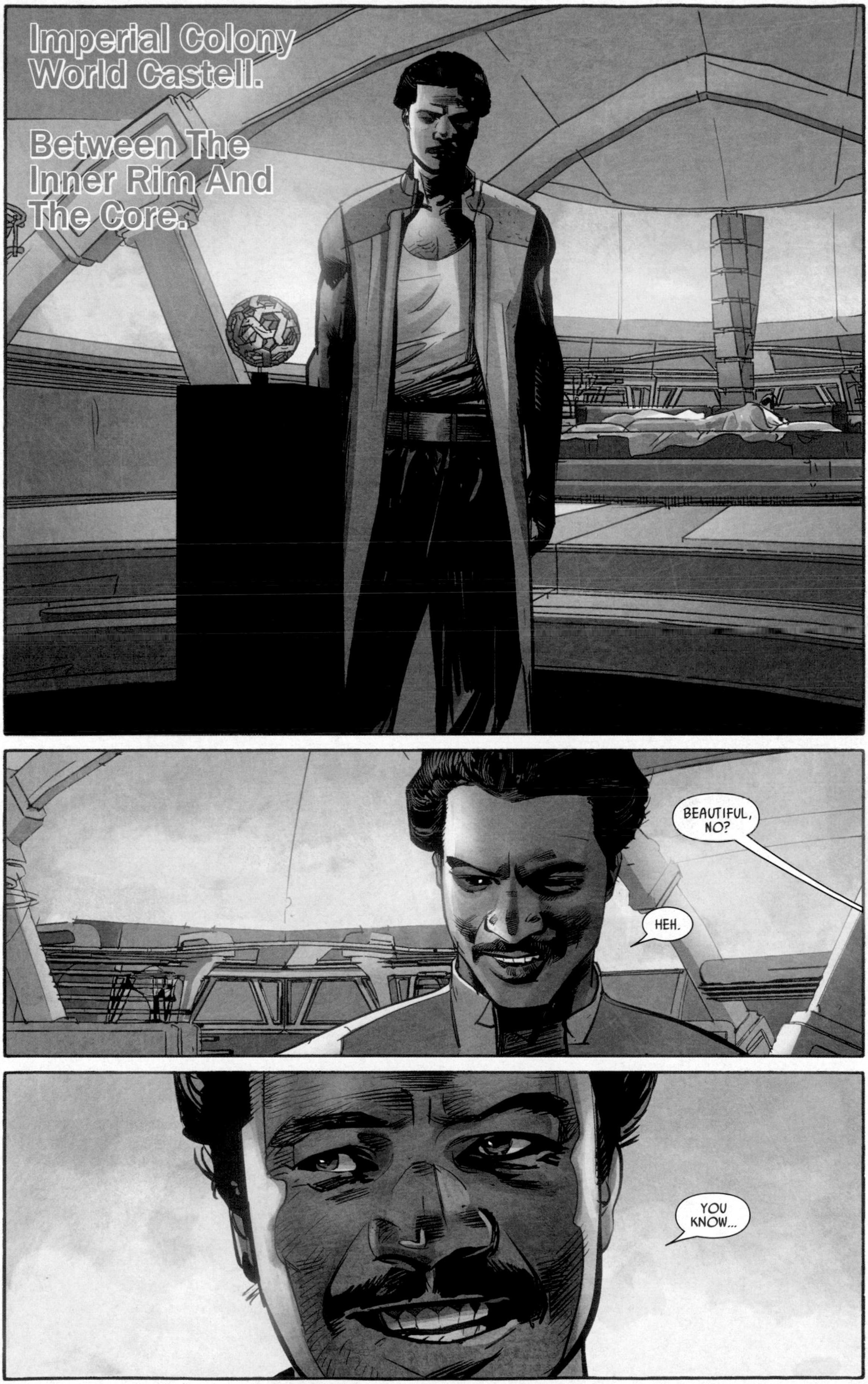
Imperial Colony World Castell.
Between The Inner Rim And The Core.
BEAUTIFUL, NO?
HEH.
YOU KNOW...

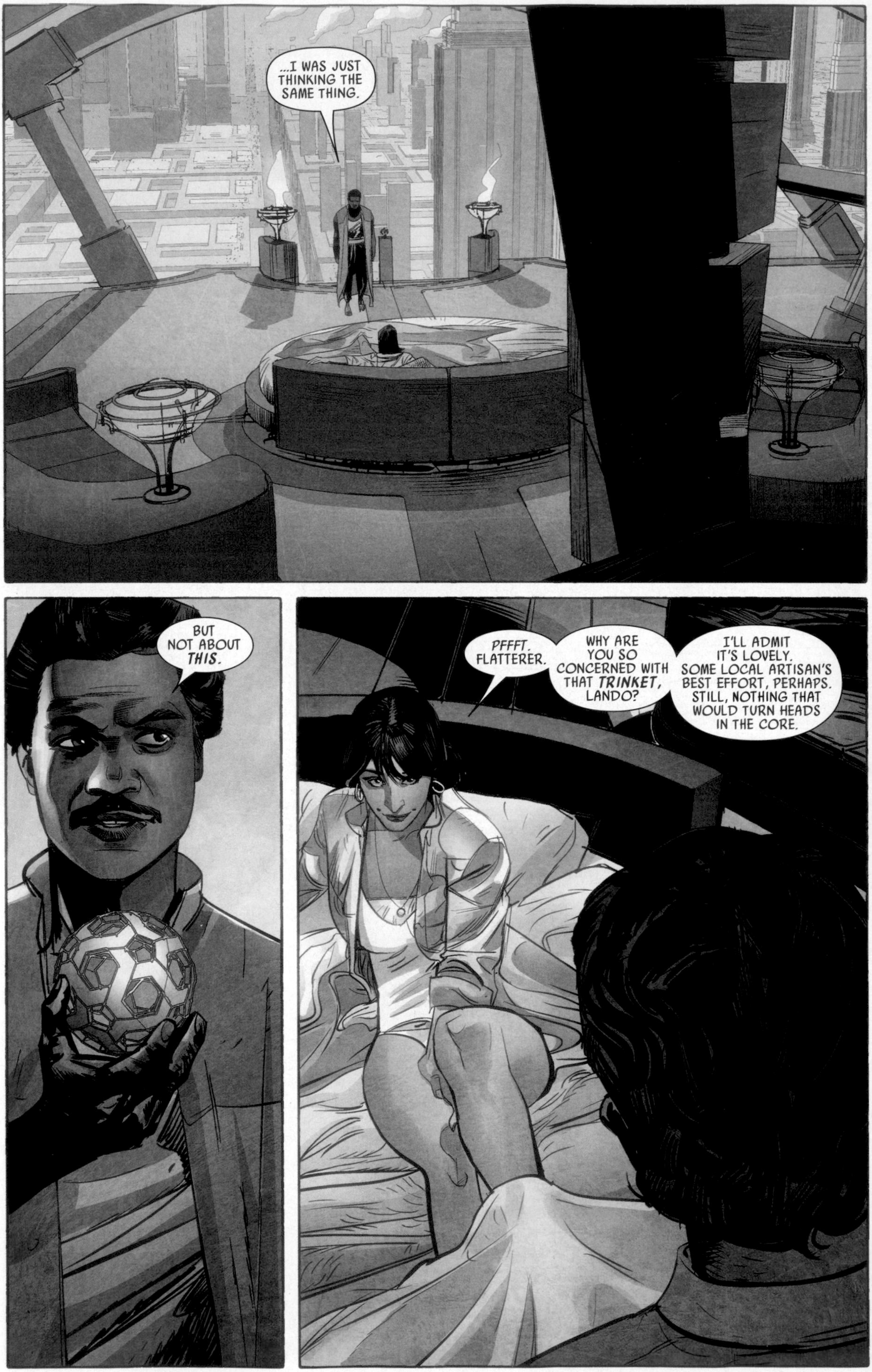
...I WAS JUST THINKING THE SAME THING.
BUT NOT ABOUT *THIS*.
PFFFT. FLATTERER.
WHY ARE YOU SO CONCERNED WITH THAT *TRINKET*, LANDO?
I'LL ADMIT IT'S LOVELY. SOME LOCAL ARTISAN'S BEST EFFORT, PERHAPS. STILL, NOTHING THAT WOULD TURN HEADS IN THE CORE.

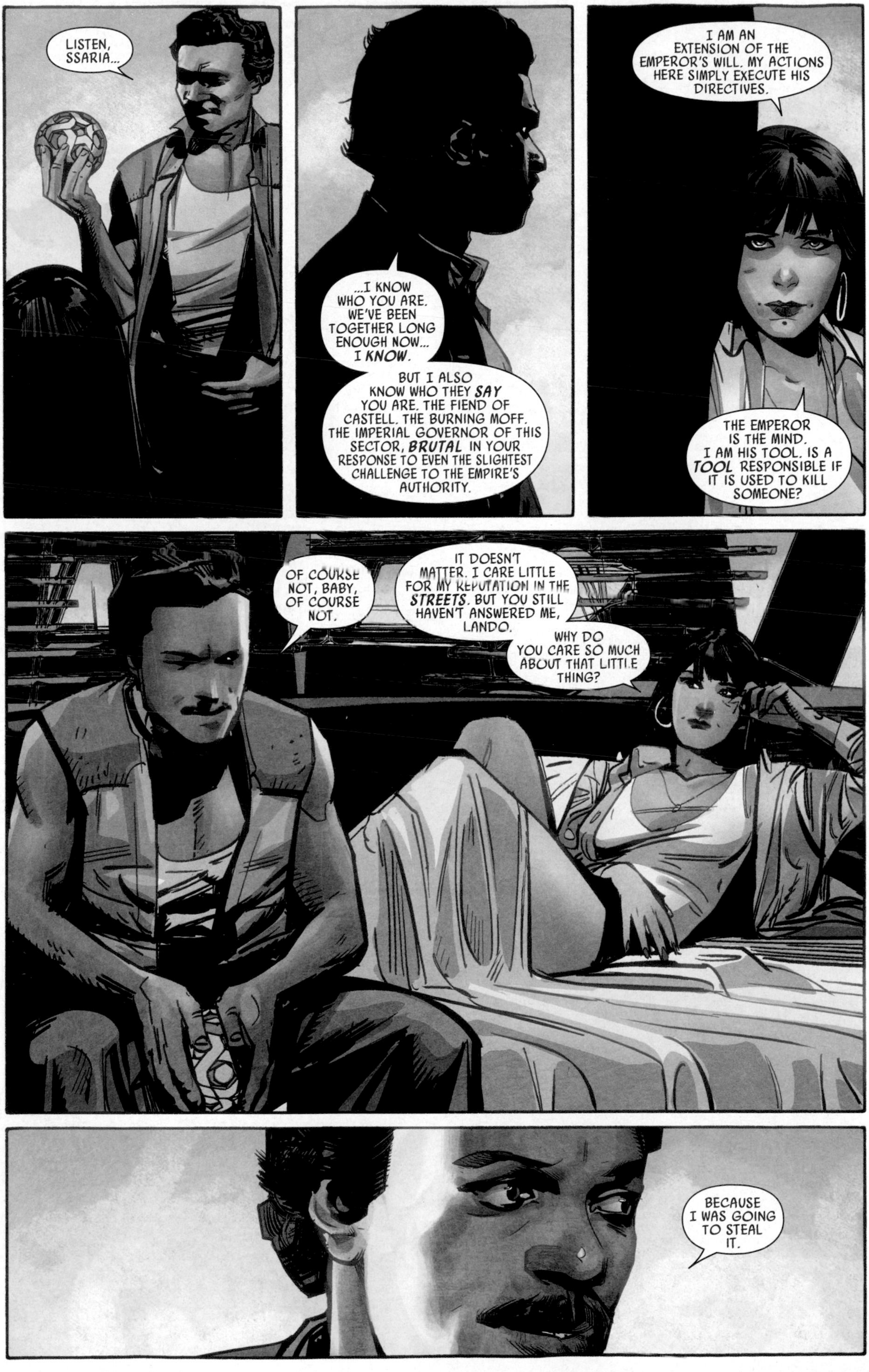
LISTEN, SSARIA...
...I KNOW WHO YOU ARE. WE'VE BEEN TOGETHER LONG ENOUGH NOW... I KNOW.
BUT I ALSO KNOW WHO THEY SAY YOU ARE. THE FIEND OF CASTELL. THE BURNING MOFF. THE IMPERIAL GOVERNOR OF THIS SECTOR, BRUTAL IN YOUR RESPONSE TO EVEN THE SLIGHTEST CHALLENGE TO THE EMPIRE'S AUTHORITY.
I AM AN EXTENSION OF THE EMPEROR'S WILL. MY ACTIONS HERE SIMPLY EXECUTE HIS DIRECTIVES.
THE EMPEROR IS THE MIND. I AM HIS TOOL. IS A TOOL RESPONSIBLE IF IT IS USED TO KILL SOMEONE?
OF COURSE NOT, BABY, OF COURSE NOT.
IT DOESN'T MATTER. I CARE LITTLE FOR MY REPUTATION IN THE STREETS. BUT YOU STILL HAVEN'T ANSWERED ME, LANDO.
WHY DO YOU CARE SO MUCH ABOUT THAT LITTLE THING?
BECAUSE I WAS GOING TO STEAL IT.

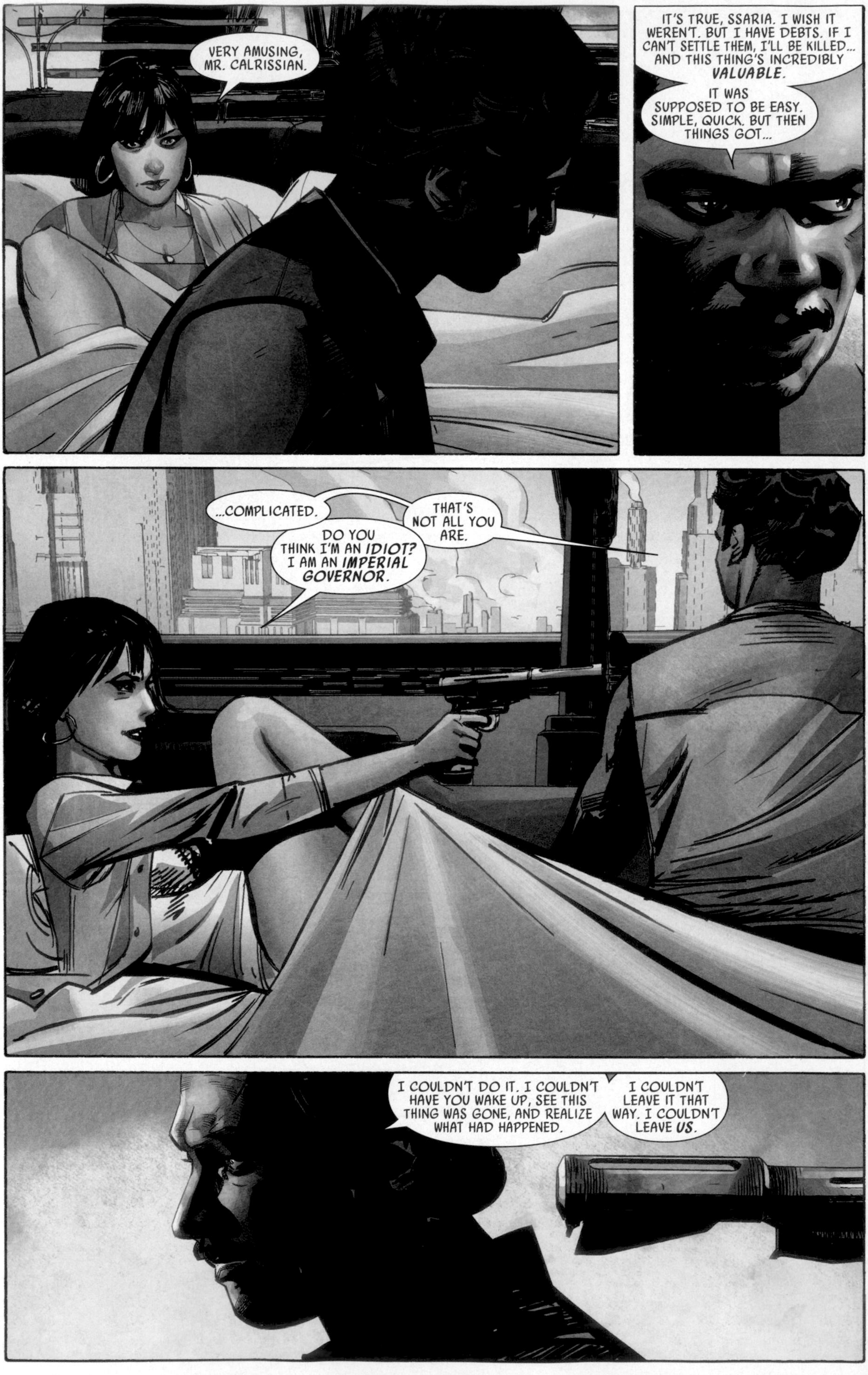
VERY AMUSING, MR. CALRISSIAN.
IT'S TRUE, SSARIA. I WISH IT WEREN'T. BUT I HAVE DEBTS. IF I CAN'T SETTLE THEM, I'LL BE KILLED... AND THIS THING'S INCREDIBLY *VALUABLE*.
IT WAS SUPPOSED TO BE EASY. SIMPLE, QUICK. BUT THEN THINGS GOT...
...COMPLICATED.
DO YOU THINK I'M AN *IDIOT?* I AM AN *IMPERIAL GOVERNOR*.
THAT'S NOT ALL YOU ARE.
I COULDN'T DO IT. I COULDN'T HAVE YOU WAKE UP, SEE THIS THING WAS GONE, AND REALIZE WHAT HAD HAPPENED.
I COULDN'T LEAVE IT THAT WAY. I COULDN'T LEAVE *US*.

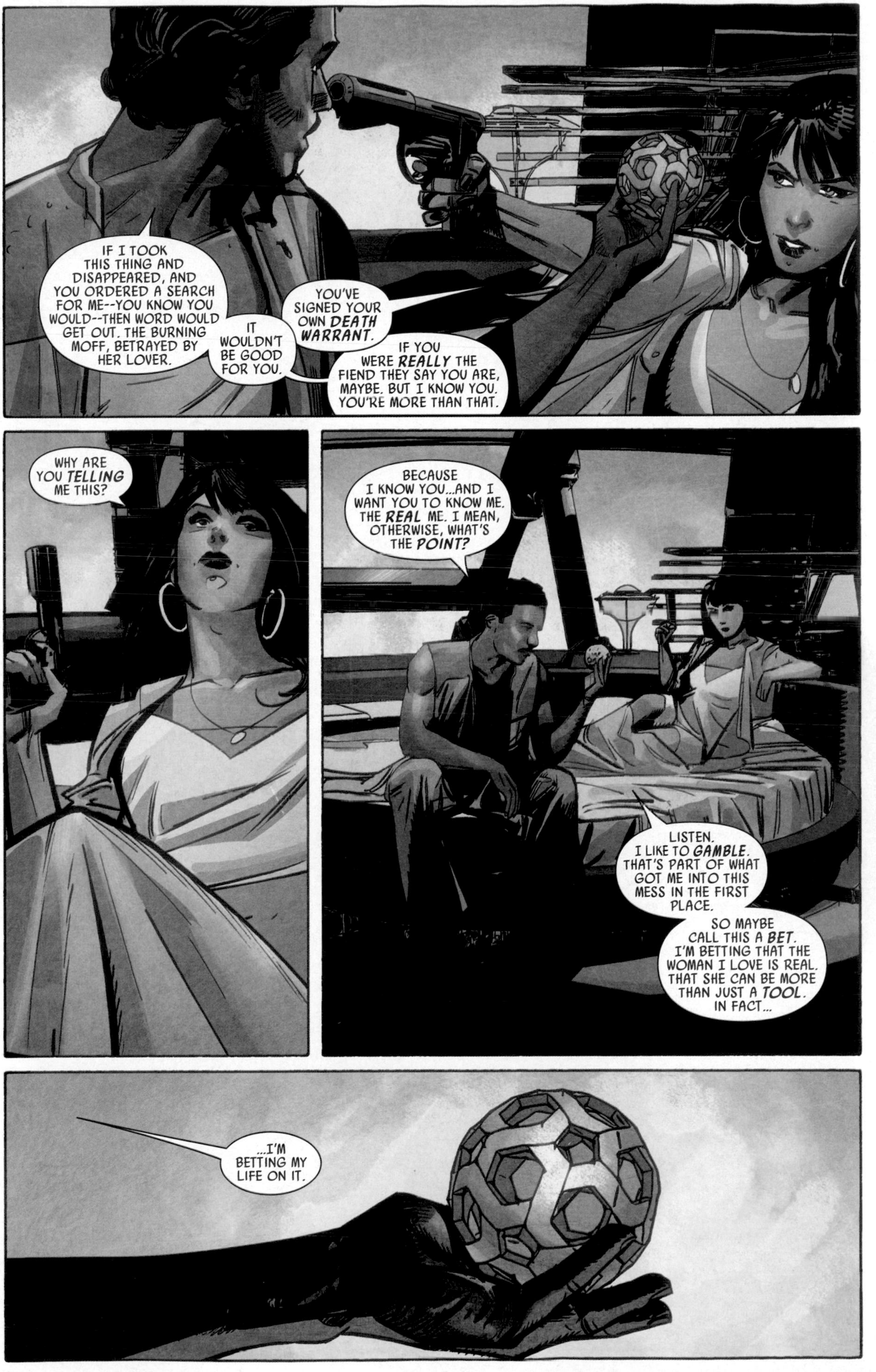
IF I TOOK THIS THING AND DISAPPEARED, AND YOU ORDERED A SEARCH FOR ME--YOU KNOW YOU WOULD--THEN WORD WOULD GET OUT. THE BURNING MOFF, BETRAYED BY HER LOVER.
IT WOULDN'T BE GOOD FOR YOU.
YOU'VE SIGNED YOUR OWN DEATH WARRANT.
IF YOU WERE REALLY THE FIEND THEY SAY YOU ARE, MAYBE. BUT I KNOW YOU. YOU'RE MORE THAN THAT.
WHY ARE YOU TELLING ME THIS?
BECAUSE I KNOW YOU...AND I WANT YOU TO KNOW ME. THE REAL ME. I MEAN, OTHERWISE, WHAT'S THE POINT?
LISTEN. I LIKE TO GAMBLE. THAT'S PART OF WHAT GOT ME INTO THIS MESS IN THE FIRST PLACE.
SO MAYBE CALL THIS A BET. I'M BETTING THAT THE WOMAN I LOVE IS REAL. THAT SHE CAN BE MORE THAN JUST A TOOL. IN FACT...
...I'M BETTING MY LIFE ON IT.

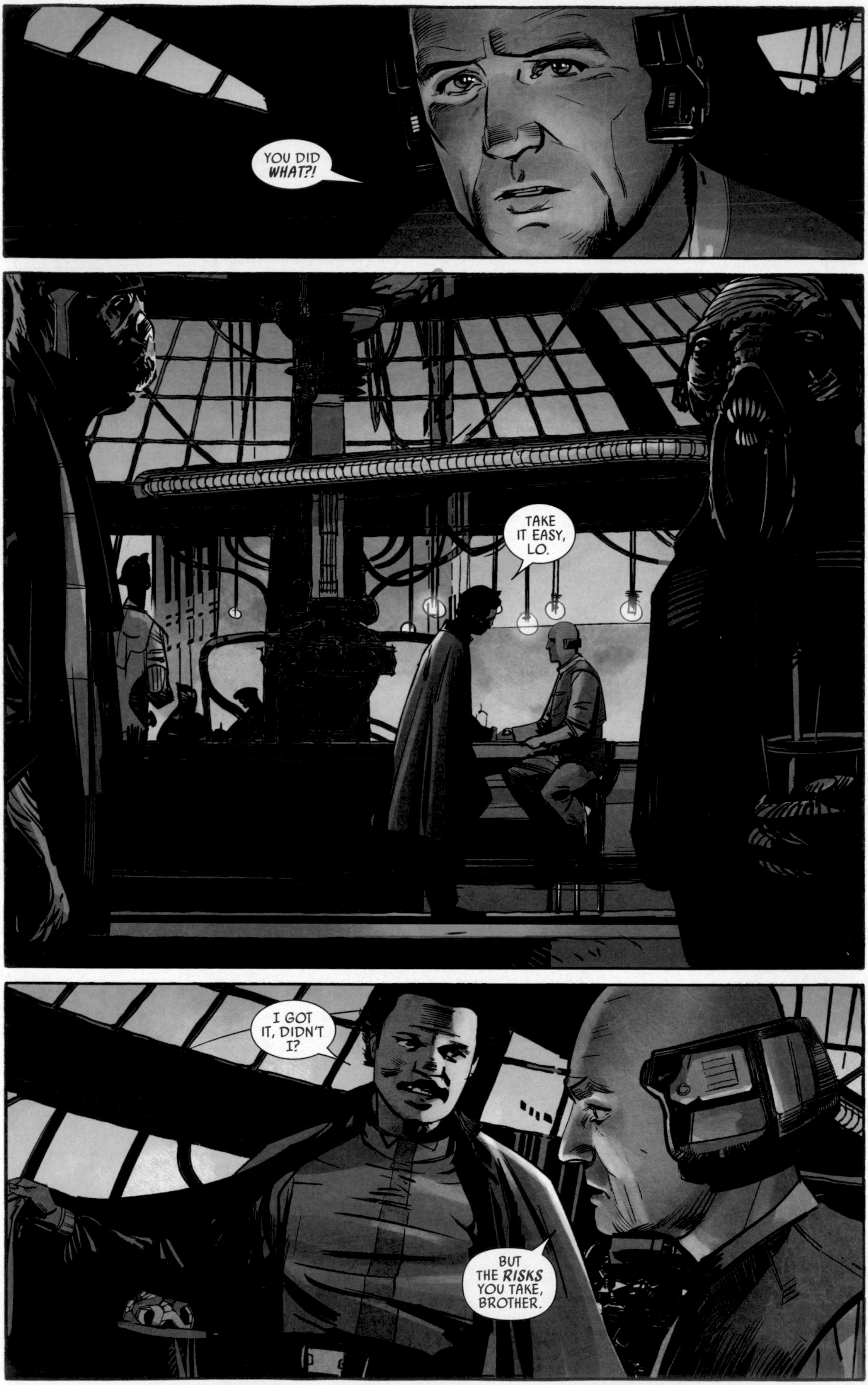
YOU DID WHAT?!
TAKE IT EASY, LO.
I GOT IT, DIDN'T I?
BUT THE RISKS YOU TAKE, BROTHER.

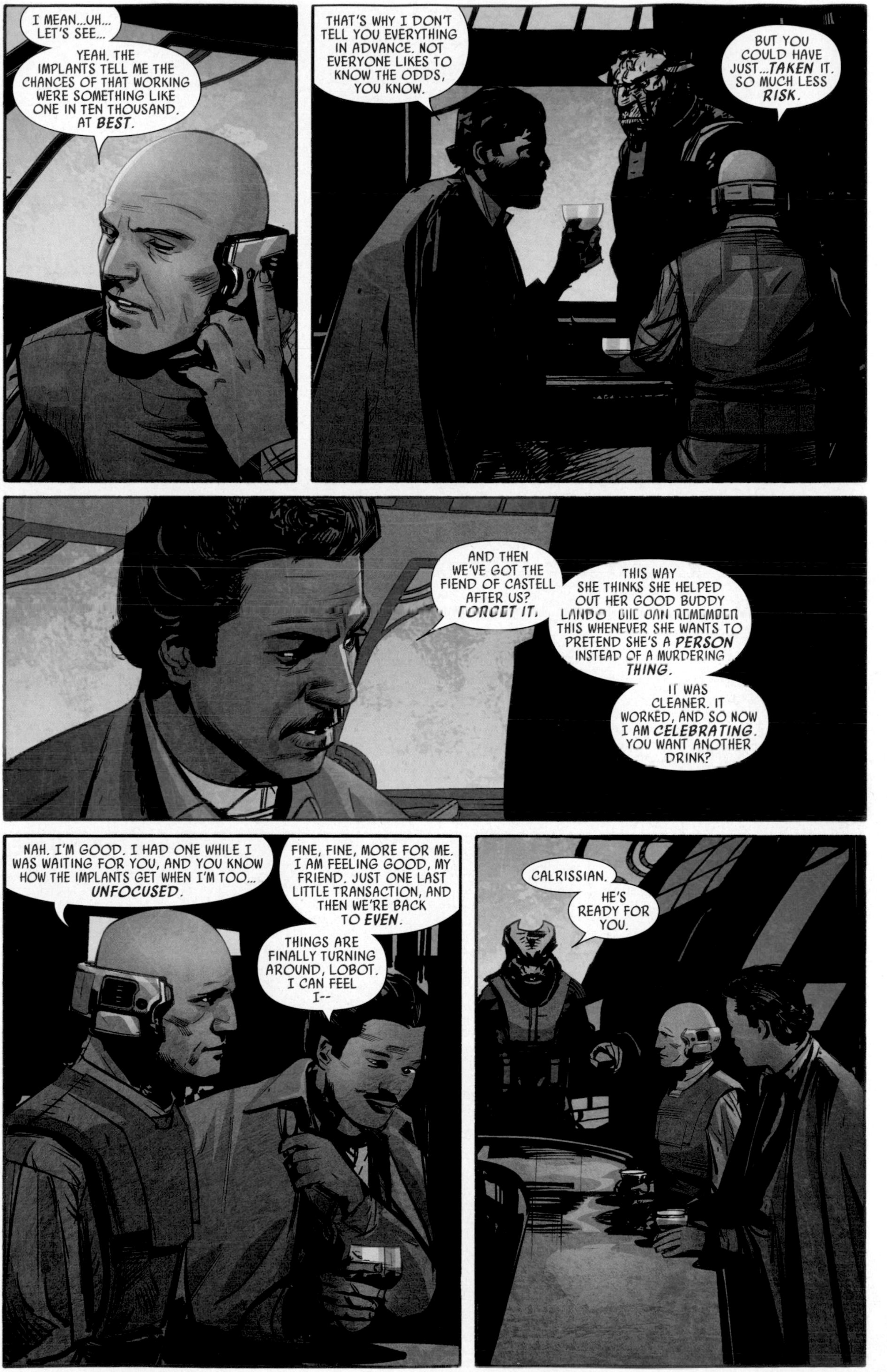
I MEAN...UH... LET'S SEE...
YEAH. THE IMPLANTS TELL ME THE CHANCES OF THAT WORKING WERE SOMETHING LIKE ONE IN TEN THOUSAND. AT **BEST**.
THAT'S WHY I DON'T TELL YOU EVERYTHING IN ADVANCE. NOT EVERYONE LIKES TO KNOW THE ODDS, YOU KNOW.
BUT YOU COULD HAVE JUST...**TAKEN** IT. SO MUCH LESS **RISK**.
AND THEN WE'VE GOT THE FIEND OF CASTELL AFTER US? **FORGET IT.**
THIS WAY SHE THINKS SHE HELPED OUT HER GOOD BUDDY LANDO. SHE CAN REMEMBER THIS WHENEVER SHE WANTS TO PRETEND SHE'S A **PERSON** INSTEAD OF A MURDERING **THING.**
IT WAS CLEANER. IT WORKED, AND SO NOW I AM **CELEBRATING**. YOU WANT ANOTHER DRINK?
NAH. I'M GOOD. I HAD ONE WHILE I WAS WAITING FOR YOU, AND YOU KNOW HOW THE IMPLANTS GET WHEN I'M TOO... **UNFOCUSED**.
FINE, FINE, MORE FOR ME. I AM FEELING GOOD, MY FRIEND. JUST ONE LAST LITTLE TRANSACTION, AND THEN WE'RE BACK TO **EVEN**.
THINGS ARE FINALLY TURNING AROUND, LOBOT. I CAN FEEL I--
CALRISSIAN.
HE'S READY FOR YOU.

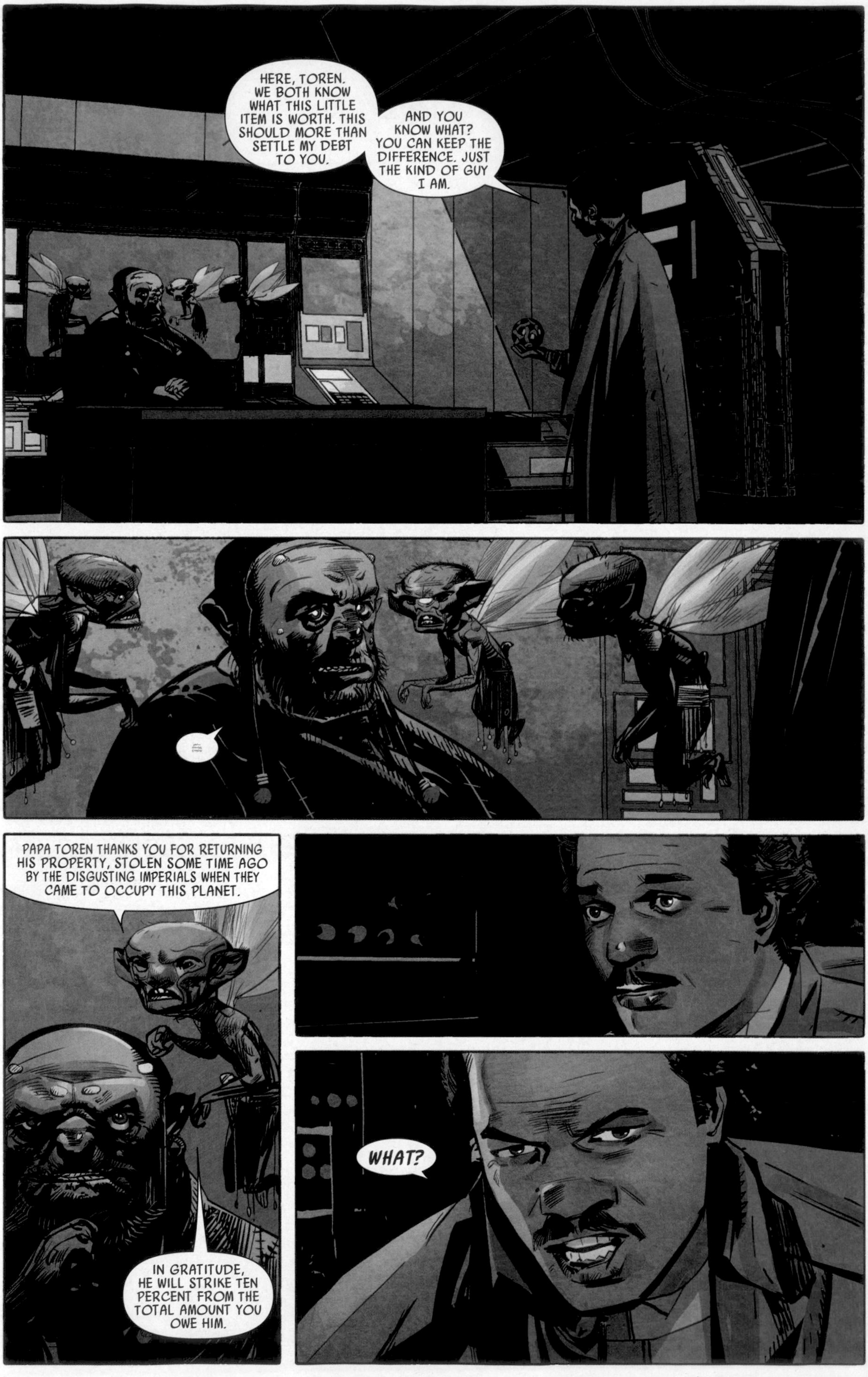
HERE, TOREN. WE BOTH KNOW WHAT THIS LITTLE ITEM IS WORTH. THIS SHOULD MORE THAN SETTLE MY DEBT TO YOU.
AND YOU KNOW WHAT? YOU CAN KEEP THE DIFFERENCE. JUST THE KIND OF GUY I AM.
PAPA TOREN THANKS YOU FOR RETURNING HIS PROPERTY, STOLEN SOME TIME AGO BY THE DISGUSTING IMPERIALS WHEN THEY CAME TO OCCUPY THIS PLANET.
IN GRATITUDE, HE WILL STRIKE TEN PERCENT FROM THE TOTAL AMOUNT YOU OWE HIM.
WHAT?

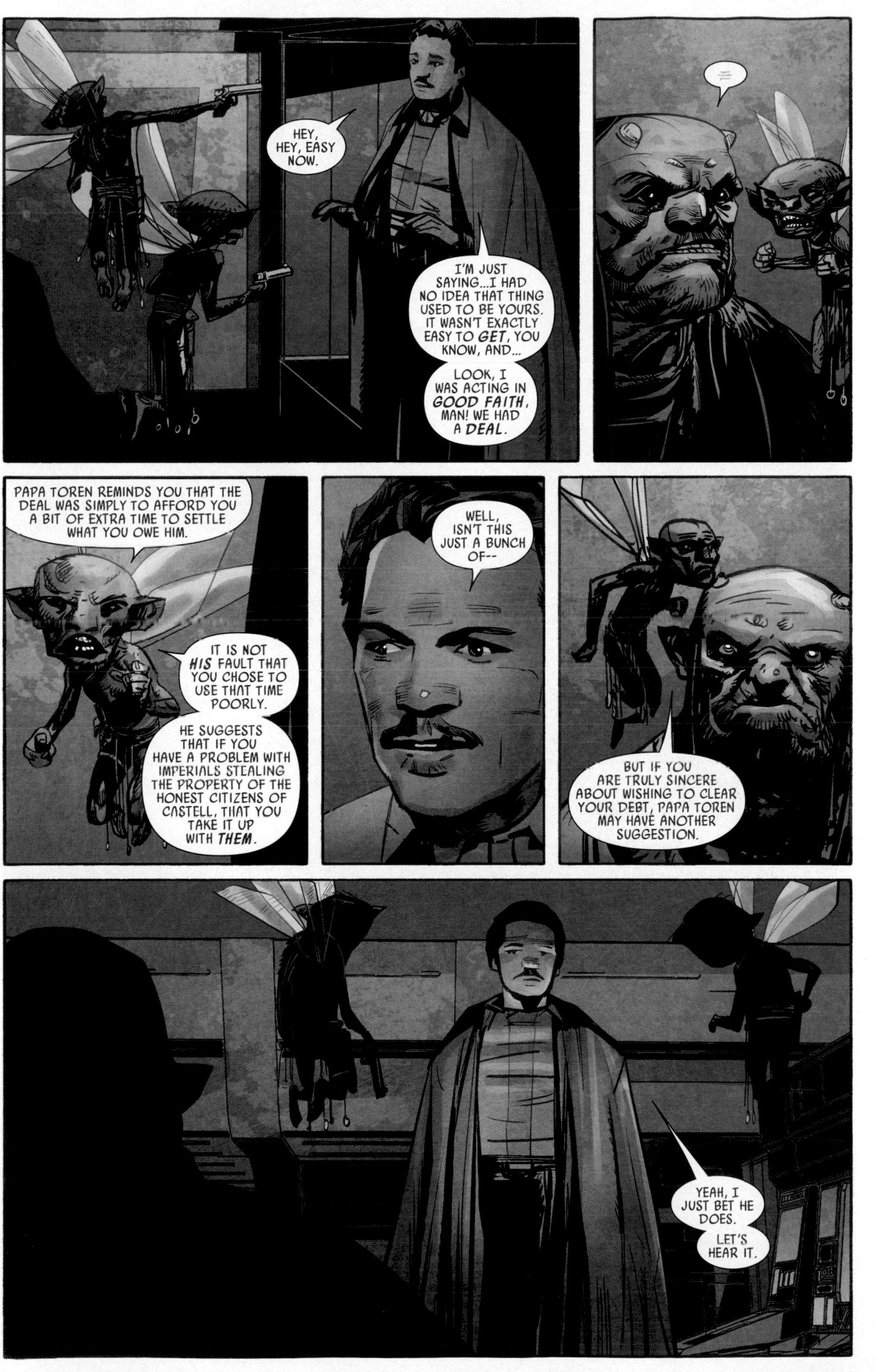
HEY, HEY, EASY NOW.
I'M JUST SAYING...I HAD NO IDEA THAT THING USED TO BE YOURS. IT WASN'T EXACTLY EASY TO GET, YOU KNOW, AND...
LOOK, I WAS ACTING IN GOOD FAITH, MAN! WE HAD A DEAL.
PAPA TOREN REMINDS YOU THAT THE DEAL WAS SIMPLY TO AFFORD YOU A BIT OF EXTRA TIME TO SETTLE WHAT YOU OWE HIM.
IT IS NOT HIS FAULT THAT YOU CHOSE TO USE THAT TIME POORLY.
HE SUGGESTS THAT IF YOU HAVE A PROBLEM WITH IMPERIALS STEALING THE PROPERTY OF THE HONEST CITIZENS OF CASTELL, THAT YOU TAKE IT UP WITH THEM.
WELL, ISN'T THIS JUST A BUNCH OF--
BUT IF YOU ARE TRULY SINCERE ABOUT WISHING TO CLEAR YOUR DEBT, PAPA TOREN MAY HAVE ANOTHER SUGGESTION.
YEAH, I JUST BET HE DOES.
LET'S HEAR IT.

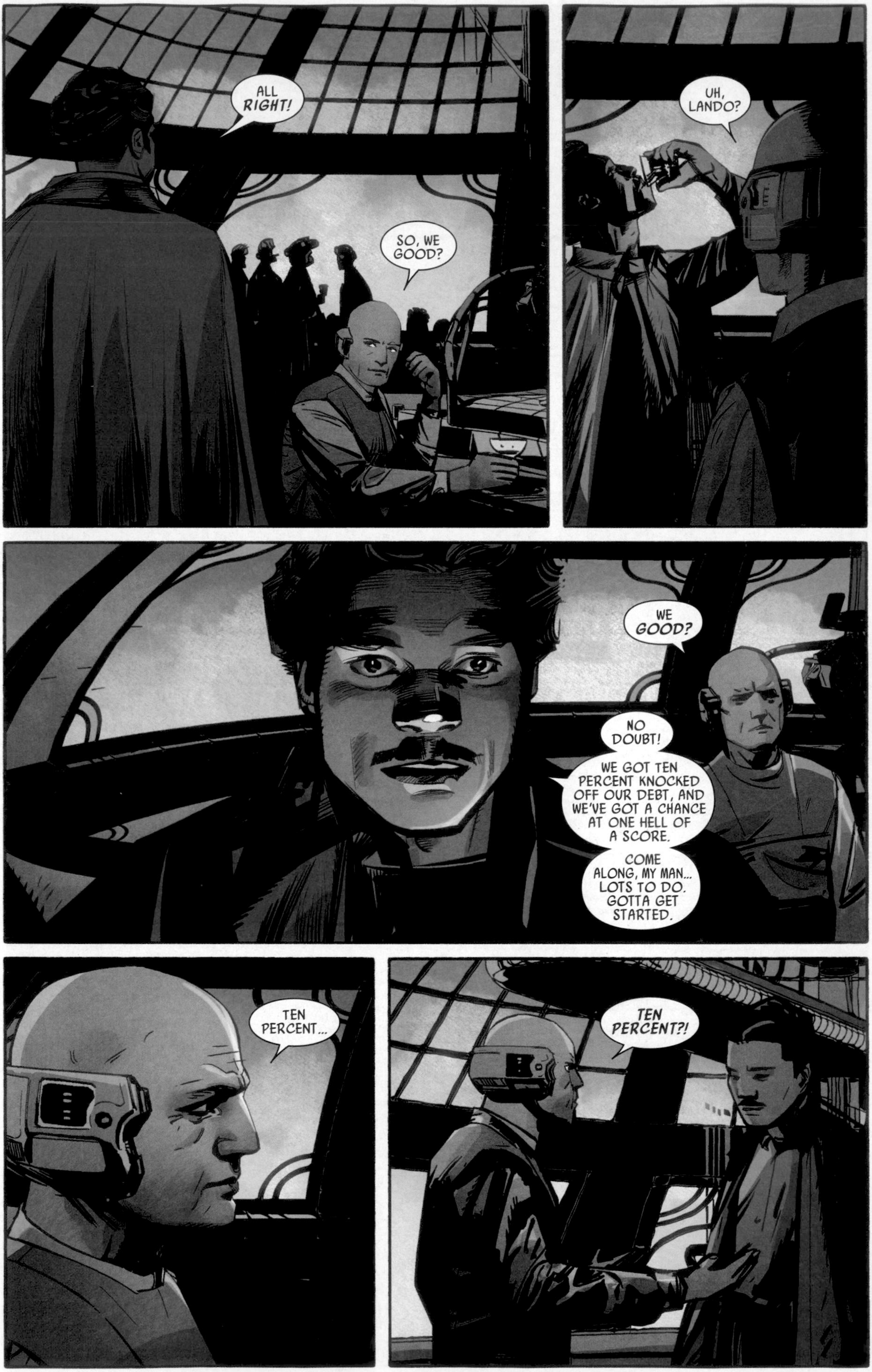
ALL RIGHT!
SO, WE GOOD?
UH, LANDO?
WE GOOD?
NO DOUBT!
WE GOT TEN PERCENT KNOCKED OFF OUR DEBT, AND WE'VE GOT A CHANCE AT ONE HELL OF A SCORE.
COME ALONG, MY MAN... LOTS TO DO. GOTTA GET STARTED.
TEN PERCENT...
TEN PERCENT?!

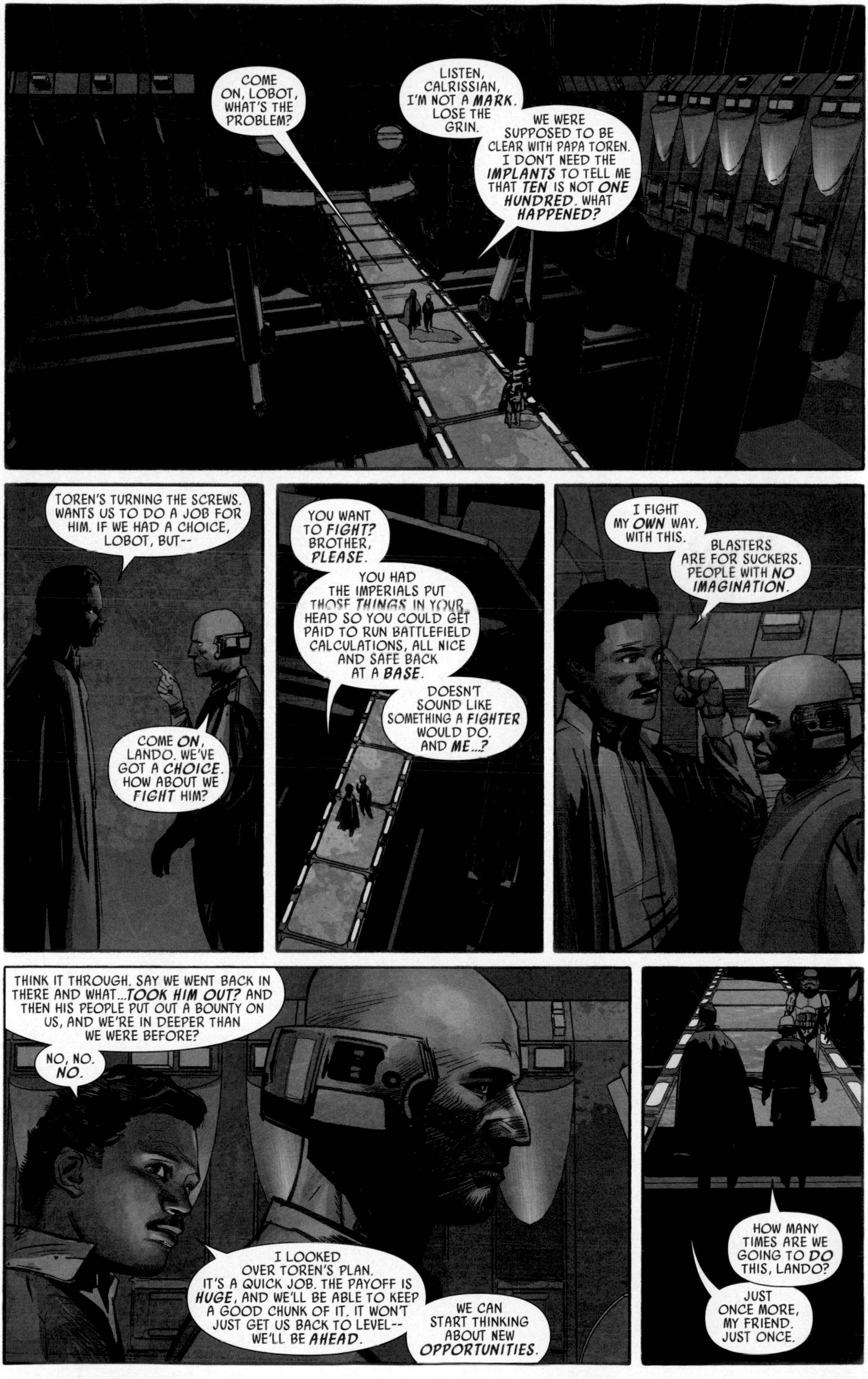
COME ON, LOBOT, WHAT'S THE PROBLEM?
LISTEN, CALRISSIAN, I'M NOT A MARK. LOSE THE GRIN.
WE WERE SUPPOSED TO BE CLEAR WITH PAPA TOREN. I DON'T NEED THE IMPLANTS TO TELL ME THAT TEN IS NOT ONE HUNDRED. WHAT HAPPENED?
TOREN'S TURNING THE SCREWS. WANTS US TO DO A JOB FOR HIM. IF WE HAD A CHOICE, LOBOT, BUT--
COME ON, LANDO. WE'VE GOT A CHOICE. HOW ABOUT WE FIGHT HIM?
YOU WANT TO FIGHT? BROTHER, PLEASE.
YOU HAD THE IMPERIALS PUT THOSE THINGS IN YOUR HEAD SO YOU COULD GET PAID TO RUN BATTLEFIELD CALCULATIONS, ALL NICE AND SAFE BACK AT A BASE.
DOESN'T SOUND LIKE SOMETHING A FIGHTER WOULD DO. AND ME...?
I FIGHT MY OWN WAY. WITH THIS.
BLASTERS ARE FOR SUCKERS. PEOPLE WITH NO IMAGINATION.
THINK IT THROUGH. SAY WE WENT BACK IN THERE AND WHAT...TOOK HIM OUT? AND THEN HIS PEOPLE PUT OUT A BOUNTY ON US, AND WE'RE IN DEEPER THAN WE WERE BEFORE?
NO, NO. NO.
I LOOKED OVER TOREN'S PLAN. IT'S A QUICK JOB. THE PAYOFF IS HUGE, AND WE'LL BE ABLE TO KEEP A GOOD CHUNK OF IT. IT WON'T JUST GET US BACK TO LEVEL-- WE'LL BE AHEAD.
WE CAN START THINKING ABOUT NEW OPPORTUNITIES.
HOW MANY TIMES ARE WE GOING TO DO THIS, LANDO?
JUST ONCE MORE, MY FRIEND. JUST ONCE.

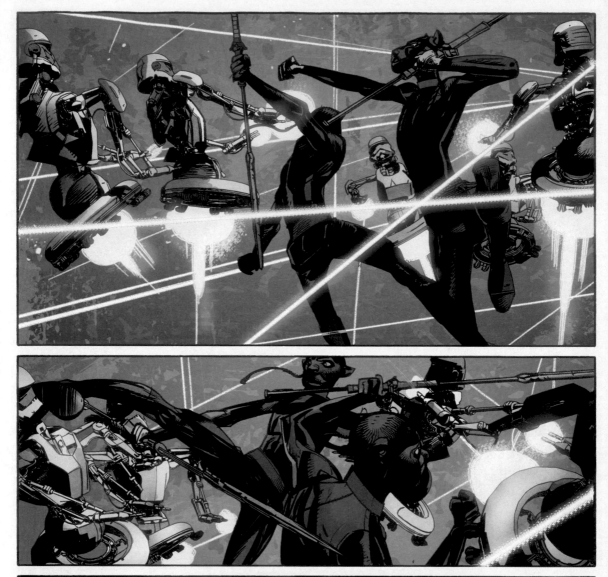

SHKKK!

SHKKK!

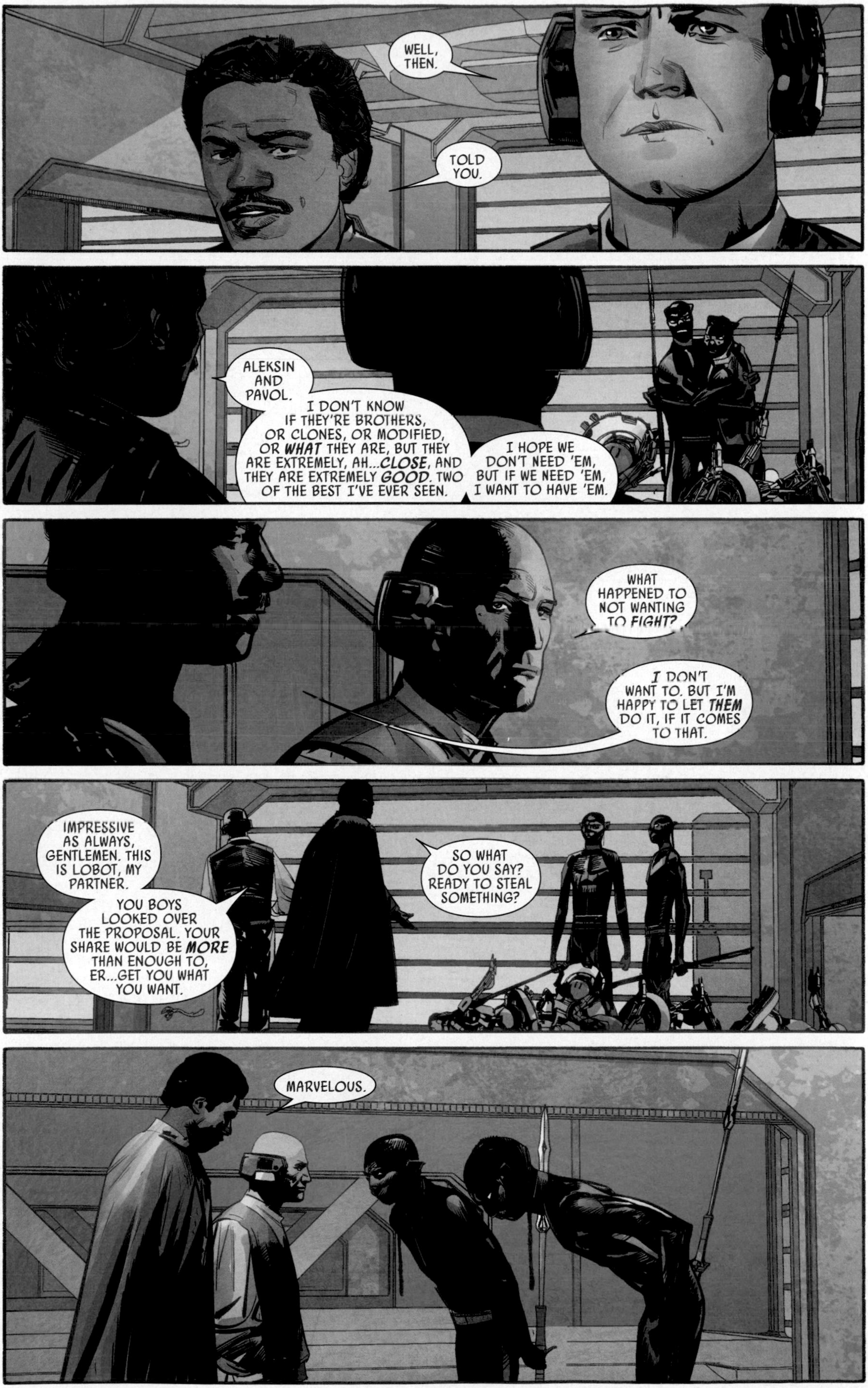
WELL, THEN.
TOLD YOU.
ALEKSIN AND PAVOL.
I DON'T KNOW IF THEY'RE BROTHERS, OR CLONES, OR MODIFIED, OR WHAT THEY ARE, BUT THEY ARE EXTREMELY, AH...CLOSE, AND THEY ARE EXTREMELY GOOD. TWO OF THE BEST I'VE EVER SEEN.
I HOPE WE DON'T NEED 'EM, BUT IF WE NEED 'EM, I WANT TO HAVE 'EM.
WHAT HAPPENED TO NOT WANTING TO FIGHT?
I DON'T WANT TO. BUT I'M HAPPY TO LET THEM DO IT, IF IT COMES TO THAT.
IMPRESSIVE AS ALWAYS, GENTLEMEN. THIS IS LOBOT, MY PARTNER.
YOU BOYS LOOKED OVER THE PROPOSAL. YOUR SHARE WOULD BE MORE THAN ENOUGH TO, ER...GET YOU WHAT YOU WANT.
SO WHAT DO YOU SAY? READY TO STEAL SOMETHING?
MARVELOUS.

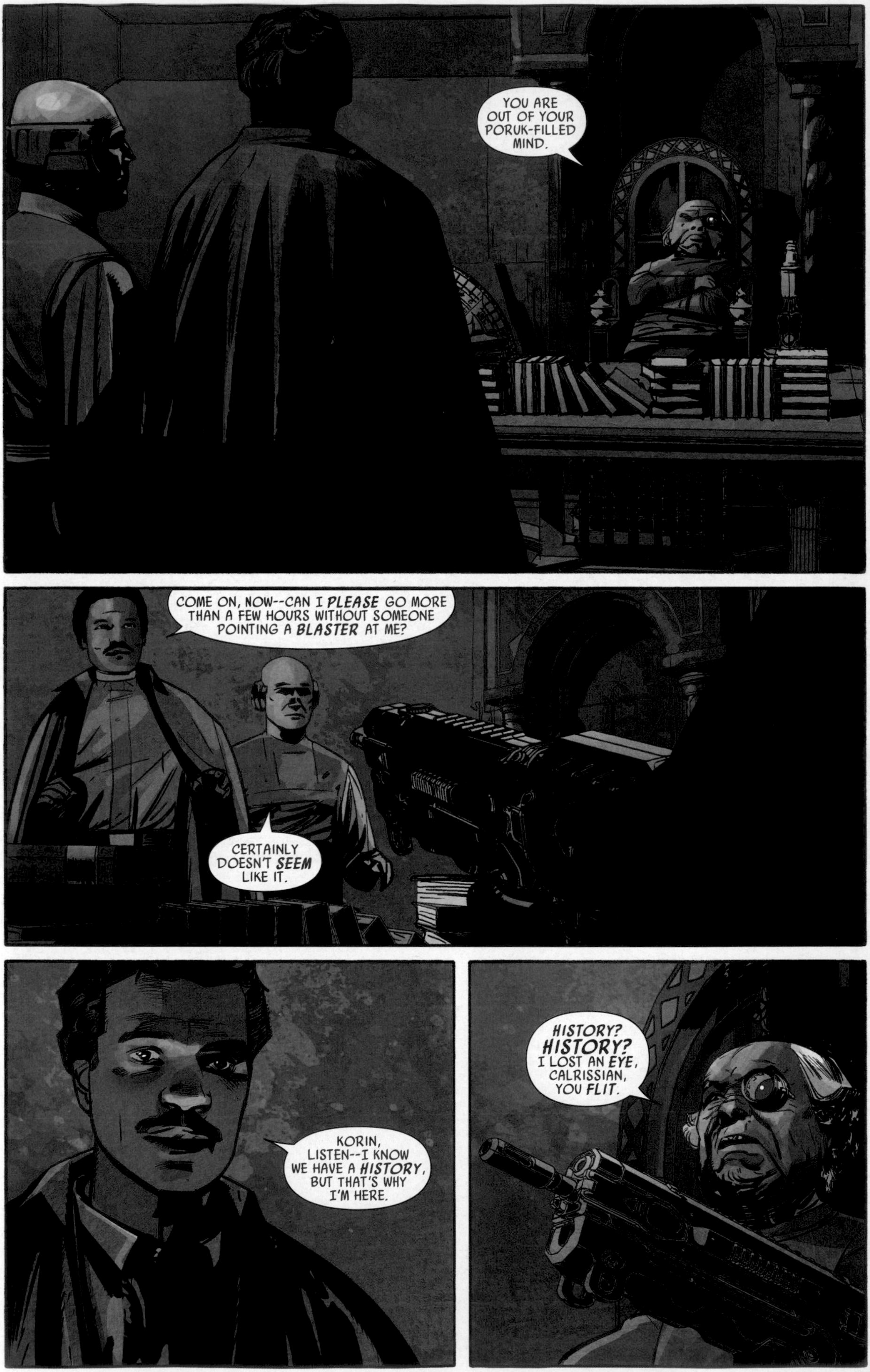
YOU ARE OUT OF YOUR PORUK-FILLED MIND.
COME ON, NOW--CAN I PLEASE GO MORE THAN A FEW HOURS WITHOUT SOMEONE POINTING A BLASTER AT ME?
CERTAINLY DOESN'T SEEM LIKE IT.
KORIN, LISTEN--I KNOW WE HAVE A HISTORY, BUT THAT'S WHY I'M HERE.
HISTORY? HISTORY? I LOST AN EYE, CALRISSIAN, YOU FLIT.

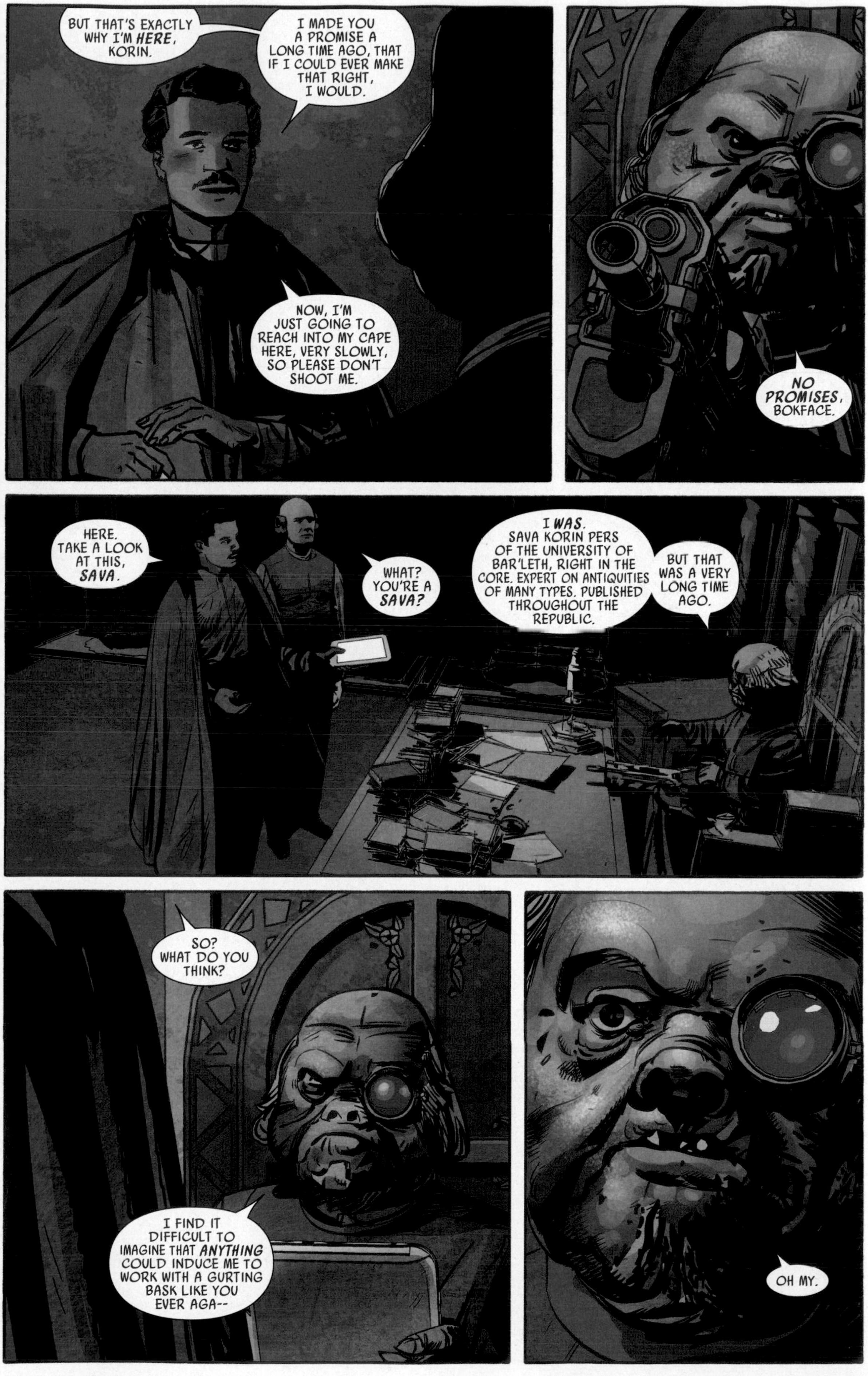
BUT THAT'S EXACTLY WHY I'M *HERE*, KORIN.
I MADE YOU A PROMISE A LONG TIME AGO, THAT IF I COULD EVER MAKE THAT RIGHT, I WOULD.
NOW, I'M JUST GOING TO REACH INTO MY CAPE HERE, VERY SLOWLY, SO PLEASE DON'T SHOOT ME.
NO PROMISES, BOKFACE.
HERE. TAKE A LOOK AT THIS, *SAVA*.
WHAT? YOU'RE A *SAVA?*
I *WAS*. SAVA KORIN PERS OF THE UNIVERSITY OF BAR'LETH, RIGHT IN THE CORE. EXPERT ON ANTIQUITIES OF MANY TYPES. PUBLISHED THROUGHOUT THE REPUBLIC.
BUT THAT WAS A VERY LONG TIME AGO.
SO? WHAT DO YOU THINK?
I FIND IT DIFFICULT TO IMAGINE THAT *ANYTHING* COULD INDUCE ME TO WORK WITH A GURTING BASK LIKE YOU EVER AGA--
OH MY.

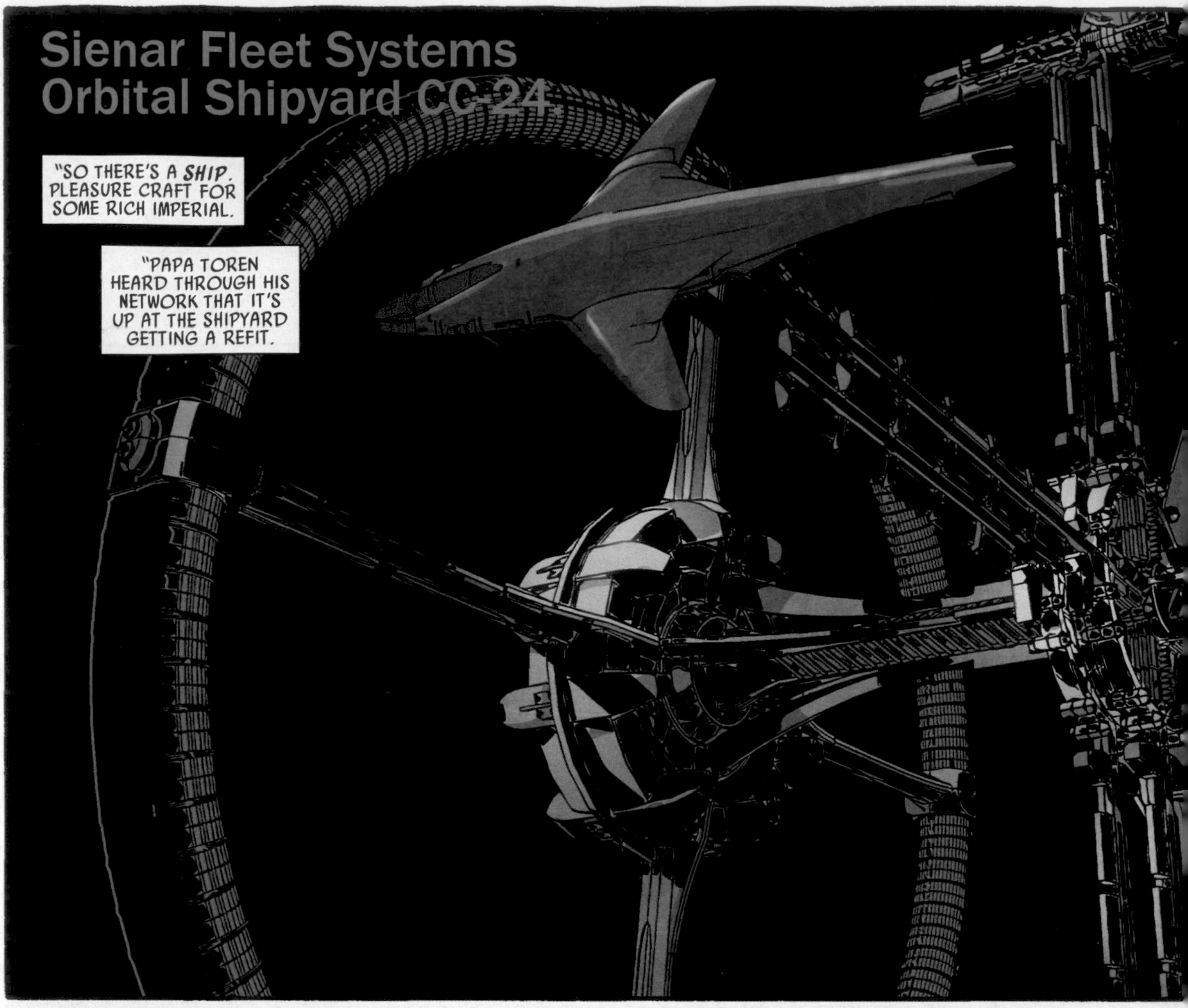
Sienar Fleet Systems
Orbital Shipyard CC-24.
"SO THERE'S A SHIP. PLEASURE CRAFT FOR SOME RICH IMPERIAL.
"PAPA TOREN HEARD THROUGH HIS NETWORK THAT IT'S UP AT THE SHIPYARD GETTING A REFIT.
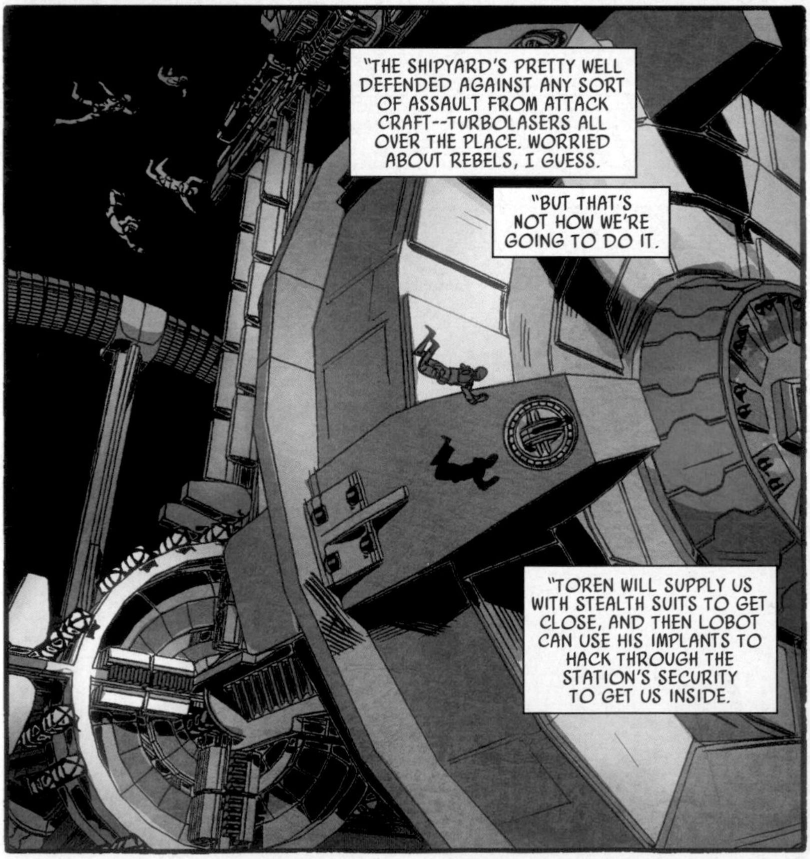
"THE SHIPYARD'S PRETTY WELL DEFENDED AGAINST ANY SORT OF ASSAULT FROM ATTACK CRAFT--TURBOLASERS ALL OVER THE PLACE. WORRIED ABOUT REBELS, I GUESS.
"BUT THAT'S NOT HOW WE'RE GOING TO DO IT.
"TOREN WILL SUPPLY US WITH STEALTH SUITS TO GET CLOSE, AND THEN LOBOT CAN USE HIS IMPLANTS TO HACK THROUGH THE STATION'S SECURITY TO GET US INSIDE.
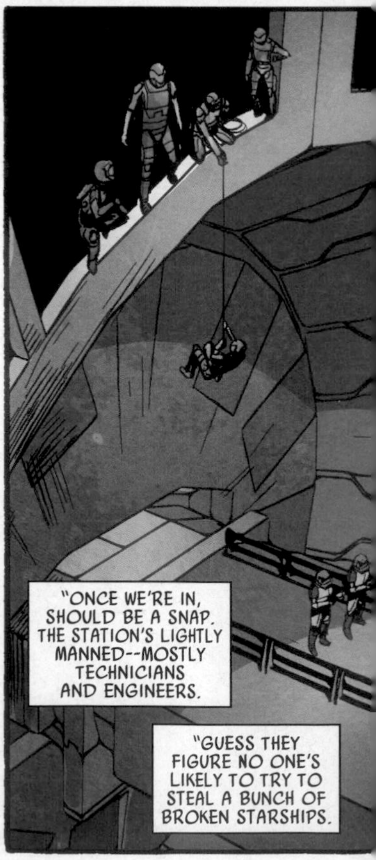
"ONCE WE'RE IN, SHOULD BE A SNAP. THE STATION'S LIGHTLY MANNED--MOSTLY TECHNICIANS AND ENGINEERS.
"GUESS THEY FIGURE NO ONE'S LIKELY TO TRY TO STEAL A BUNCH OF BROKEN STARSHIPS.

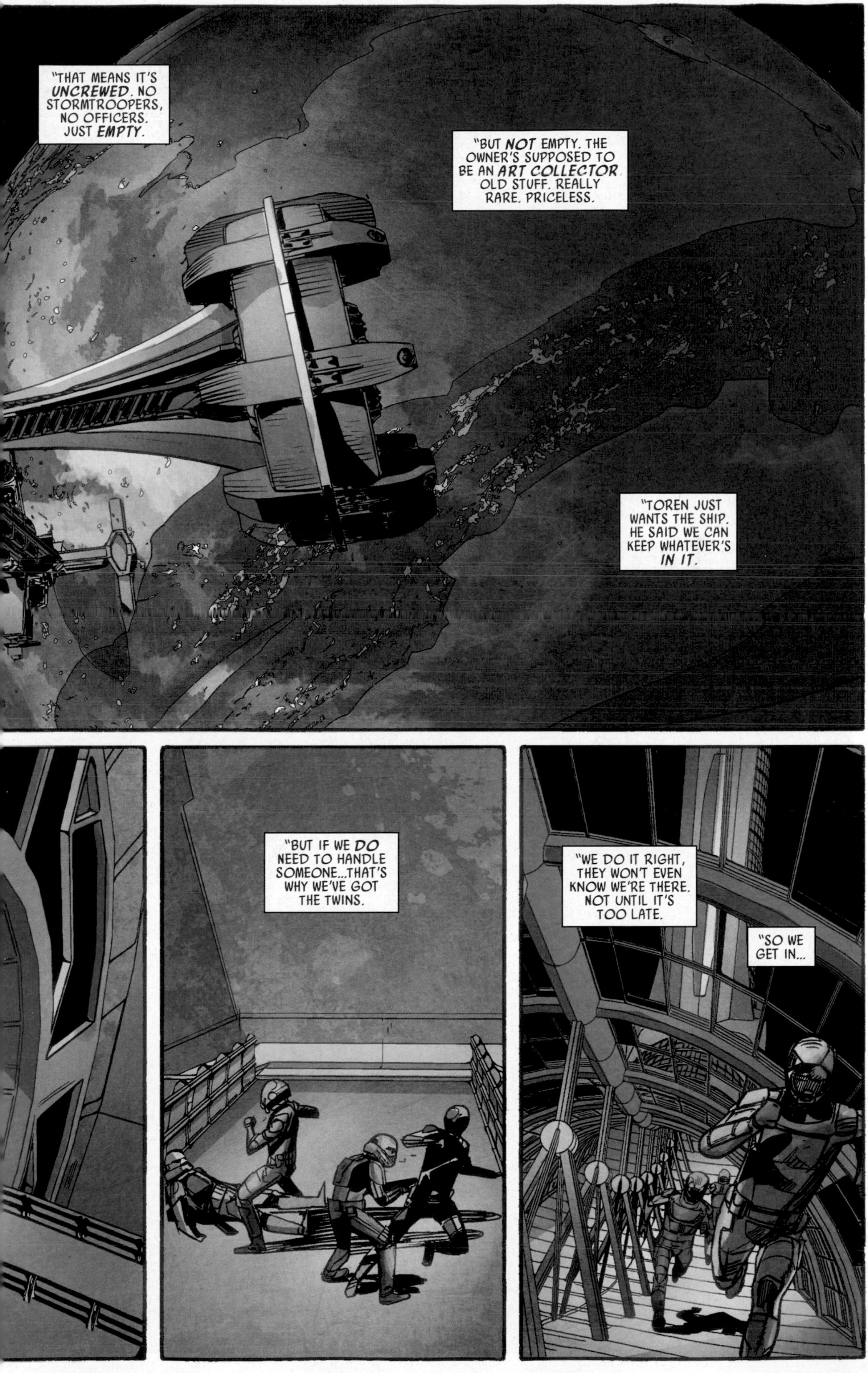
"THAT MEANS IT'S UNCREWED. NO STORMTROOPERS, NO OFFICERS. JUST EMPTY.
"BUT NOT EMPTY. THE OWNER'S SUPPOSED TO BE AN ART COLLECTOR OLD STUFF. REALLY RARE. PRICELESS.
"TOREN JUST WANTS THE SHIP. HE SAID WE CAN KEEP WHATEVER'S IN IT.
"BUT IF WE DO NEED TO HANDLE SOMEONE...THAT'S WHY WE'VE GOT THE TWINS.
"WE DO IT RIGHT, THEY WON'T EVEN KNOW WE'RE THERE. NOT UNTIL IT'S TOO LATE.
"SO WE GET IN...

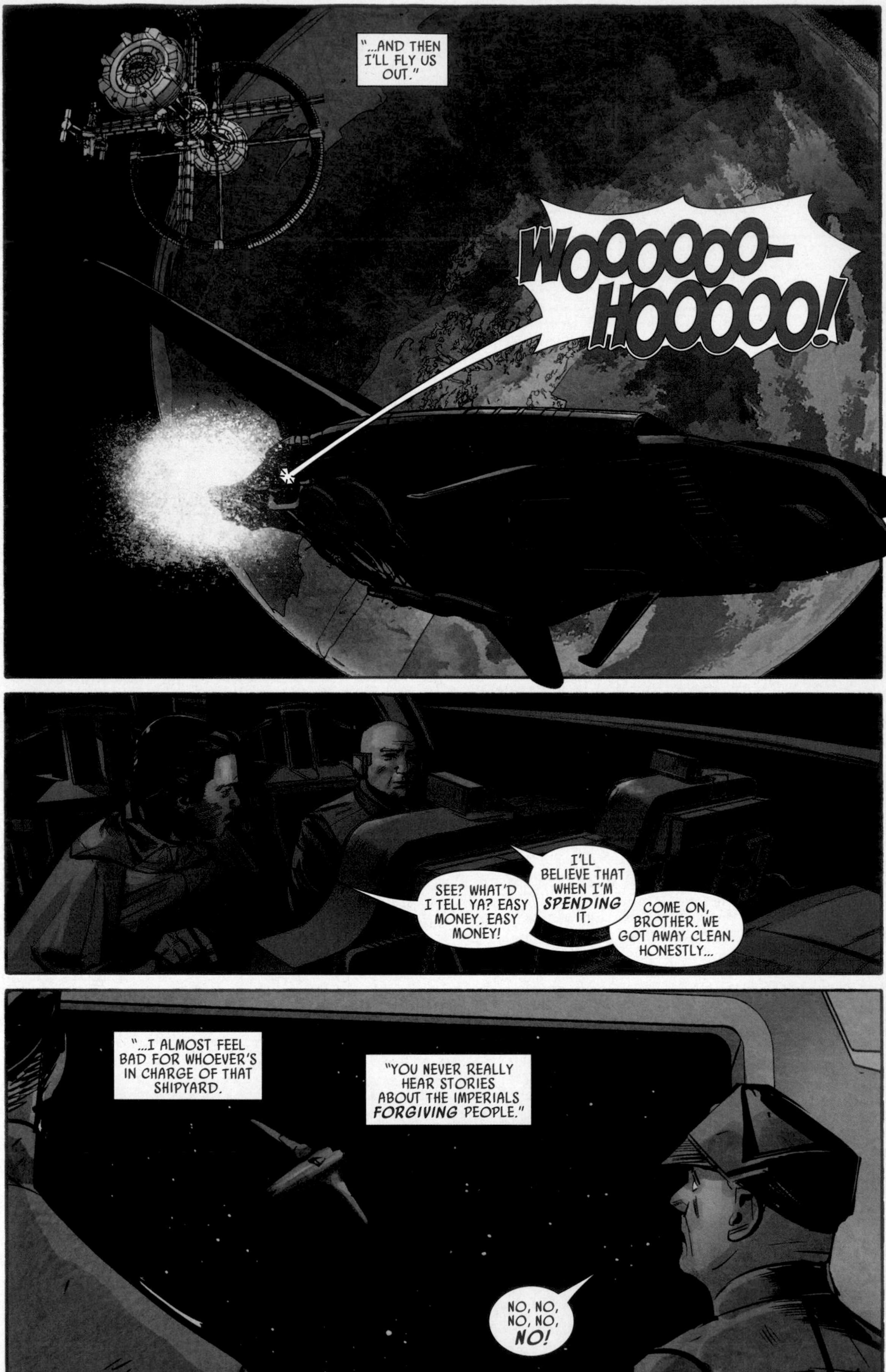
"...AND THEN I'LL FLY US OUT."
WOOOOOO-HOOOOO!
SEE? WHAT'D I TELL YA? EASY MONEY. EASY MONEY!
I'LL BELIEVE THAT WHEN I'M SPENDING IT.
COME ON, BROTHER. WE GOT AWAY CLEAN. HONESTLY...
"...I ALMOST FEEL BAD FOR WHOEVER'S IN CHARGE OF THAT SHIPYARD.
"YOU NEVER REALLY HEAR STORIES ABOUT THE IMPERIALS FORGIVING PEOPLE."
NO, NO, NO, NO, NO!

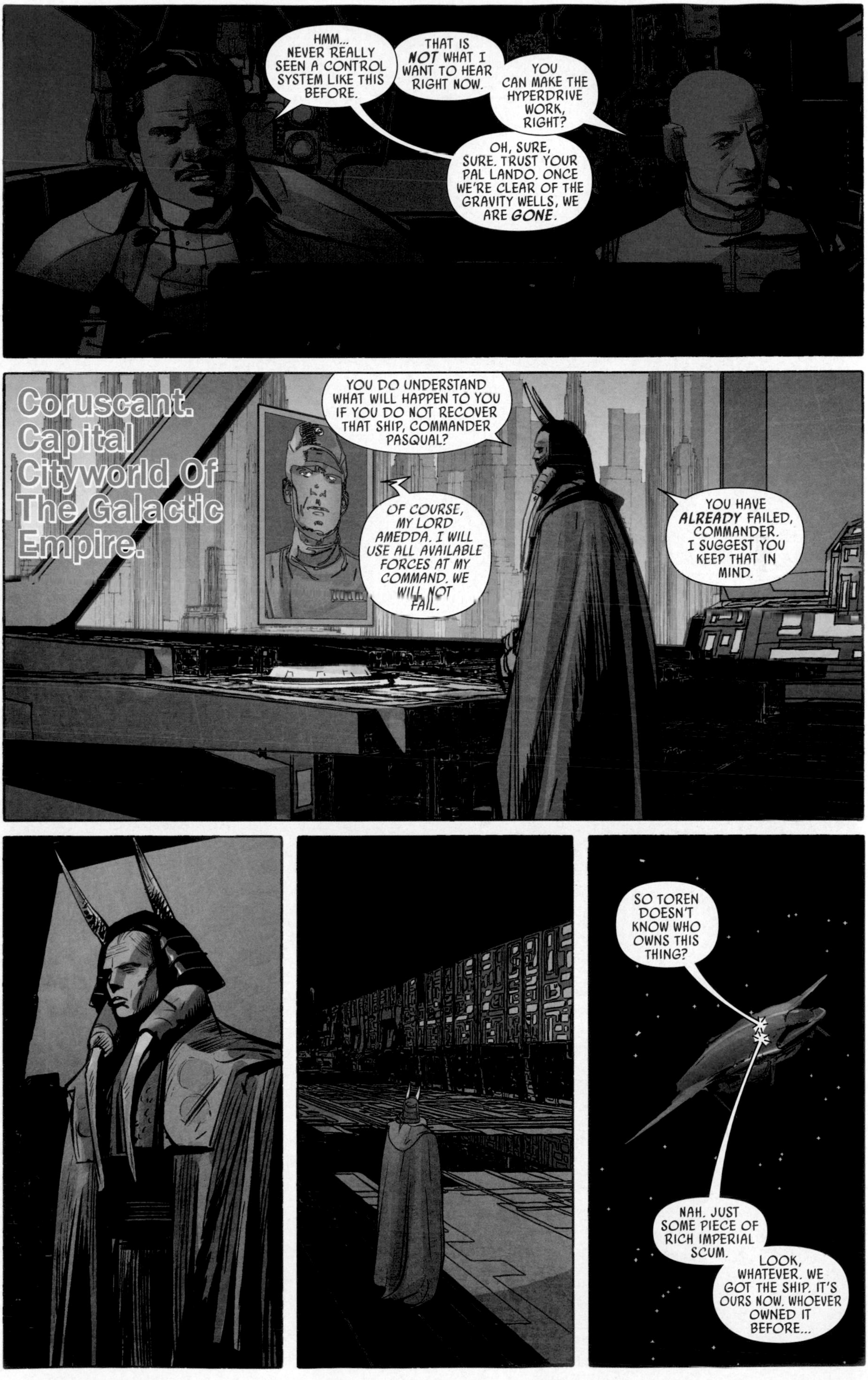
HMM... NEVER REALLY SEEN A CONTROL SYSTEM LIKE THIS BEFORE.
THAT IS NOT WHAT I WANT TO HEAR RIGHT NOW.
YOU CAN MAKE THE HYPERDRIVE WORK, RIGHT?
OH, SURE, SURE. TRUST YOUR PAL LANDO. ONCE WE'RE CLEAR OF THE GRAVITY WELLS, WE ARE GONE.
Coruscant. Capital Cityworld Of The Galactic Empire.
YOU DO UNDERSTAND WHAT WILL HAPPEN TO YOU IF YOU DO NOT RECOVER THAT SHIP, COMMANDER PASQUAL?
OF COURSE, MY LORD AMEDDA. I WILL USE ALL AVAILABLE FORCES AT MY COMMAND. WE WILL NOT FAIL.
YOU HAVE ALREADY FAILED, COMMANDER. I SUGGEST YOU KEEP THAT IN MIND.
SO TOREN DOESN'T KNOW WHO OWNS THIS THING?
NAH. JUST SOME PIECE OF RICH IMPERIAL SCUM.
LOOK, WHATEVER. WE GOT THE SHIP. IT'S OURS NOW. WHOEVER OWNED IT BEFORE...

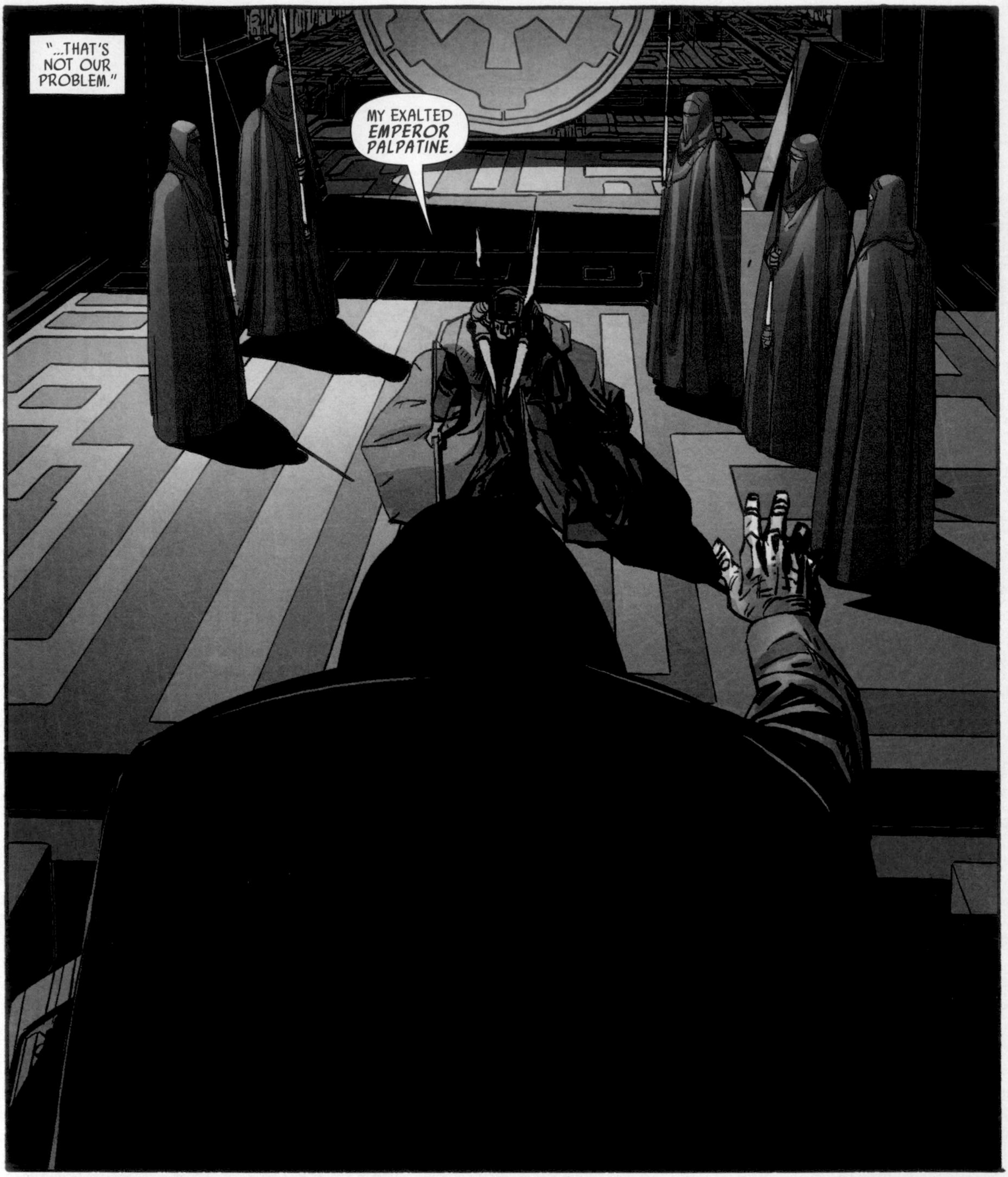
"...THAT'S NOT OUR PROBLEM."
MY EXALTED EMPEROR PALPATINE.
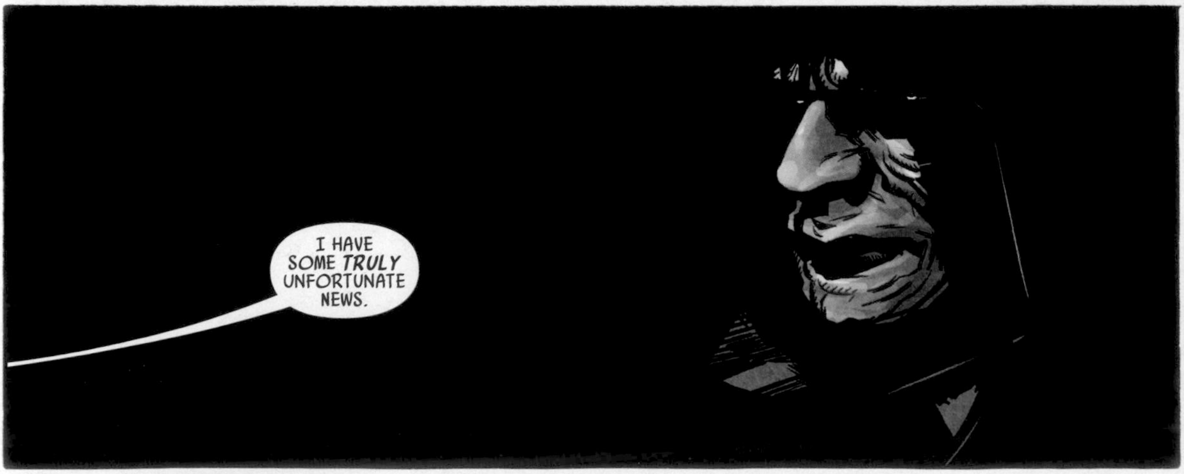
I HAVE SOME TRULY UNFORTUNATE NEWS.

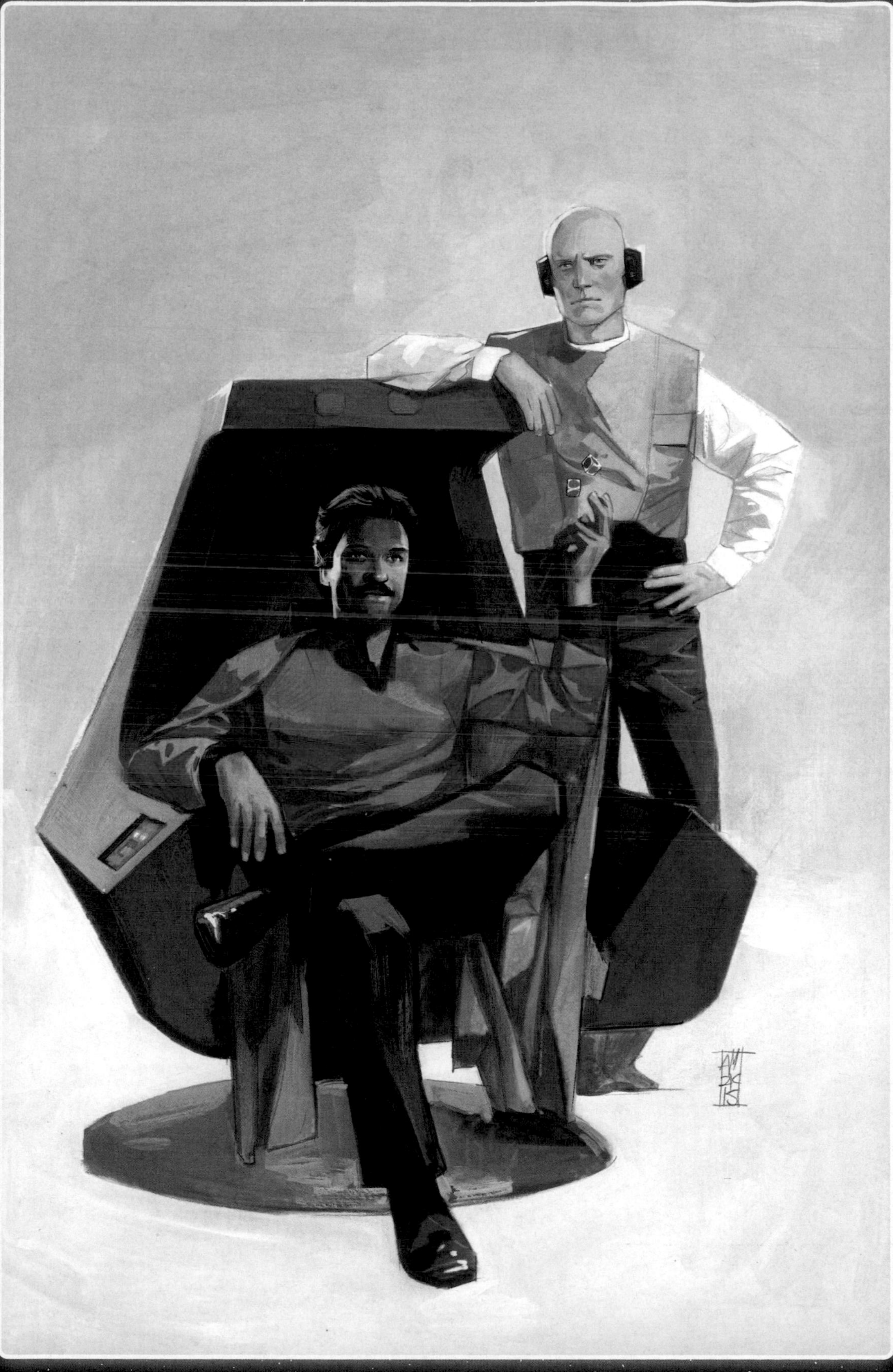

2

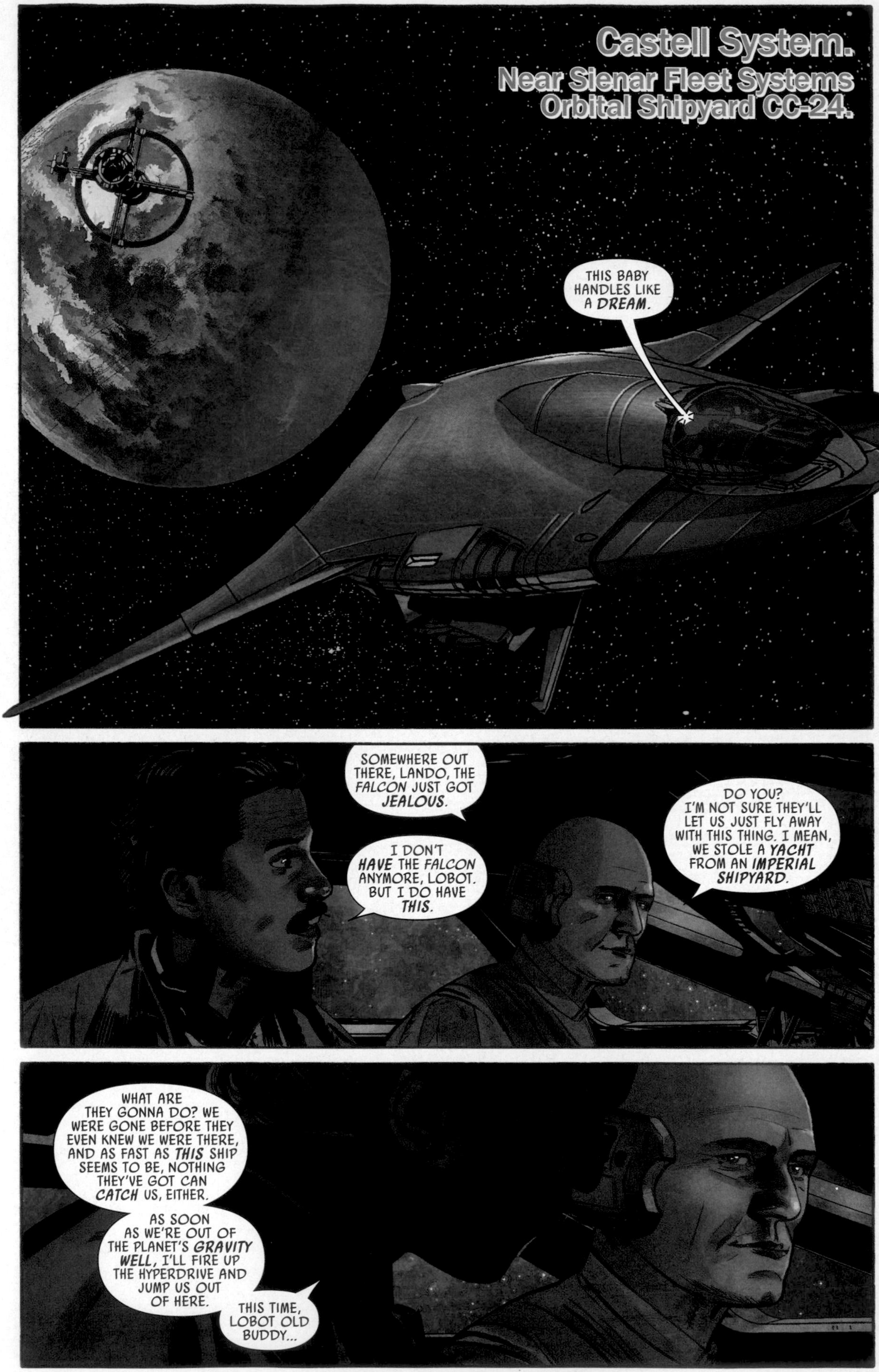
Castell System.
Near Sienar Fleet Systems Orbital Shipyard CC-24.
THIS BABY HANDLES LIKE A DREAM.
SOMEWHERE OUT THERE, LANDO, THE FALCON JUST GOT JEALOUS.
I DON'T HAVE THE FALCON ANYMORE, LOBOT. BUT I DO HAVE THIS.
DO YOU? I'M NOT SURE THEY'LL LET US JUST FLY AWAY WITH THIS THING. I MEAN, WE STOLE A YACHT FROM AN IMPERIAL SHIPYARD.
WHAT ARE THEY GONNA DO? WE WERE GONE BEFORE THEY EVEN KNEW WE WERE THERE, AND AS FAST AS THIS SHIP SEEMS TO BE, NOTHING THEY'VE GOT CAN CATCH US, EITHER.
AS SOON AS WE'RE OUT OF THE PLANET'S GRAVITY WELL, I'LL FIRE UP THE HYPERDRIVE AND JUMP US OUT OF HERE.
THIS TIME, LOBOT OLD BUDDY...

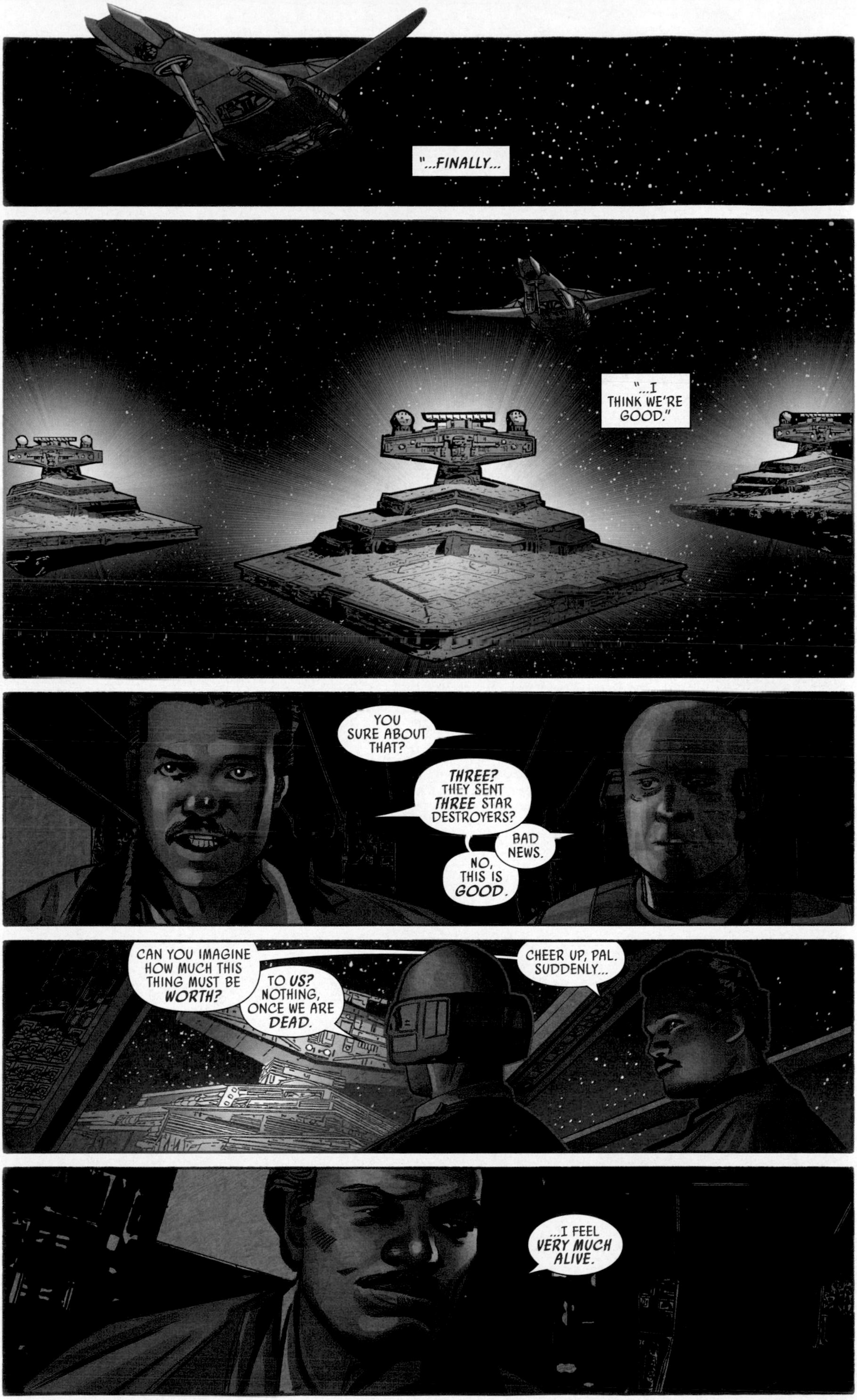
"...FINALLY...
"...I THINK WE'RE GOOD."
YOU SURE ABOUT THAT?
THREE? THEY SENT THREE STAR DESTROYERS?
BAD NEWS.
NO, THIS IS GOOD.
CAN YOU IMAGINE HOW MUCH THIS THING MUST BE WORTH?
TO US? NOTHING, ONCE WE ARE DEAD.
CHEER UP, PAL. SUDDENLY...
...I FEEL VERY MUCH ALIVE.

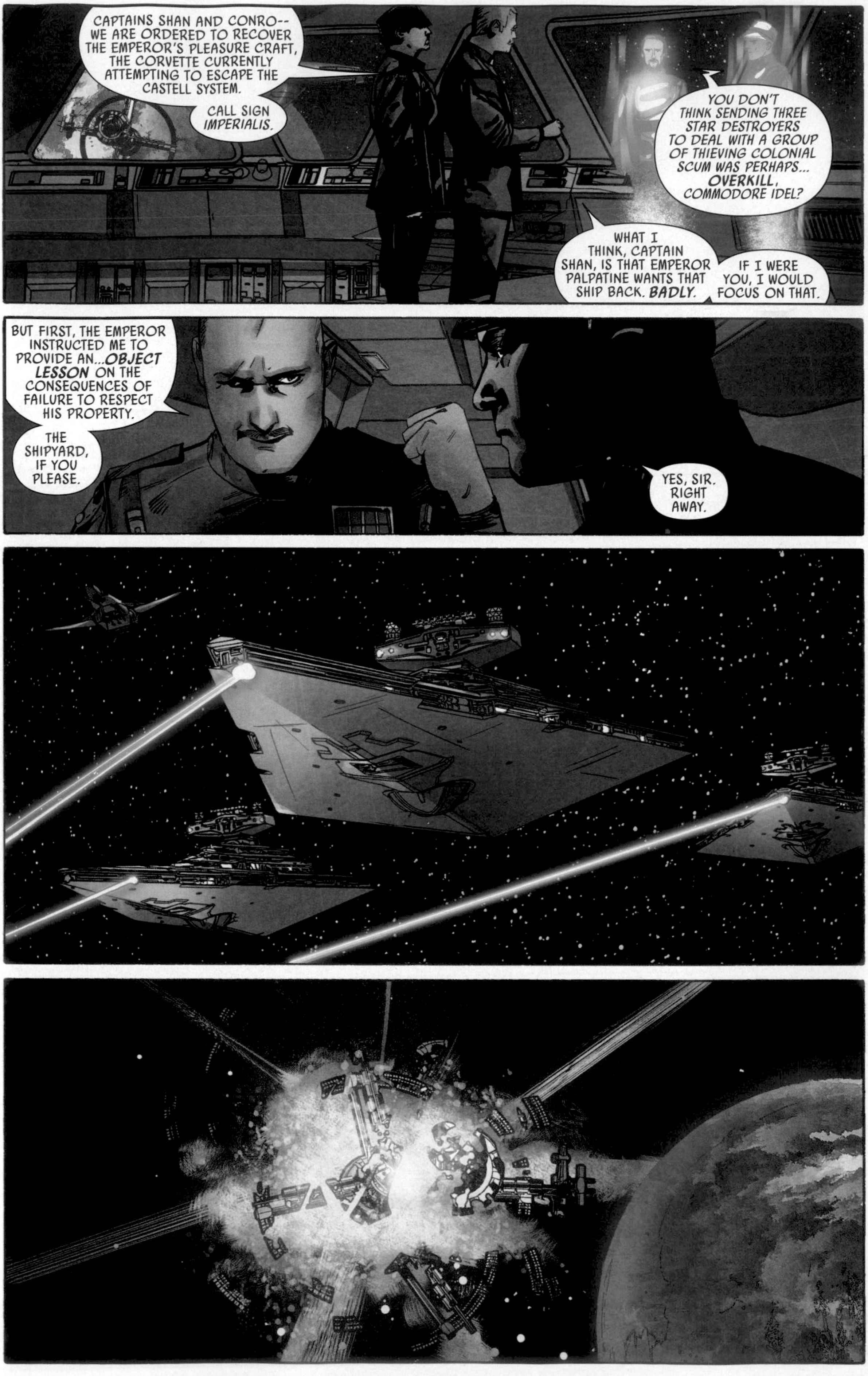
CAPTAINS SHAN AND CONRO-- WE ARE ORDERED TO RECOVER THE EMPEROR'S PLEASURE CRAFT, THE CORVETTE CURRENTLY ATTEMPTING TO ESCAPE THE CASTELL SYSTEM.
CALL SIGN IMPERIALIS.
YOU DON'T THINK SENDING THREE STAR DESTROYERS TO DEAL WITH A GROUP OF THIEVING COLONIAL SCUM WAS PERHAPS... OVERKILL, COMMODORE IDEL?
WHAT I THINK, CAPTAIN SHAN, IS THAT EMPEROR PALPATINE WANTS THAT SHIP BACK. BADLY.
IF I WERE YOU, I WOULD FOCUS ON THAT.
BUT FIRST, THE EMPEROR INSTRUCTED ME TO PROVIDE AN...OBJECT LESSON ON THE CONSEQUENCES OF FAILURE TO RESPECT HIS PROPERTY.
THE SHIPYARD, IF YOU PLEASE.
YES, SIR. RIGHT AWAY.

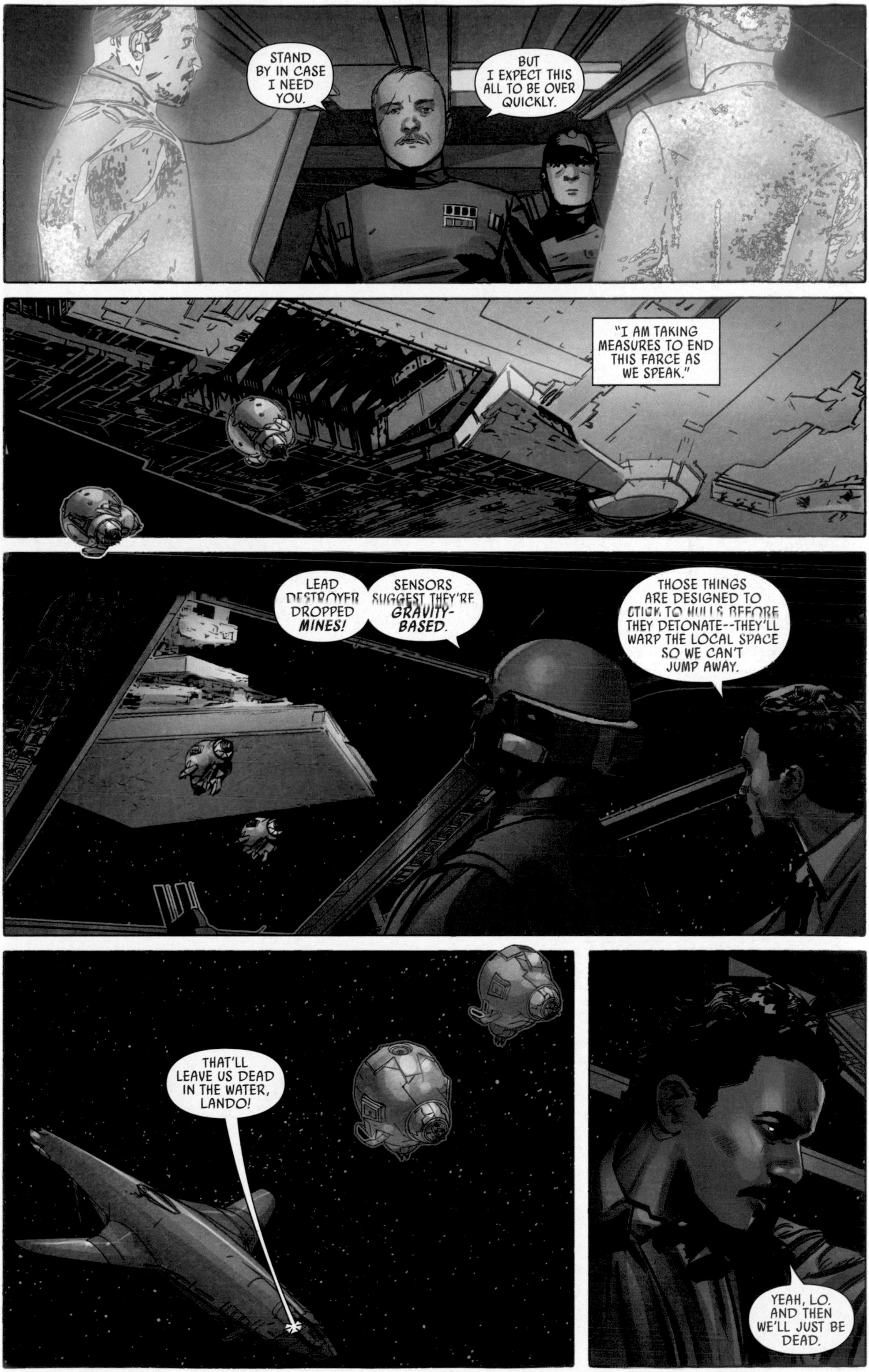
STAND BY IN CASE I NEED YOU.
BUT I EXPECT THIS ALL TO BE OVER QUICKLY.
"I AM TAKING MEASURES TO END THIS FARCE AS WE SPEAK."
LEAD DESTROYER DROPPED MINES!
SENSORS SUGGEST THEY'RE GRAVITY-BASED.
THOSE THINGS ARE DESIGNED TO STICK TO HULLS BEFORE THEY DETONATE--THEY'LL WARP THE LOCAL SPACE SO WE CAN'T JUMP AWAY.
THAT'LL LEAVE US DEAD IN THE WATER, LANDO!
YEAH, LO. AND THEN WE'LL JUST BE DEAD.

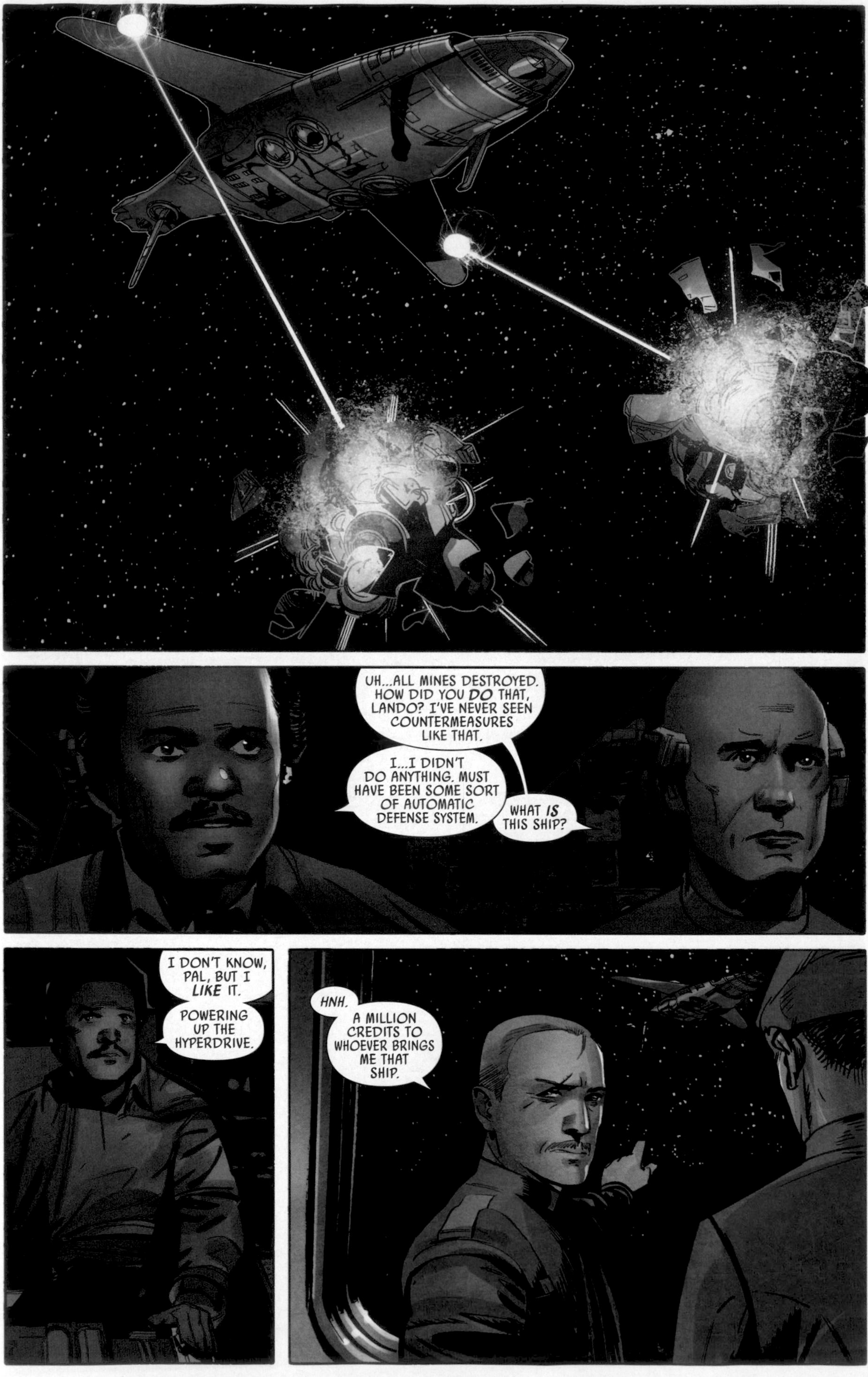
UH...ALL MINES DESTROYED. HOW DID YOU DO THAT, LANDO? I'VE NEVER SEEN COUNTERMEASURES LIKE THAT.
I...I DIDN'T DO ANYTHING. MUST HAVE BEEN SOME SORT OF AUTOMATIC DEFENSE SYSTEM.
WHAT IS THIS SHIP?
I DON'T KNOW, PAL, BUT I LIKE IT.
POWERING UP THE HYPERDRIVE.
HNH.
A MILLION CREDITS TO WHOEVER BRINGS ME THAT SHIP.

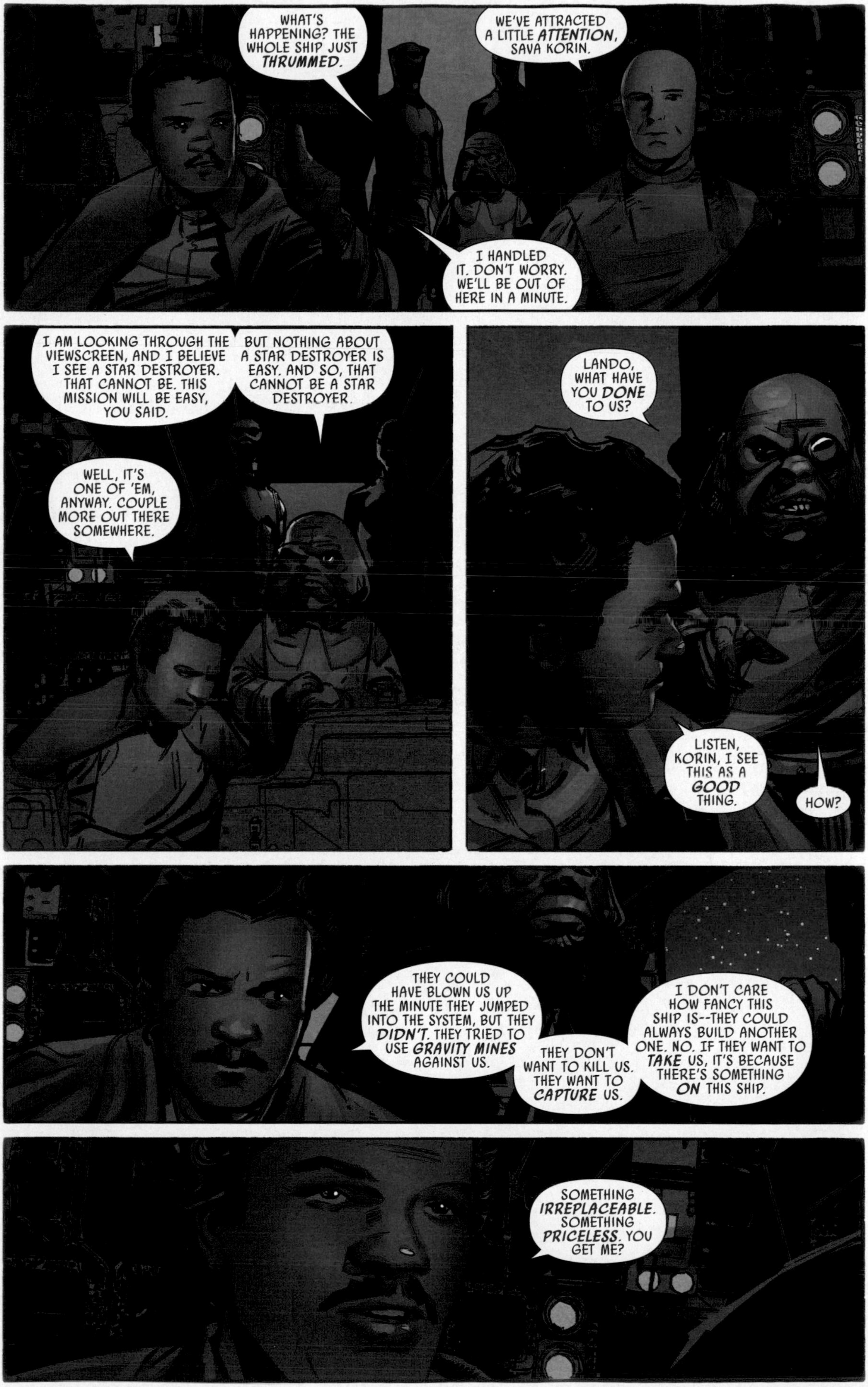
WHAT'S HAPPENING? THE WHOLE SHIP JUST THRUMMED.
WE'VE ATTRACTED A LITTLE ATTENTION, SAVA KORIN.
I HANDLED IT. DON'T WORRY. WE'LL BE OUT OF HERE IN A MINUTE.
I AM LOOKING THROUGH THE VIEWSCREEN, AND I BELIEVE I SEE A STAR DESTROYER. THAT CANNOT BE. THIS MISSION WILL BE EASY, YOU SAID.
BUT NOTHING ABOUT A STAR DESTROYER IS EASY. AND SO, THAT CANNOT BE A STAR DESTROYER.
WELL, IT'S ONE OF 'EM, ANYWAY. COUPLE MORE OUT THERE SOMEWHERE.
LANDO, WHAT HAVE YOU DONE TO US?
LISTEN, KORIN, I SEE THIS AS A GOOD THING.
HOW?
THEY COULD HAVE BLOWN US UP THE MINUTE THEY JUMPED INTO THE SYSTEM, BUT THEY DIDN'T. THEY TRIED TO USE GRAVITY MINES AGAINST US.
THEY DON'T WANT TO KILL US. THEY WANT TO CAPTURE US.
I DON'T CARE HOW FANCY THIS SHIP IS--THEY COULD ALWAYS BUILD ANOTHER ONE. NO. IF THEY WANT TO TAKE US, IT'S BECAUSE THERE'S SOMETHING ON THIS SHIP.
SOMETHING IRREPLACEABLE. SOMETHING PRICELESS. YOU GET ME?

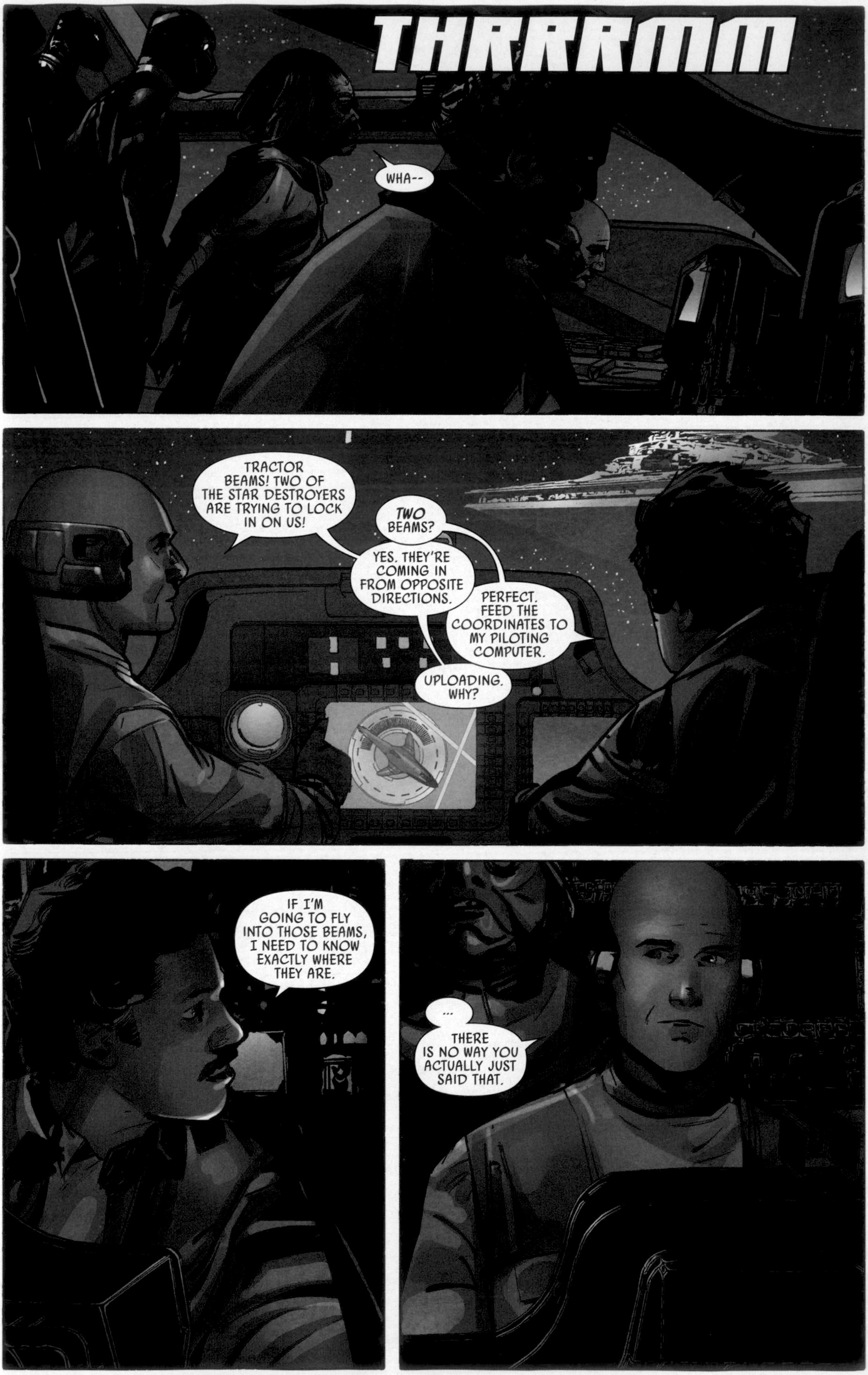
THRRRMM
WHA--
TRACTOR BEAMS! TWO OF THE STAR DESTROYERS ARE TRYING TO LOCK IN ON US!
TWO BEAMS?
YES. THEY'RE COMING IN FROM OPPOSITE DIRECTIONS.
PERFECT. FEED THE COORDINATES TO MY PILOTING COMPUTER.
UPLOADING. WHY?
IF I'M GOING TO FLY INTO THOSE BEAMS, I NEED TO KNOW EXACTLY WHERE THEY ARE.
...
THERE IS NO WAY YOU ACTUALLY JUST SAID THAT.

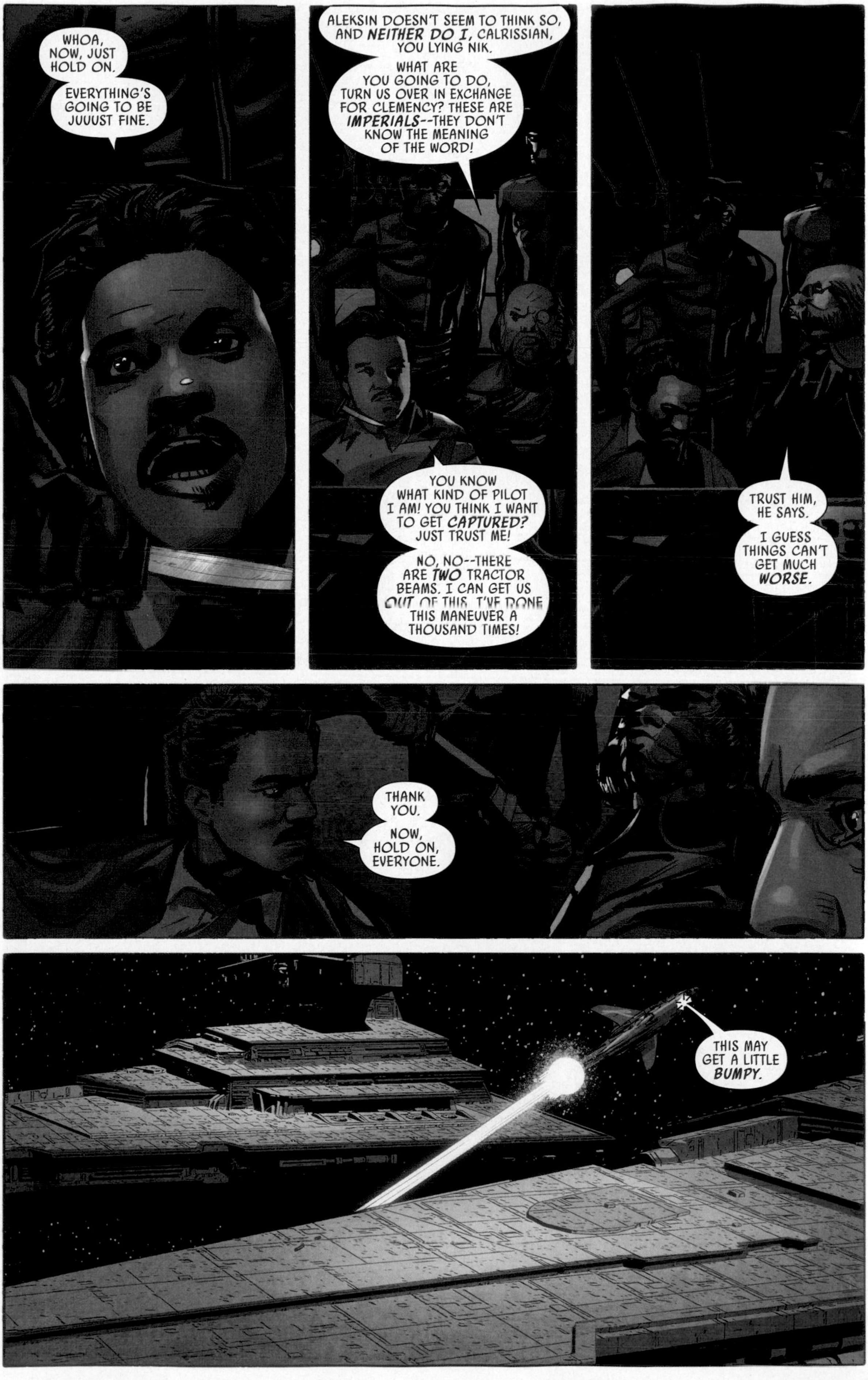
WHOA, NOW, JUST HOLD ON.
EVERYTHING'S GOING TO BE JUUUST FINE.
ALEKSIN DOESN'T SEEM TO THINK SO, AND NEITHER DO I, CALRISSIAN, YOU LYING NIK.
WHAT ARE YOU GOING TO DO, TURN US OVER IN EXCHANGE FOR CLEMENCY? THESE ARE IMPERIALS--THEY DON'T KNOW THE MEANING OF THE WORD!
YOU KNOW WHAT KIND OF PILOT I AM! YOU THINK I WANT TO GET CAPTURED? JUST TRUST ME!
NO, NO--THERE ARE TWO TRACTOR BEAMS. I CAN GET US OUT OF THIS. I'VE DONE THIS MANEUVER A THOUSAND TIMES!
TRUST HIM, HE SAYS.
I GUESS THINGS CAN'T GET MUCH WORSE.
THANK YOU.
NOW, HOLD ON, EVERYONE.
THIS MAY GET A LITTLE BUMPY.

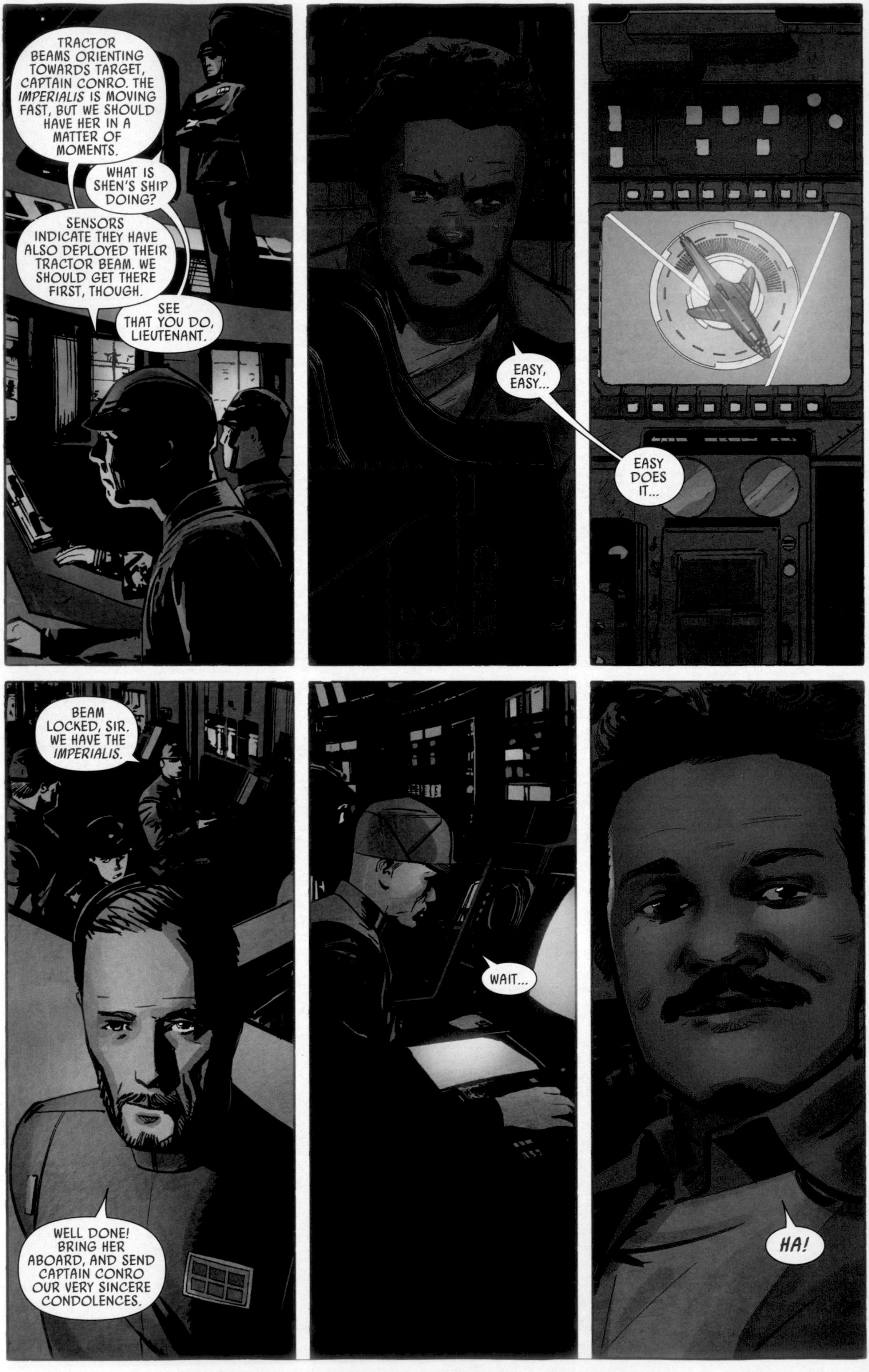
TRACTOR BEAMS ORIENTING TOWARDS TARGET, CAPTAIN CONRO. THE *IMPERIALIS* IS MOVING FAST, BUT WE SHOULD HAVE HER IN A MATTER OF MOMENTS.
WHAT IS SHEN'S SHIP DOING?
SENSORS INDICATE THEY HAVE ALSO DEPLOYED THEIR TRACTOR BEAM. WE SHOULD GET THERE FIRST, THOUGH.
SEE THAT YOU DO, LIEUTENANT.
EASY, EASY...
EASY DOES IT...
BEAM LOCKED, SIR. WE HAVE THE *IMPERIALIS*.
WELL DONE! BRING HER ABOARD, AND SEND CAPTAIN CONRO OUR VERY SINCERE CONDOLENCES.
WAIT...
HA!

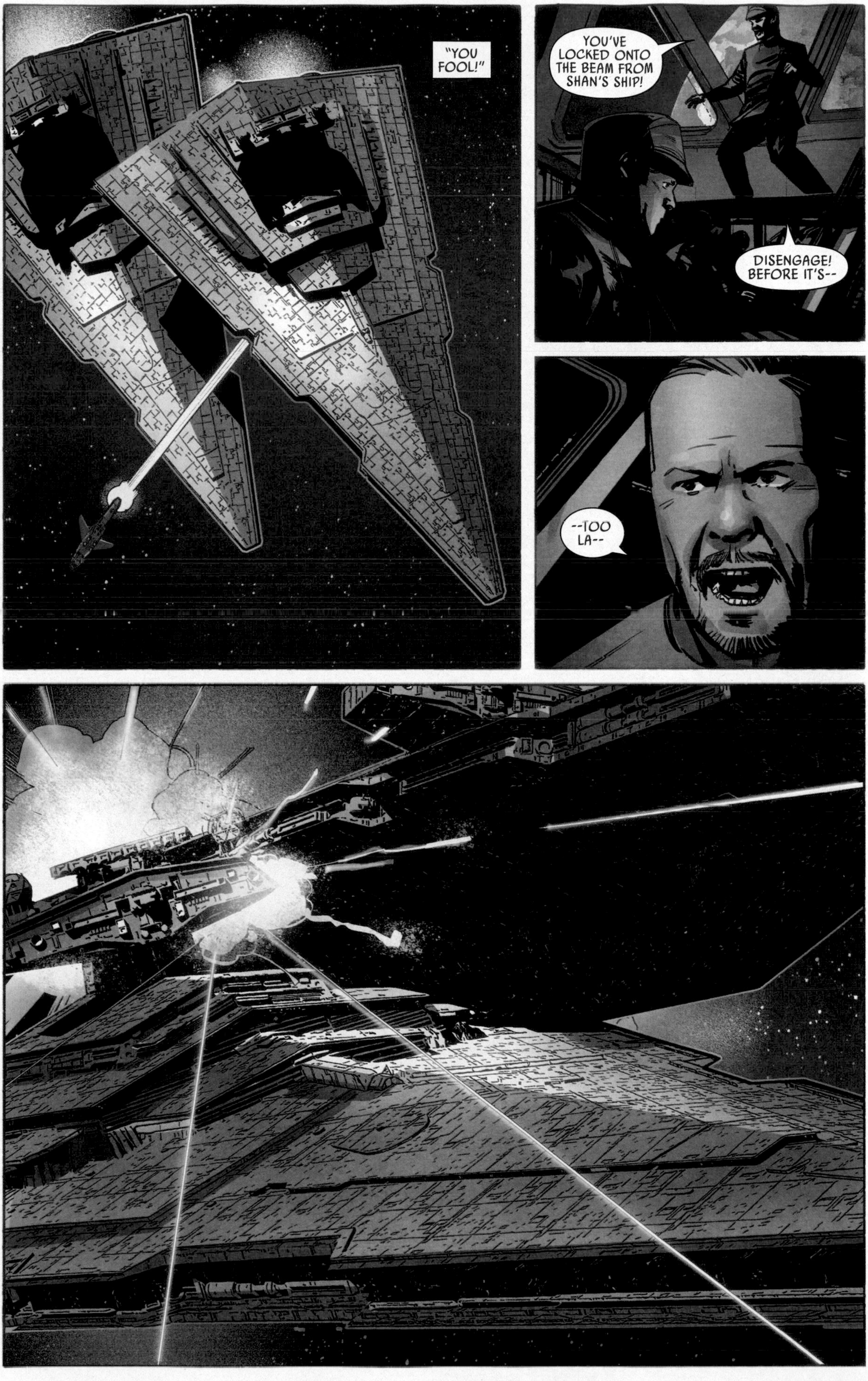
"YOU FOOL!"
YOU'VE LOCKED ONTO THE BEAM FROM SHAN'S SHIP!
DISENGAGE! BEFORE IT'S--
--TOO LA--

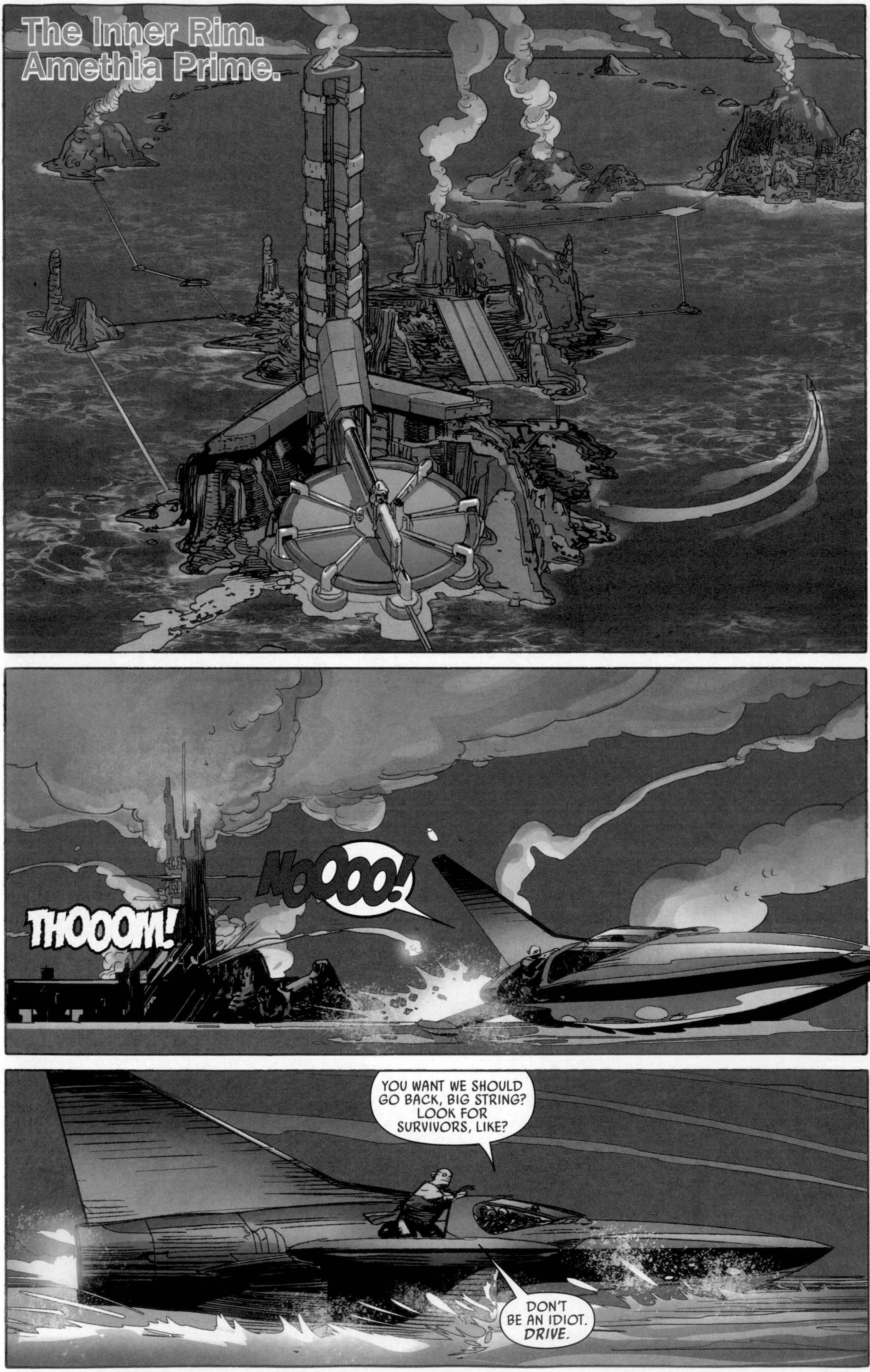
The Inner Rim.
Amethia Prime.
THOOOM!
NOOOOO!
YOU WANT WE SHOULD GO BACK, BIG STRING? LOOK FOR SURVIVORS, LIKE?
DON'T BE AN IDIOT. *DRIVE.*

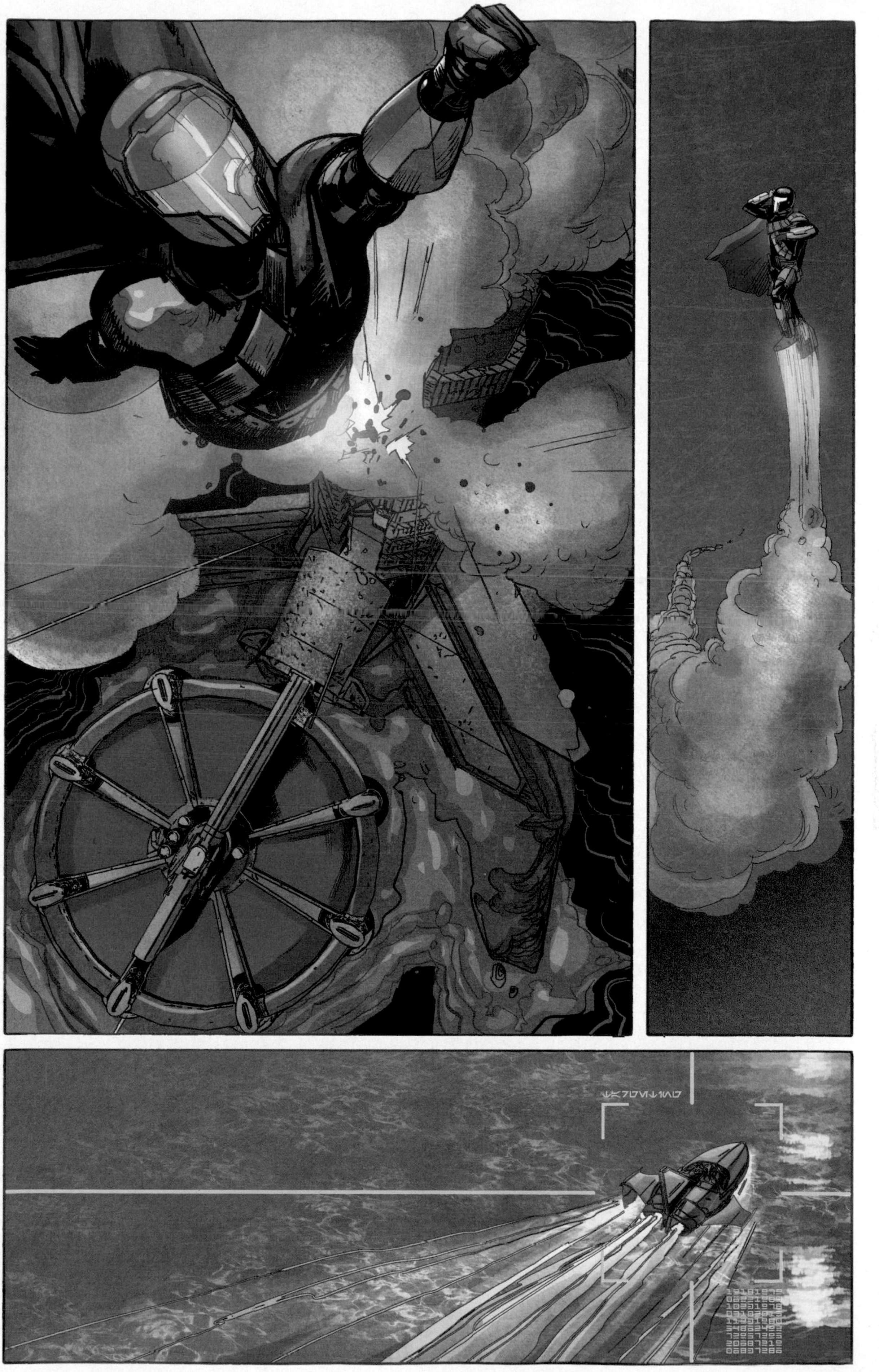

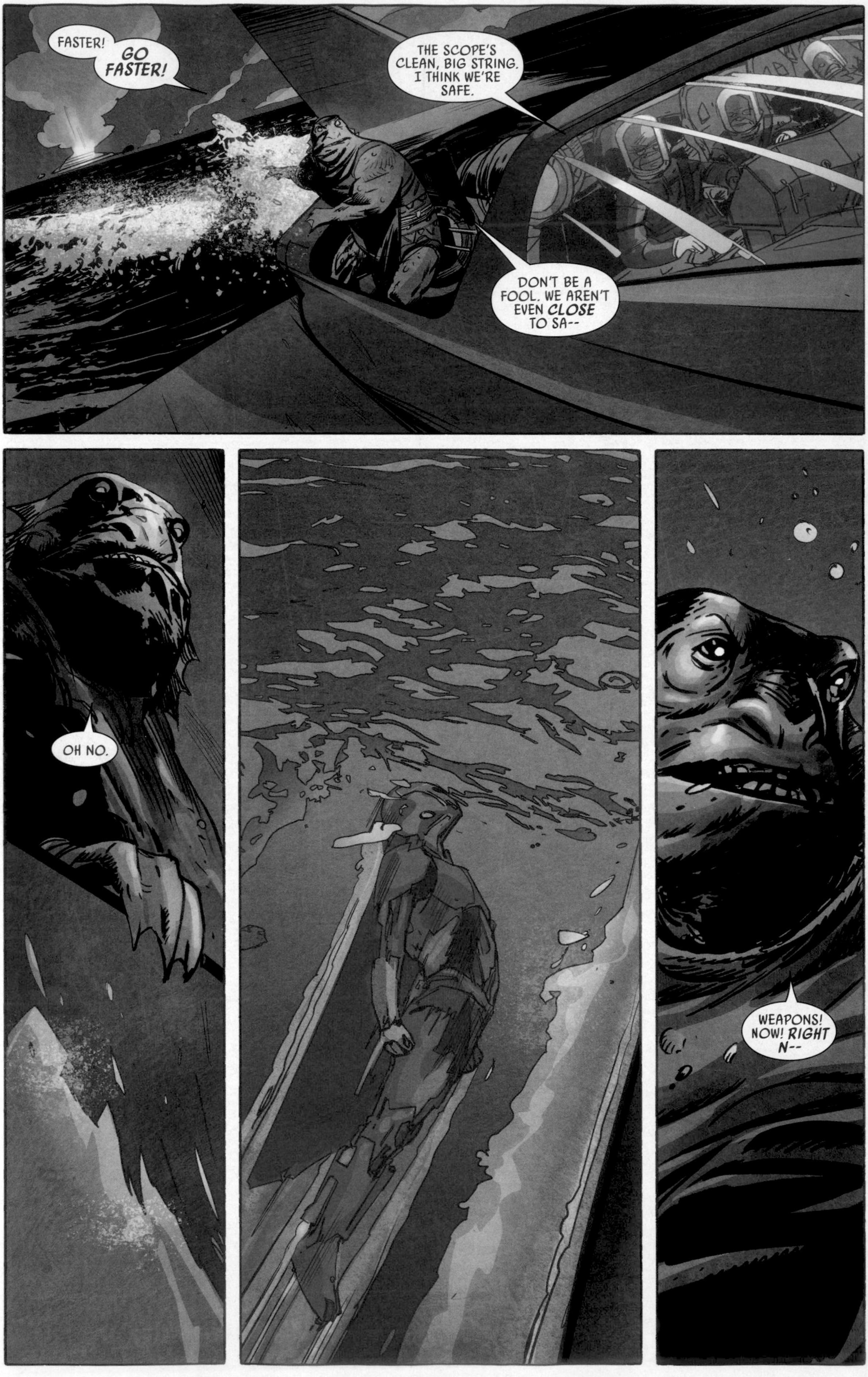
FASTER! GO FASTER!
THE SCOPE'S CLEAN, BIG STRING. I THINK WE'RE SAFE.
DON'T BE A FOOL. WE AREN'T EVEN CLOSE TO SA--
OH NO.
WEAPONS! NOW! RIGHT N--

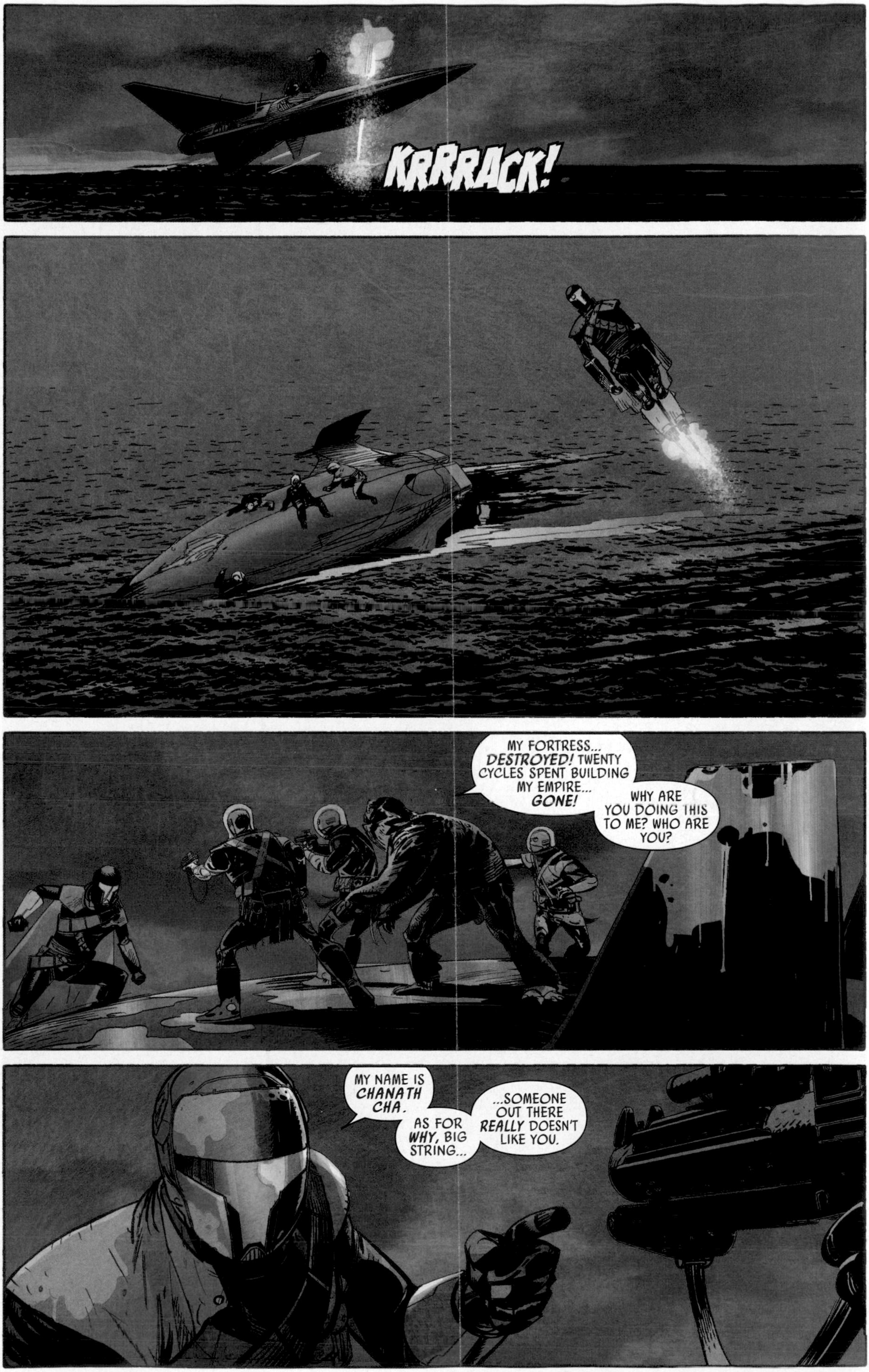
KRRRACK!
MY FORTRESS... DESTROYED! TWENTY CYCLES SPENT BUILDING MY EMPIRE... GONE!
WHY ARE YOU DOING THIS TO ME? WHO ARE YOU?
MY NAME IS CHANATH CHA.
AS FOR WHY, BIG STRING...
...SOMEONE OUT THERE REALLY DOESN'T LIKE YOU.

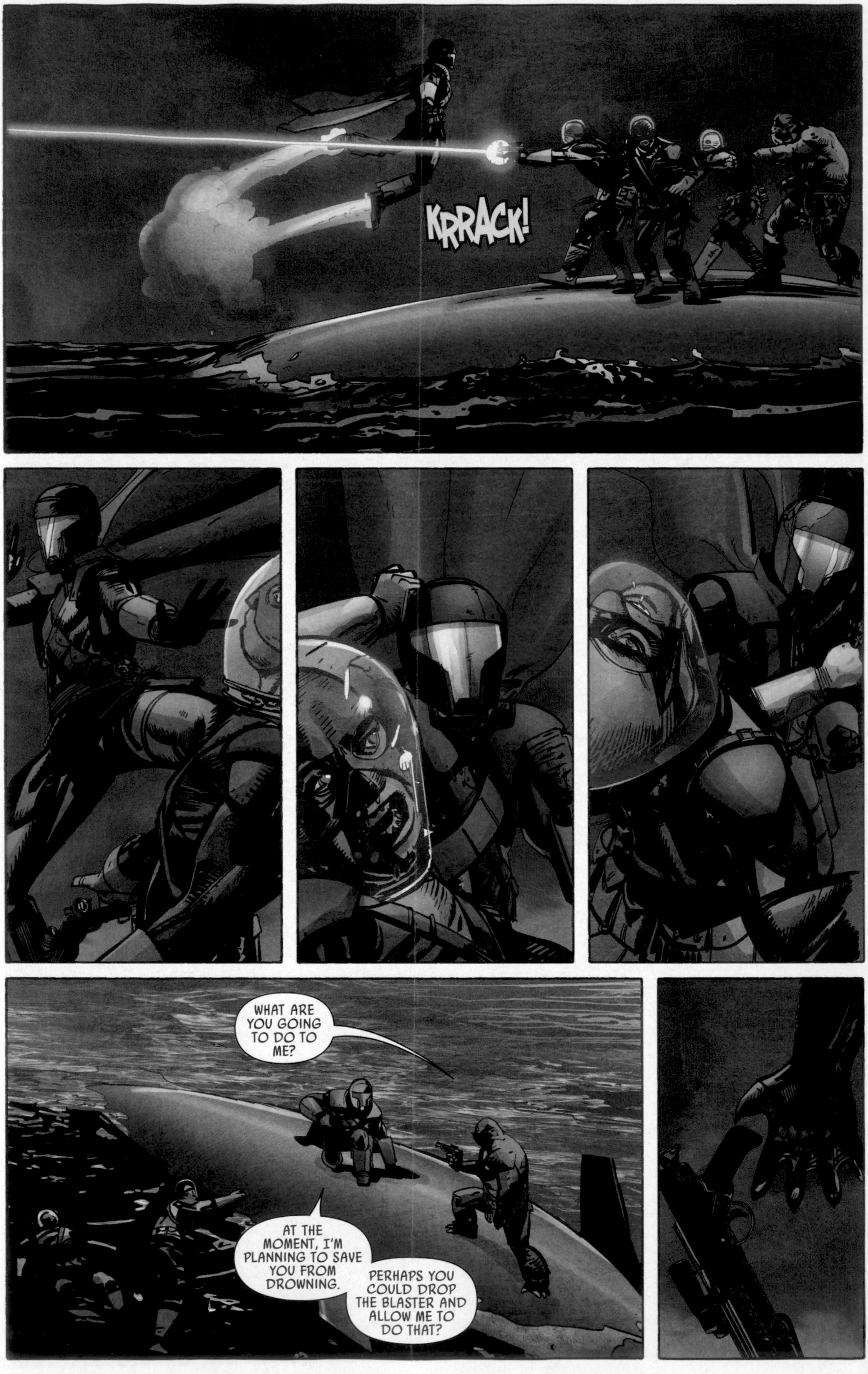
KRRACK!
WHAT ARE YOU GOING TO DO TO ME?
AT THE MOMENT, I'M PLANNING TO SAVE YOU FROM DROWNING.
PERHAPS YOU COULD DROP THE BLASTER AND ALLOW ME TO DO THAT?

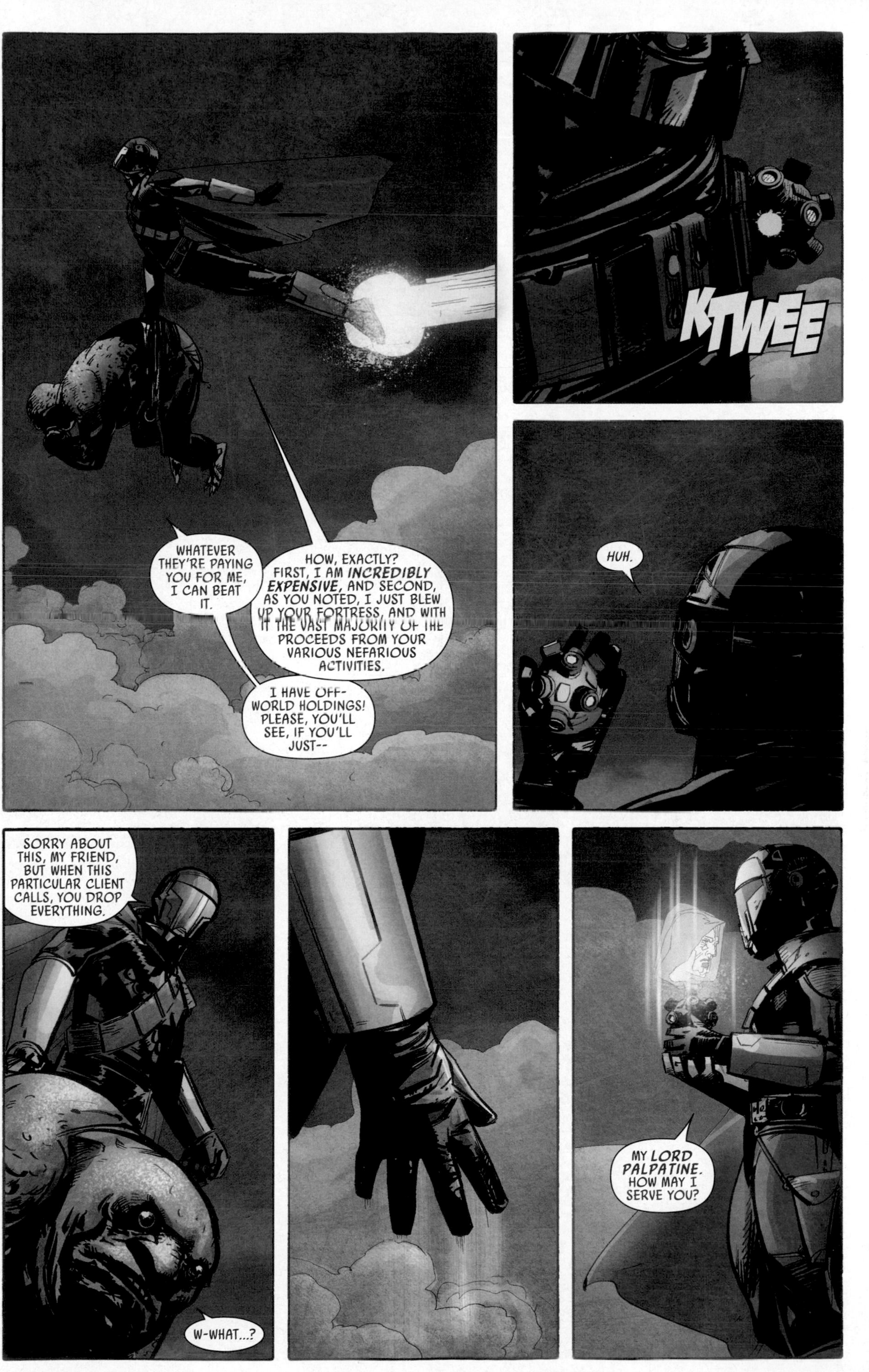
WHATEVER THEY'RE PAYING YOU FOR ME, I CAN BEAT IT.
HOW, EXACTLY? FIRST, I AM **INCREDIBLY EXPENSIVE,** AND SECOND, AS YOU NOTED, I JUST BLEW UP YOUR FORTRESS, AND WITH IT THE VAST MAJORITY OF THE PROCEEDS FROM YOUR VARIOUS NEFARIOUS ACTIVITIES.
I HAVE OFF-WORLD HOLDINGS! PLEASE, YOU'LL SEE, IF YOU'LL JUST--
KTWEE
HUH.
SORRY ABOUT THIS, MY FRIEND, BUT WHEN THIS PARTICULAR CLIENT CALLS, YOU DROP EVERYTHING.
W-WHAT...?
MY **LORD PALPATINE.** HOW MAY I SERVE YOU?

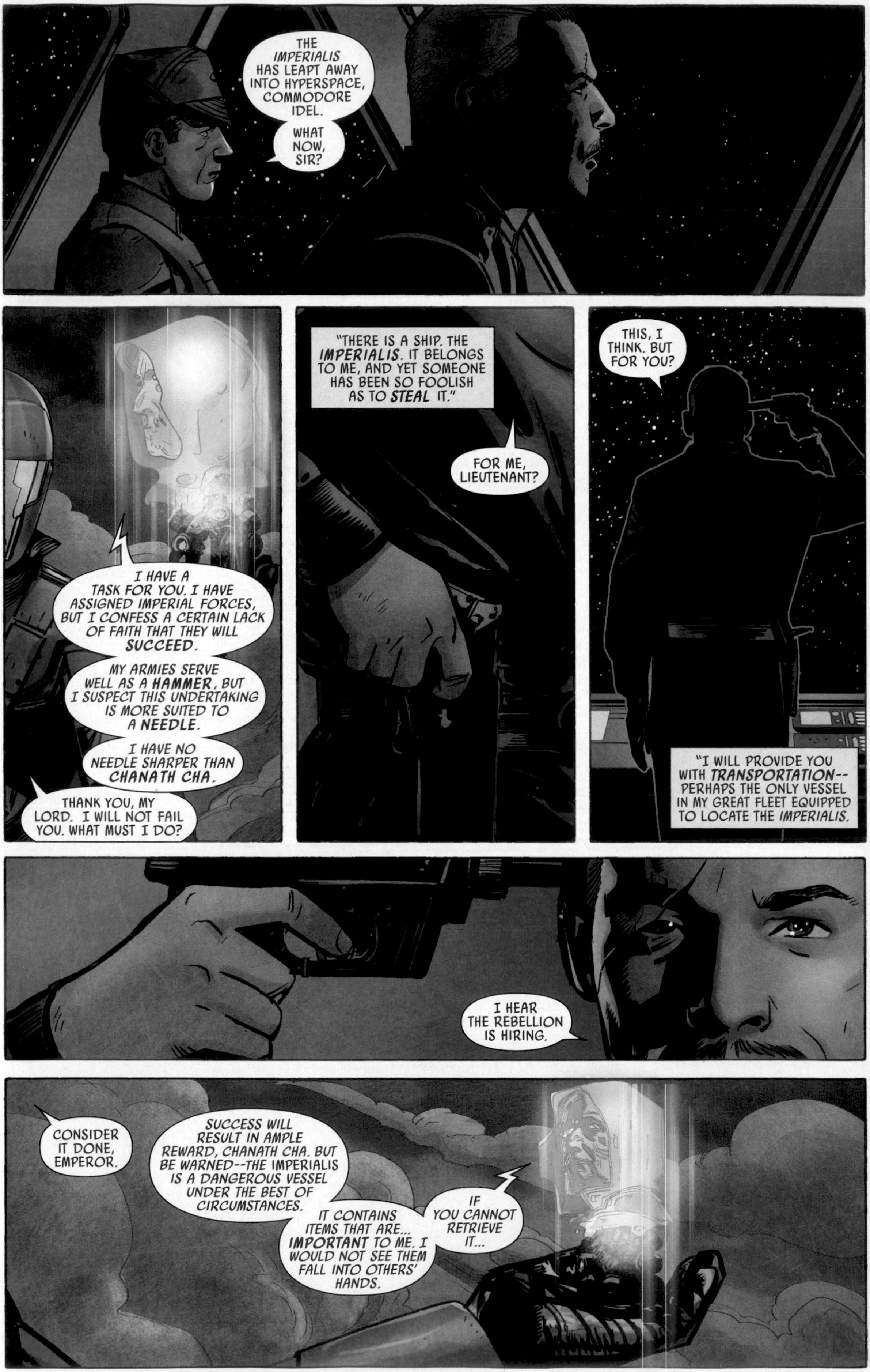
THE IMPERIALIS HAS LEAPT AWAY INTO HYPERSPACE, COMMODORE IDEL.
WHAT NOW, SIR?
I HAVE A TASK FOR YOU. I HAVE ASSIGNED IMPERIAL FORCES, BUT I CONFESS A CERTAIN LACK OF FAITH THAT THEY WILL SUCCEED.
MY ARMIES SERVE WELL AS A HAMMER, BUT I SUSPECT THIS UNDERTAKING IS MORE SUITED TO A NEEDLE.
I HAVE NO NEEDLE SHARPER THAN CHANATH CHA.
THANK YOU, MY LORD. I WILL NOT FAIL YOU. WHAT MUST I DO?
"THERE IS A SHIP. THE IMPERIALIS. IT BELONGS TO ME, AND YET SOMEONE HAS BEEN SO FOOLISH AS TO STEAL IT."
FOR ME, LIEUTENANT?
THIS, I THINK. BUT FOR YOU?
"I WILL PROVIDE YOU WITH TRANSPORTATION--PERHAPS THE ONLY VESSEL IN MY GREAT FLEET EQUIPPED TO LOCATE THE IMPERIALIS.
I HEAR THE REBELLION IS HIRING.
CONSIDER IT DONE, EMPEROR.
SUCCESS WILL RESULT IN AMPLE REWARD, CHANATH CHA. BUT BE WARNED--THE IMPERIALIS IS A DANGEROUS VESSEL UNDER THE BEST OF CIRCUMSTANCES.
IT CONTAINS ITEMS THAT ARE... IMPORTANT TO ME. I WOULD NOT SEE THEM FALL INTO OTHERS' HANDS.
IF YOU CANNOT RETRIEVE IT...

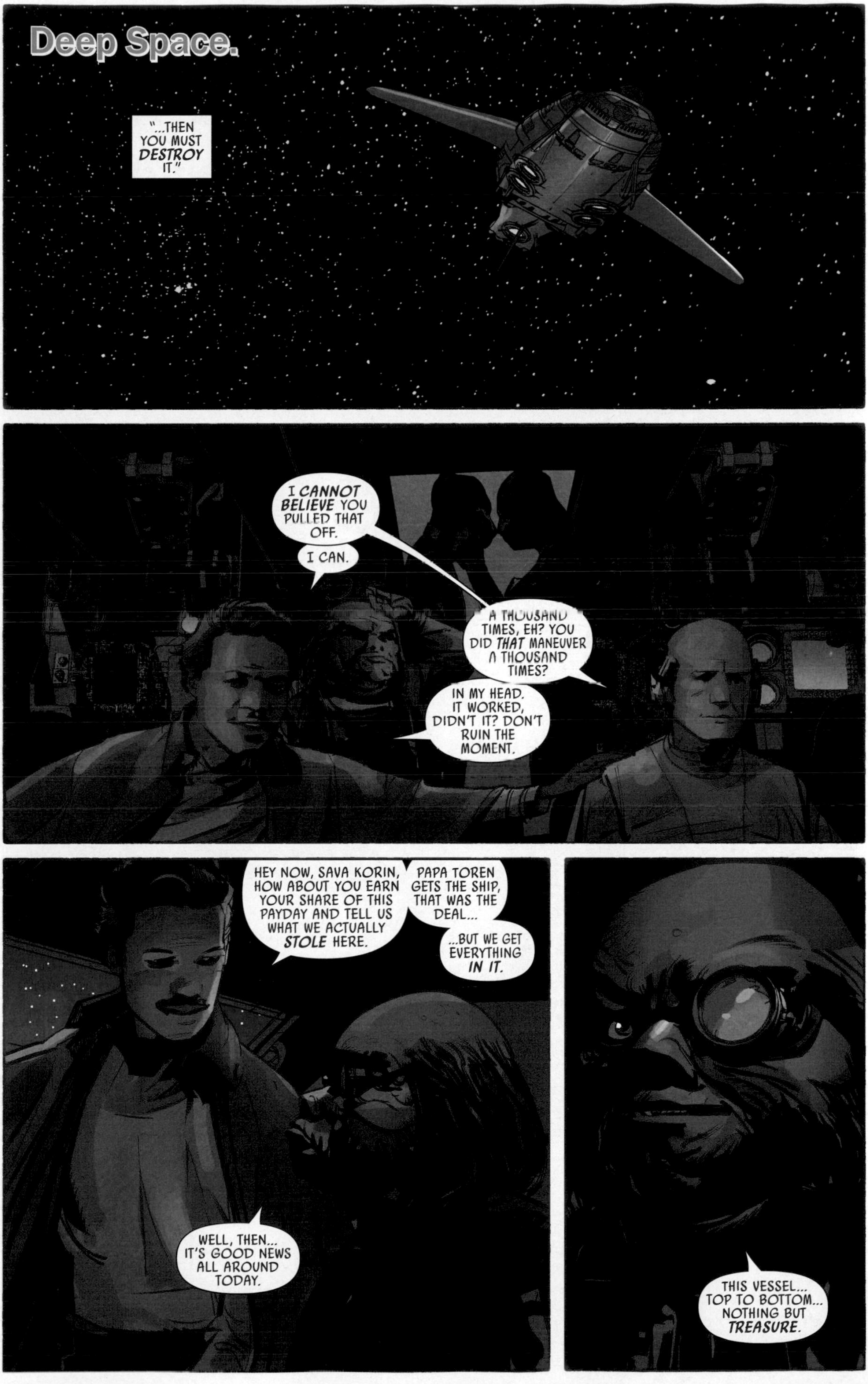
Deep Space.
"...THEN YOU MUST DESTROY IT."
I CANNOT BELIEVE YOU PULLED THAT OFF.
I CAN.
A THOUSAND TIMES, EH? YOU DID THAT MANEUVER A THOUSAND TIMES?
IN MY HEAD. IT WORKED, DIDN'T IT? DON'T RUIN THE MOMENT.
HEY NOW, SAVA KORIN, HOW ABOUT YOU EARN YOUR SHARE OF THIS PAYDAY AND TELL US WHAT WE ACTUALLY STOLE HERE.
PAPA TOREN GETS THE SHIP, THAT WAS THE DEAL...
...BUT WE GET EVERYTHING IN IT.
WELL, THEN... IT'S GOOD NEWS ALL AROUND TODAY.
THIS VESSEL... TOP TO BOTTOM... NOTHING BUT TREASURE.

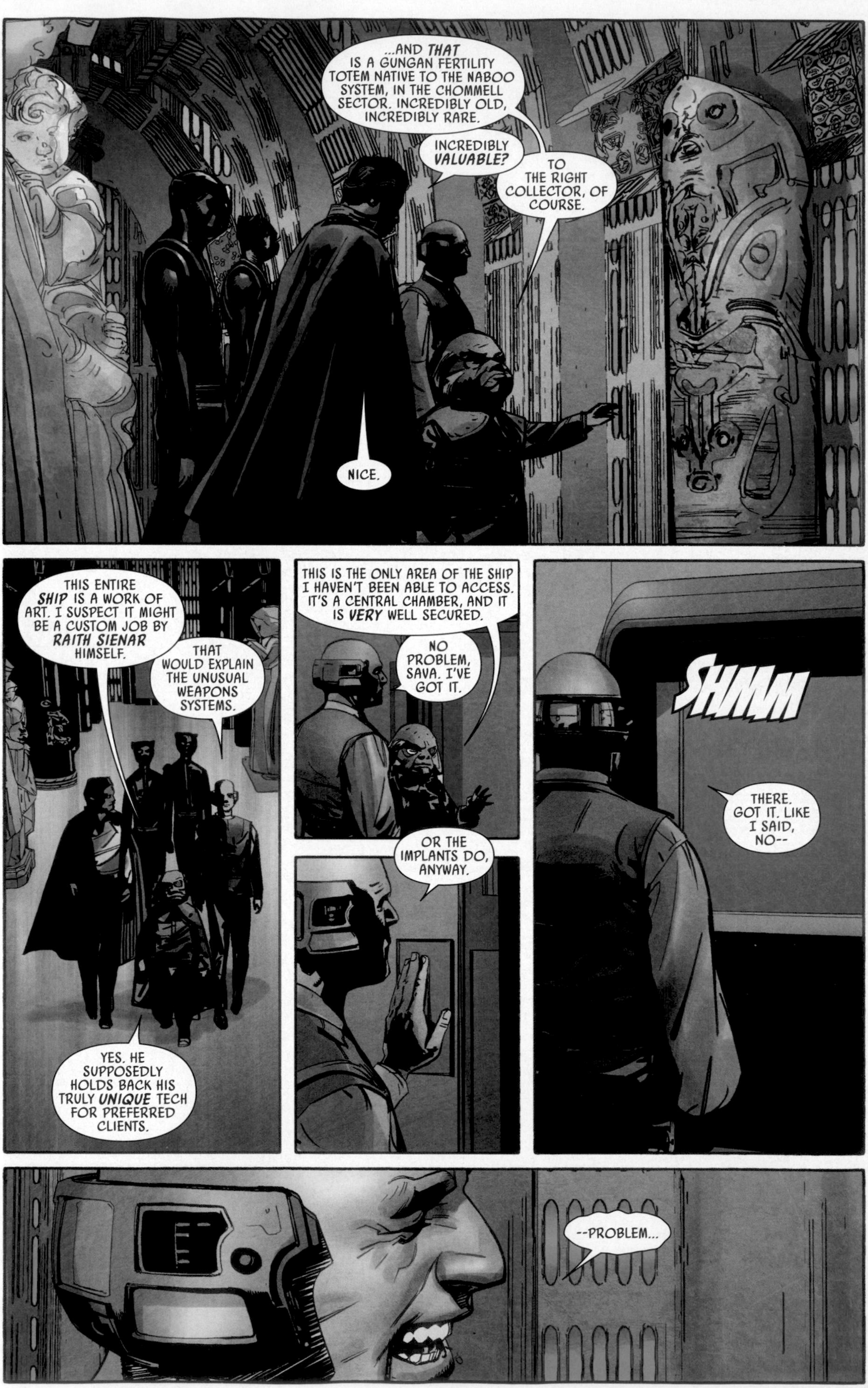
...AND THAT IS A GUNGAN FERTILITY TOTEM NATIVE TO THE NABOO SYSTEM, IN THE CHOMMELL SECTOR. INCREDIBLY OLD, INCREDIBLY RARE.
INCREDIBLY VALUABLE?
TO THE RIGHT COLLECTOR, OF COURSE.
NICE.
THIS ENTIRE SHIP IS A WORK OF ART. I SUSPECT IT MIGHT BE A CUSTOM JOB BY RAITH SIENAR HIMSELF.
THAT WOULD EXPLAIN THE UNUSUAL WEAPONS SYSTEMS.
YES. HE SUPPOSEDLY HOLDS BACK HIS TRULY UNIQUE TECH FOR PREFERRED CLIENTS.
THIS IS THE ONLY AREA OF THE SHIP I HAVEN'T BEEN ABLE TO ACCESS. IT'S A CENTRAL CHAMBER, AND IT IS VERY WELL SECURED.
NO PROBLEM, SAVA. I'VE GOT IT.
OR THE IMPLANTS DO, ANYWAY.
SHMM
THERE. GOT IT. LIKE I SAID, NO--
--PROBLEM...

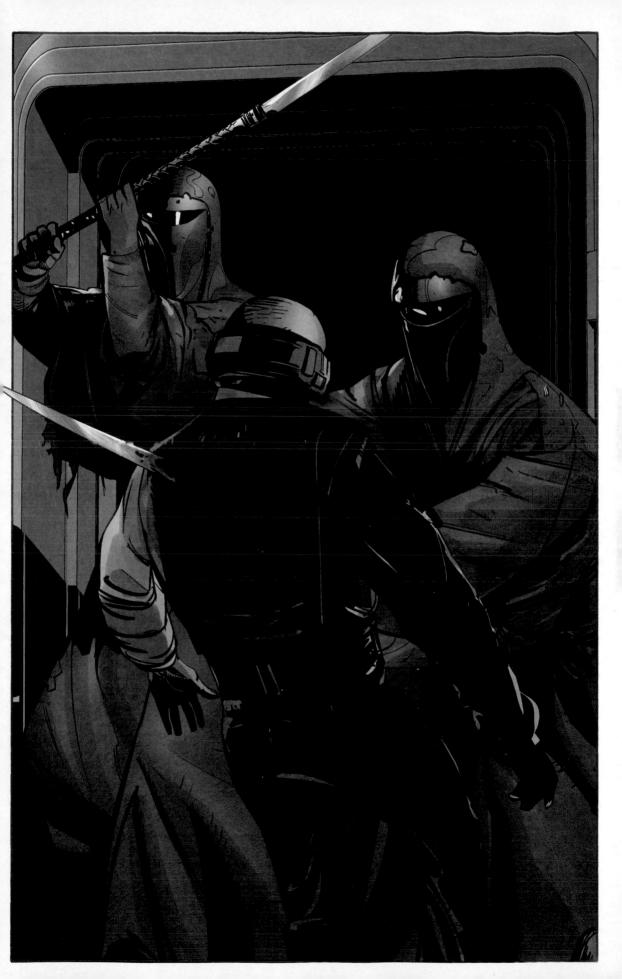

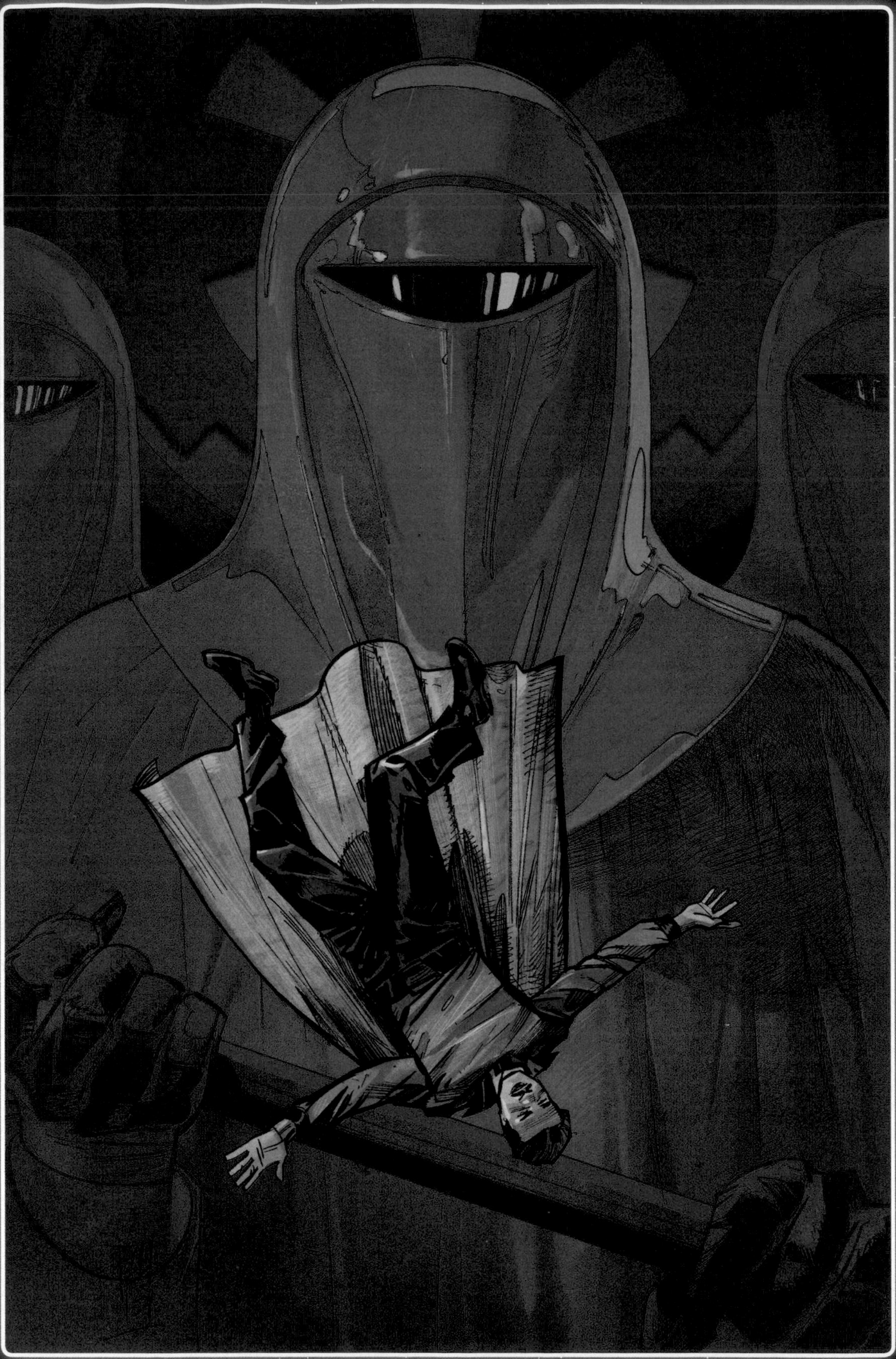

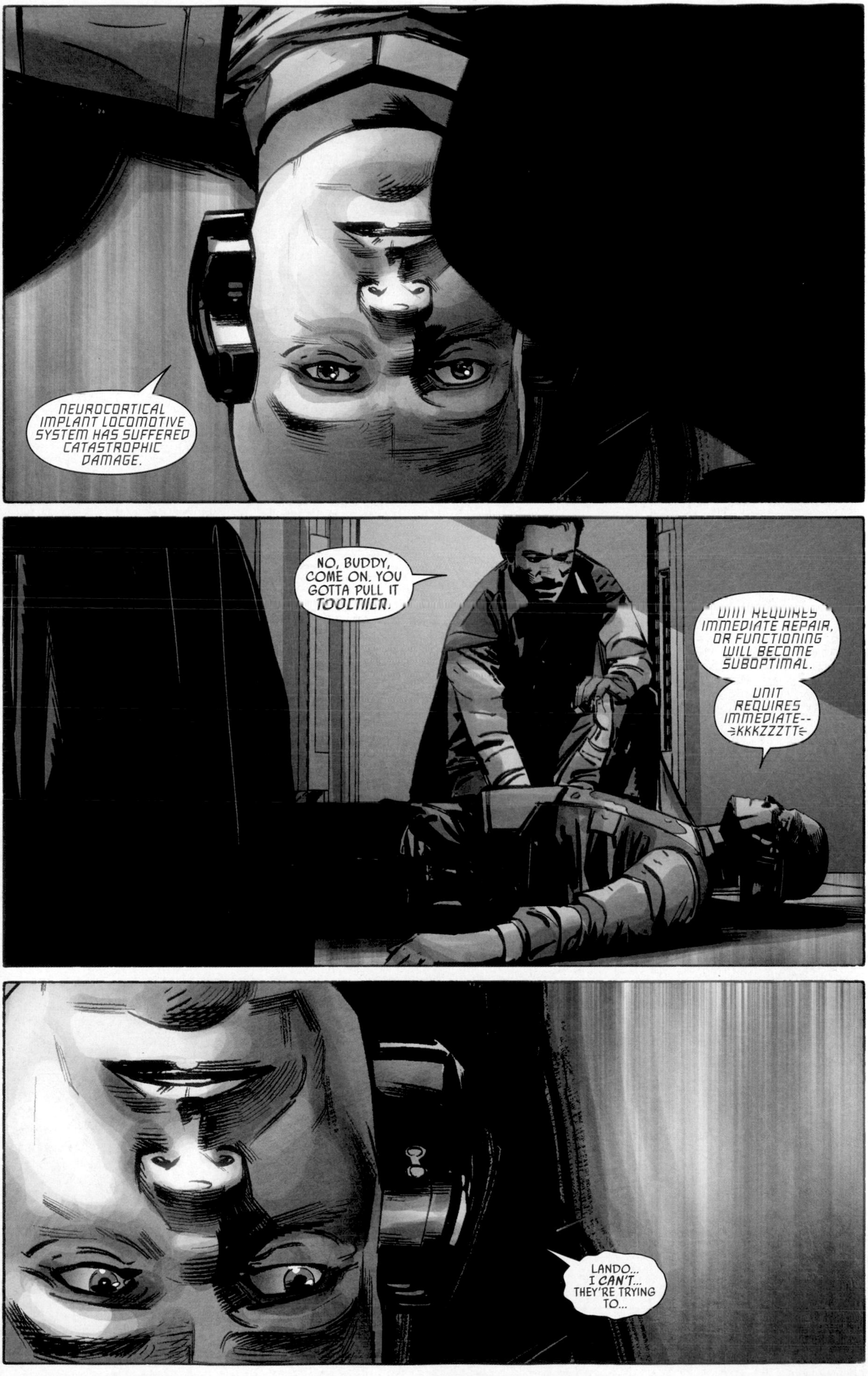
NEUROCORTICAL IMPLANT LOCOMOTIVE SYSTEM HAS SUFFERED CATASTROPHIC DAMAGE.
NO, BUDDY, COME ON. YOU GOTTA PULL IT TOGETHER.
UNIT REQUIRES IMMEDIATE REPAIR, OR FUNCTIONING WILL BECOME SUBOPTIMAL.
UNIT REQUIRES IMMEDIATE-- ⇒KKKZZZTT⇐
LANDO... I CAN'T... THEY'RE TRYING TO...

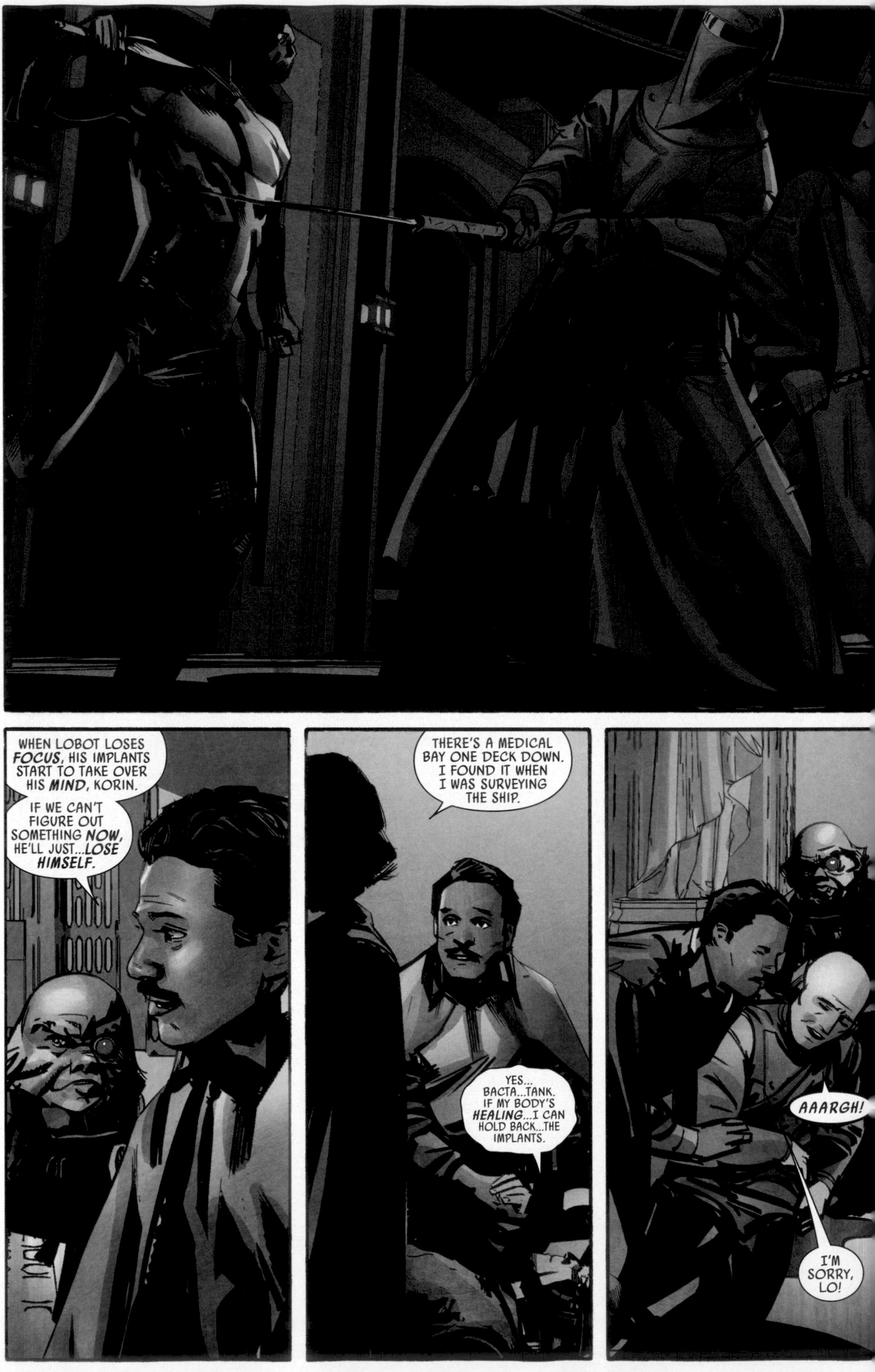
WHEN LOBOT LOSES FOCUS, HIS IMPLANTS START TO TAKE OVER HIS MIND, KORIN.
IF WE CAN'T FIGURE OUT SOMETHING NOW, HE'LL JUST...LOSE HIMSELF.
THERE'S A MEDICAL BAY ONE DECK DOWN. I FOUND IT WHEN I WAS SURVEYING THE SHIP.
YES... BACTA...TANK. IF MY BODY'S HEALING...I CAN HOLD BACK...THE IMPLANTS.
AAARGH!
I'M SORRY, LO!

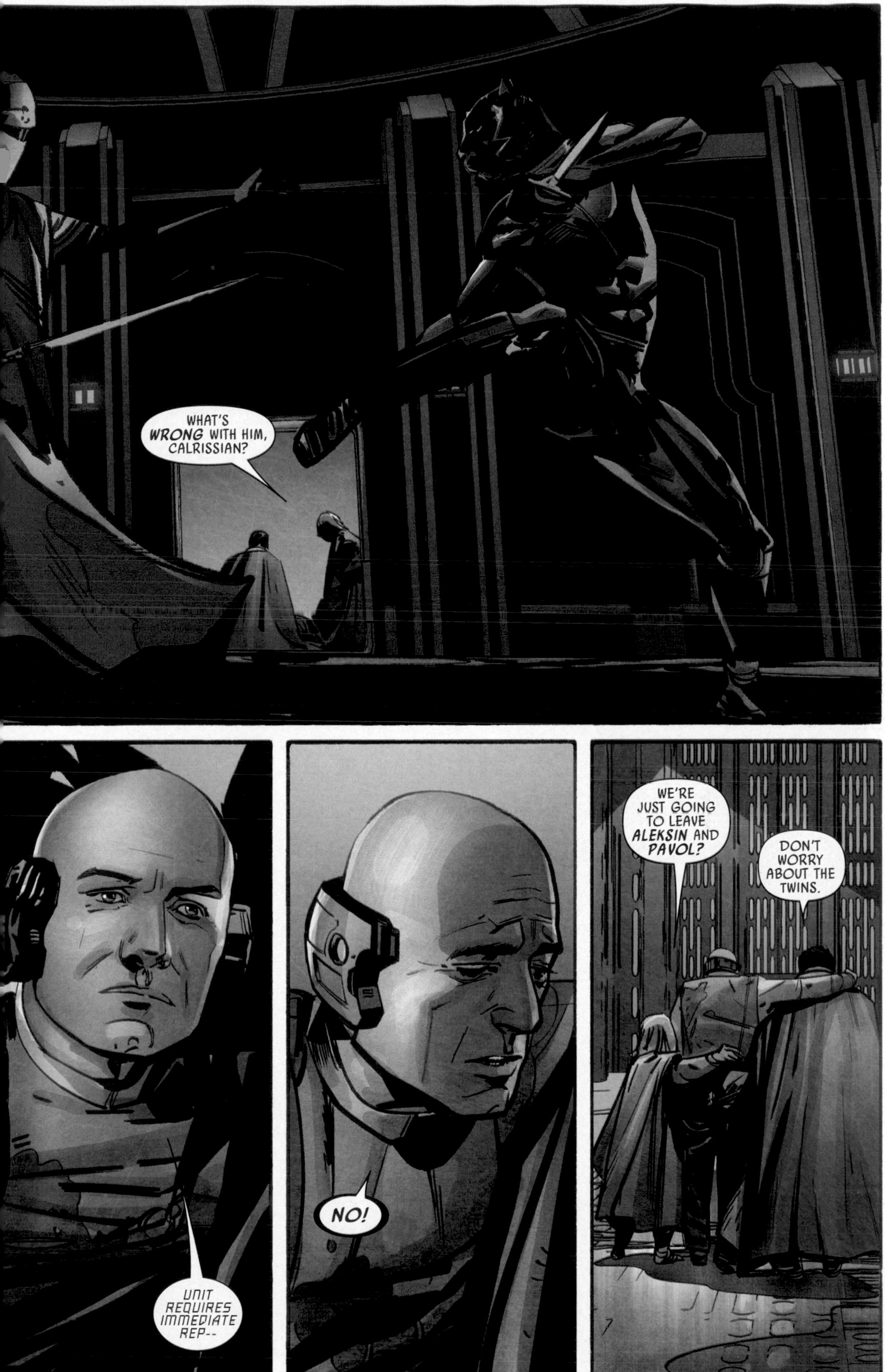
WHAT'S WRONG WITH HIM, CALRISSIAN?
UNIT REQUIRES IMMEDIATE REP--
NO!
WE'RE JUST GOING TO LEAVE ALEKSIN AND PAVOL?
DON'T WORRY ABOUT THE TWINS.

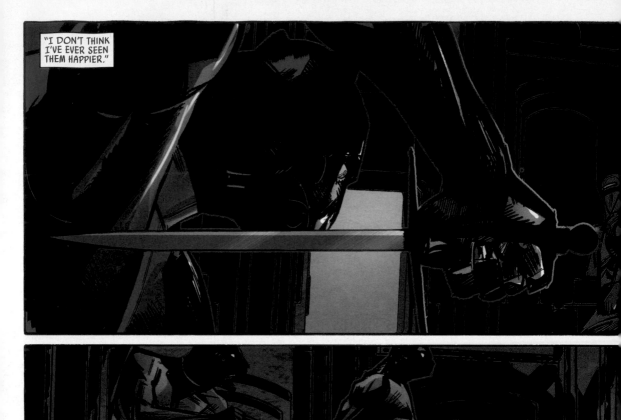

"I DON'T THINK I'VE EVER SEEN THEM HAPPIER."

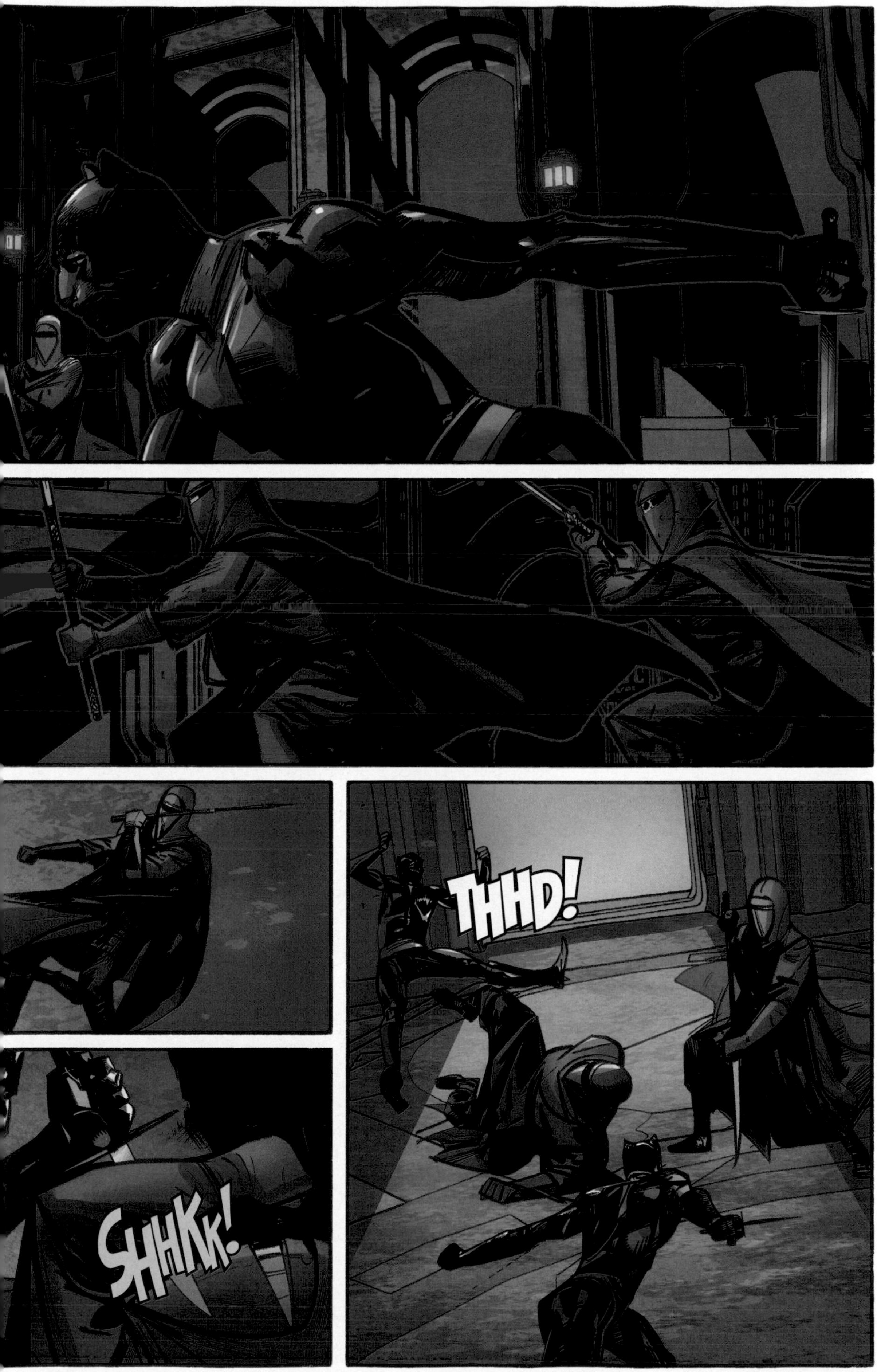
THHD!
SHHKK!

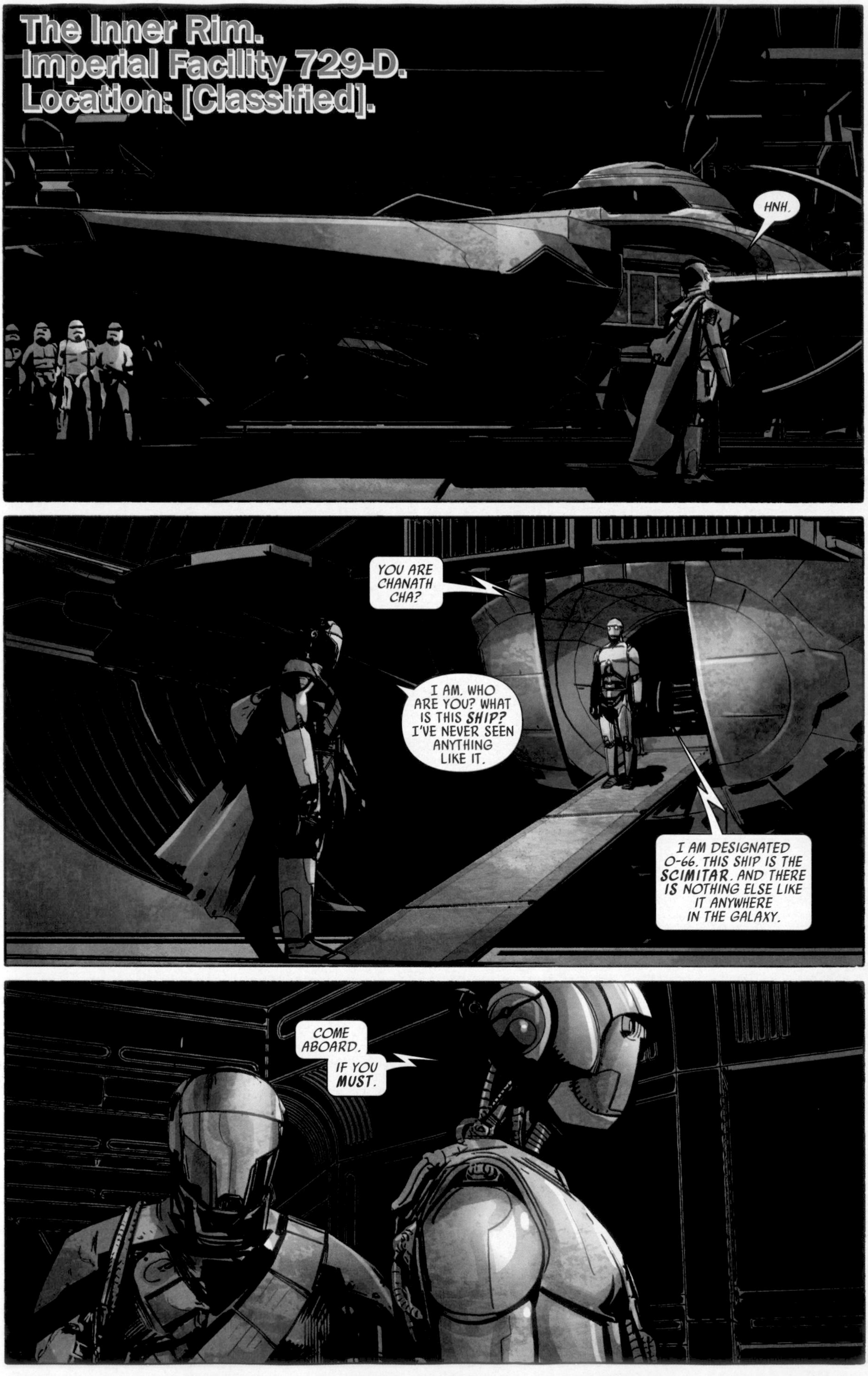
The Inner Rim.
Imperial Facility 729-D.
Location: [Classified].
HNH.
YOU ARE CHANATH CHA?
I AM. WHO ARE YOU? WHAT IS THIS SHIP? I'VE NEVER SEEN ANYTHING LIKE IT.
I AM DESIGNATED 0-66. THIS SHIP IS THE SCIMITAR. AND THERE IS NOTHING ELSE LIKE IT ANYWHERE IN THE GALAXY.
COME ABOARD.
IF YOU MUST.

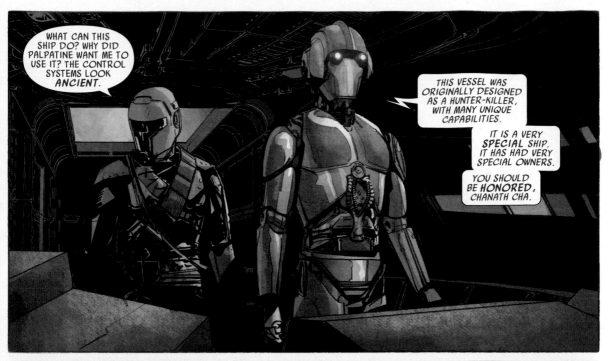

WHAT CAN THIS SHIP DO? WHY DID PALPATINE WANT ME TO USE IT? THE CONTROL SYSTEMS LOOK *ANCIENT.*

THIS VESSEL WAS ORIGINALLY DESIGNED AS A HUNTER-KILLER, WITH MANY UNIQUE CAPABILITIES.

IT IS A VERY *SPECIAL* SHIP. IT HAS HAD VERY SPECIAL OWNERS.

YOU SHOULD BE *HONORED,* CHANATH CHA.

OH, I AM. BELIEVE ME. TELL ME ABOUT THESE *CAPABILITIES.* WHAT MAKES THIS SHIP SO SPECIAL?

TECHNICAL READOUTS ARE AVAILABLE IN DATABASES 18, 24 AND 756. THE GLORIOUS EMPEROR HAS INSTRUCTED ME TO PROVIDE YOU WITH ACCESS TO EVERY--

SUMMARIZE.

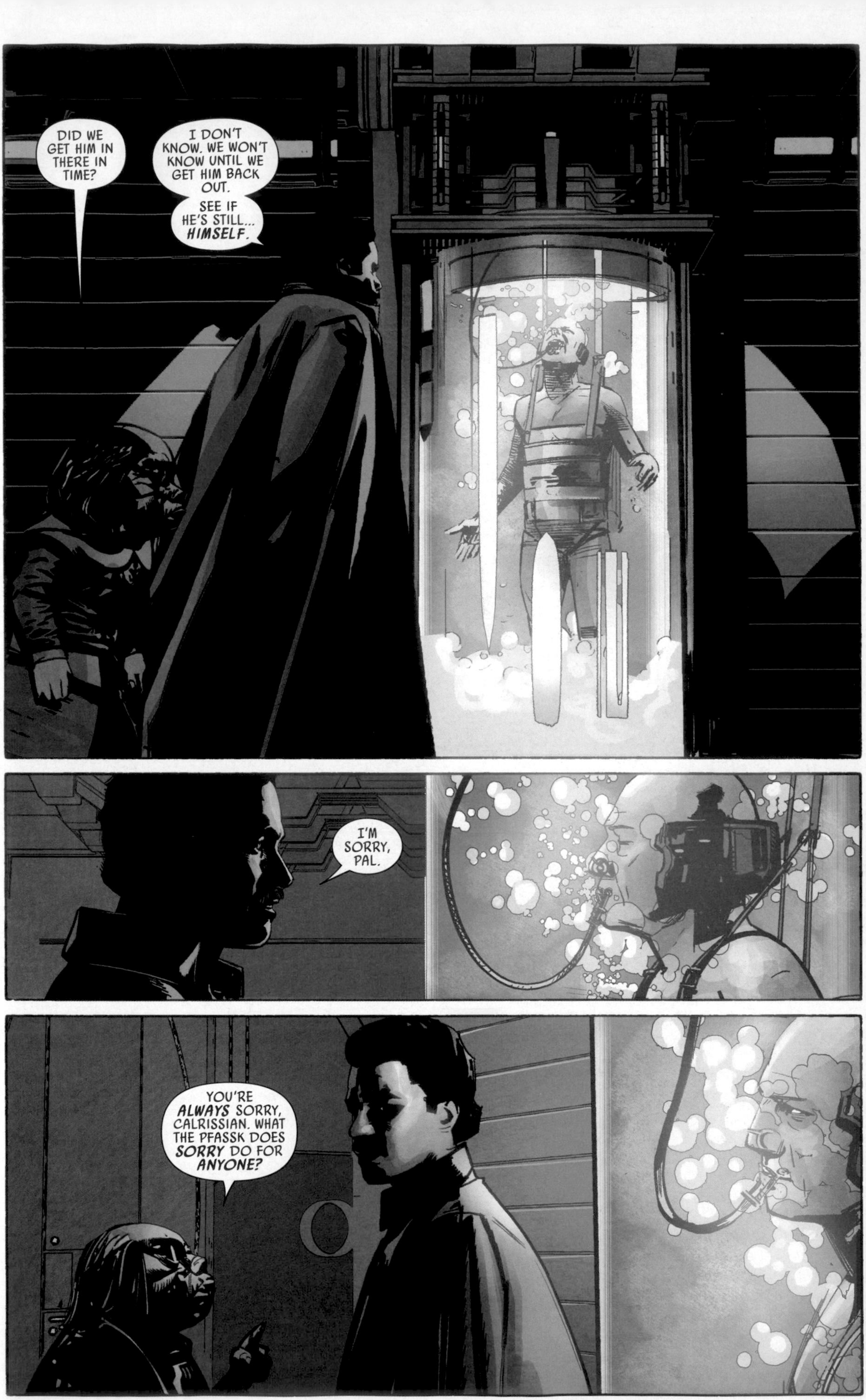

DID WE GET HIM IN THERE IN TIME?
I DON'T KNOW. WE WON'T KNOW UNTIL WE GET HIM BACK OUT.
SEE IF HE'S STILL... HIMSELF.
I'M SORRY, PAL.
YOU'RE ALWAYS SORRY, CALRISSIAN. WHAT THE PFASSK DOES SORRY DO FOR ANYONE?

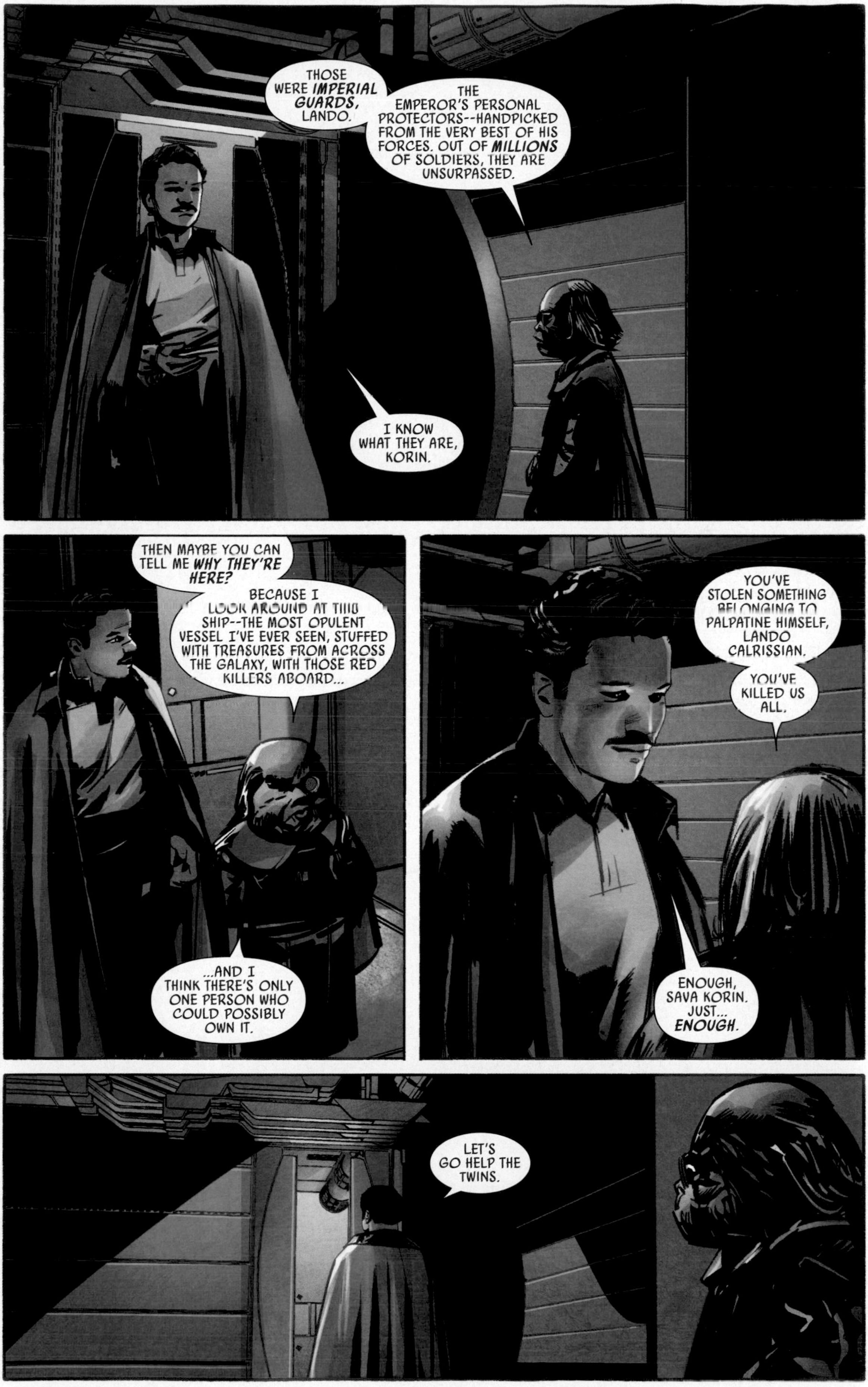
THOSE WERE IMPERIAL GUARDS, LANDO.
THE EMPEROR'S PERSONAL PROTECTORS--HANDPICKED FROM THE VERY BEST OF HIS FORCES. OUT OF MILLIONS OF SOLDIERS, THEY ARE UNSURPASSED.
I KNOW WHAT THEY ARE, KORIN.
THEN MAYBE YOU CAN TELL ME WHY THEY'RE HERE?
BECAUSE I LOOK AROUND AT THIS SHIP--THE MOST OPULENT VESSEL I'VE EVER SEEN, STUFFED WITH TREASURES FROM ACROSS THE GALAXY, WITH THOSE RED KILLERS ABOARD...
...AND I THINK THERE'S ONLY ONE PERSON WHO COULD POSSIBLY OWN IT.
YOU'VE STOLEN SOMETHING BELONGING TO PALPATINE HIMSELF, LANDO CALRISSIAN.
YOU'VE KILLED US ALL.
ENOUGH, SAVA KORIN. JUST... ENOUGH.
LET'S GO HELP THE TWINS.

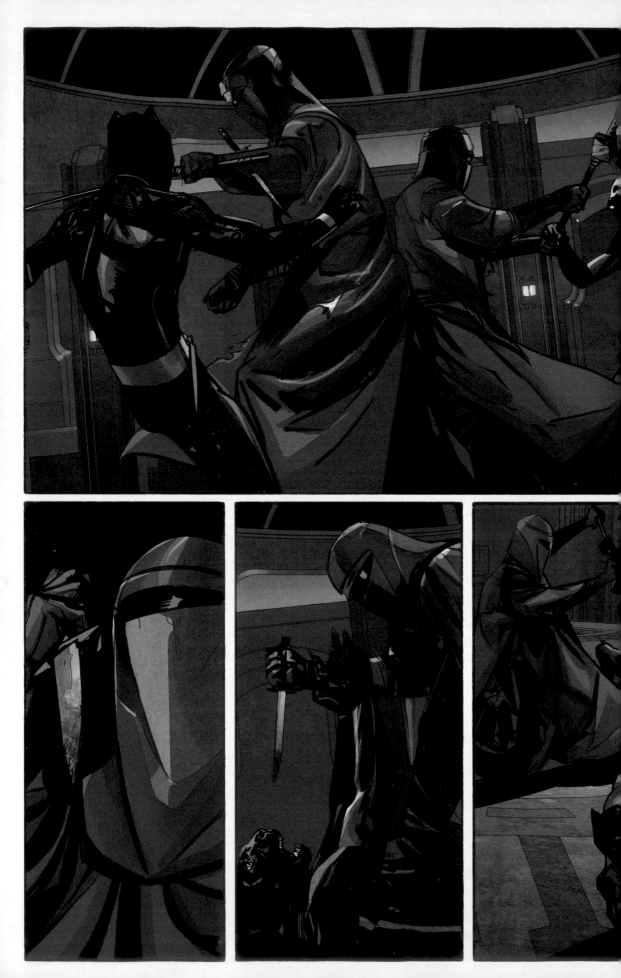

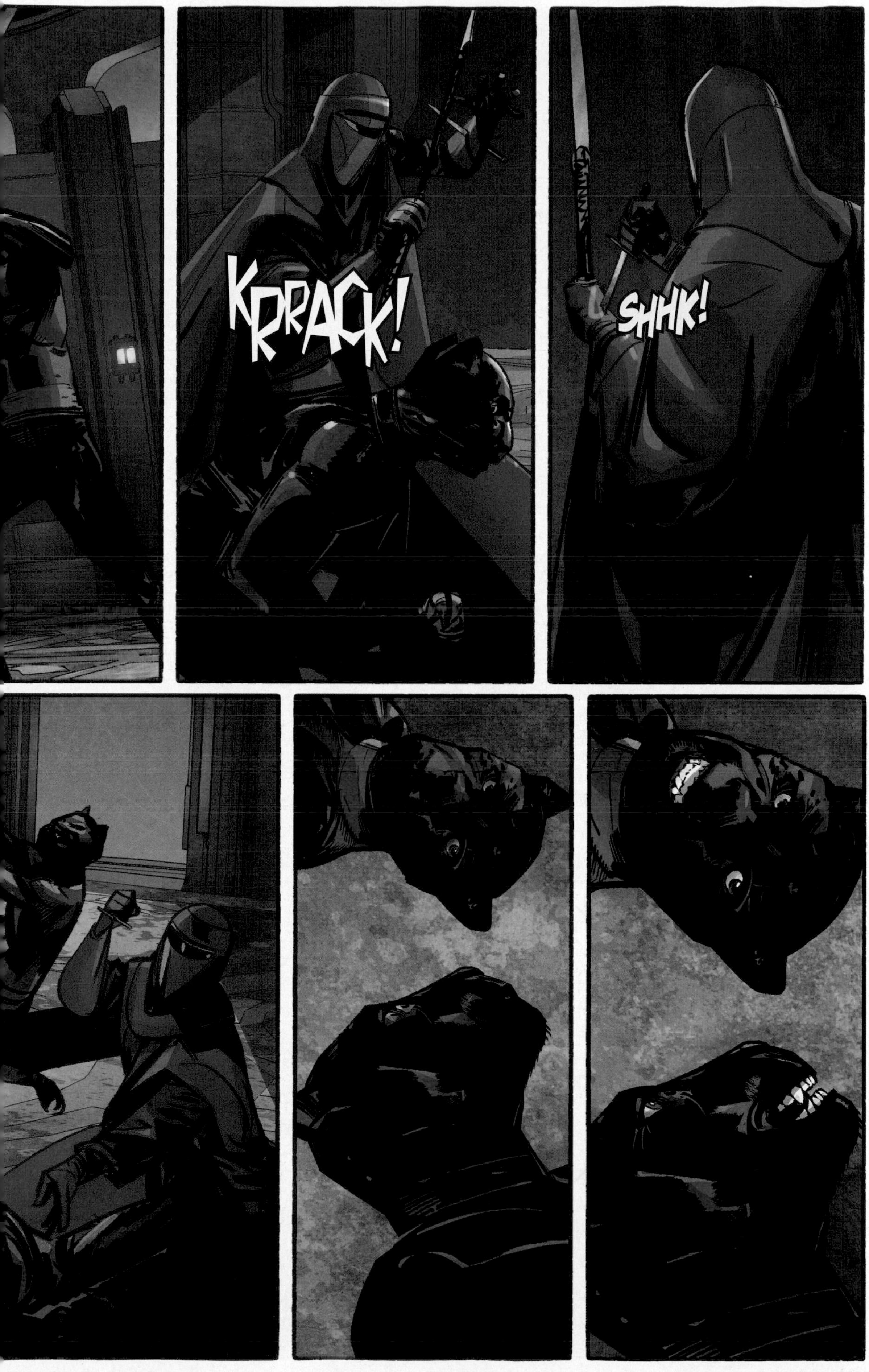
KRRACK!
SHHK!

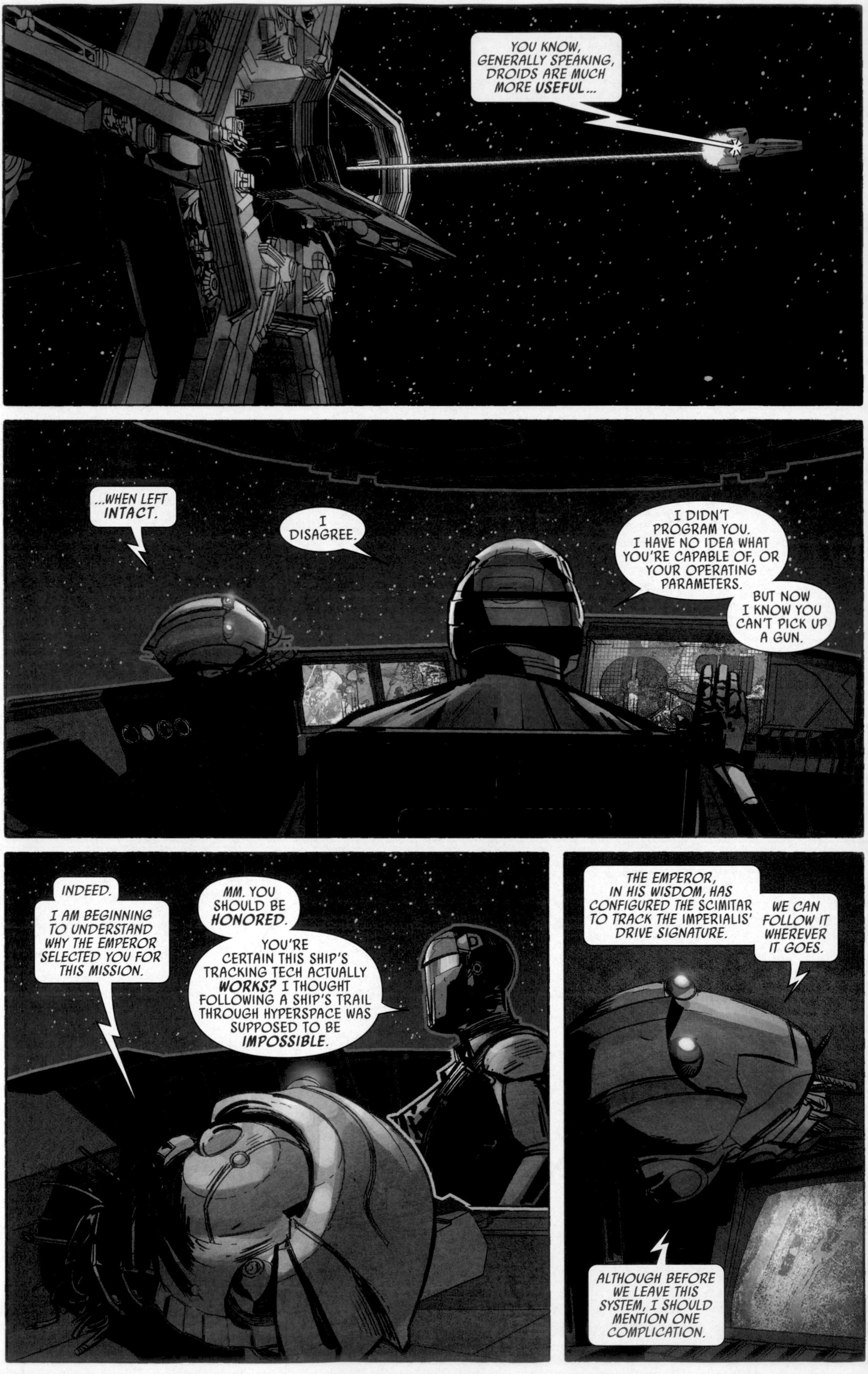

YOU KNOW, GENERALLY SPEAKING, DROIDS ARE MUCH MORE USEFUL...
...WHEN LEFT INTACT.
I DISAGREE.
I DIDN'T PROGRAM YOU. I HAVE NO IDEA WHAT YOU'RE CAPABLE OF, OR YOUR OPERATING PARAMETERS.
BUT NOW I KNOW YOU CAN'T PICK UP A GUN.
INDEED.
I AM BEGINNING TO UNDERSTAND WHY THE EMPEROR SELECTED YOU FOR THIS MISSION.
MM. YOU SHOULD BE HONORED.
YOU'RE CERTAIN THIS SHIP'S TRACKING TECH ACTUALLY WORKS? I THOUGHT FOLLOWING A SHIP'S TRAIL THROUGH HYPERSPACE WAS SUPPOSED TO BE IMPOSSIBLE.
THE EMPEROR, IN HIS WISDOM, HAS CONFIGURED THE SCIMITAR TO TRACK THE IMPERIALIS' DRIVE SIGNATURE.
WE CAN FOLLOW IT WHEREVER IT GOES.
ALTHOUGH BEFORE WE LEAVE THIS SYSTEM, I SHOULD MENTION ONE COMPLICATION.

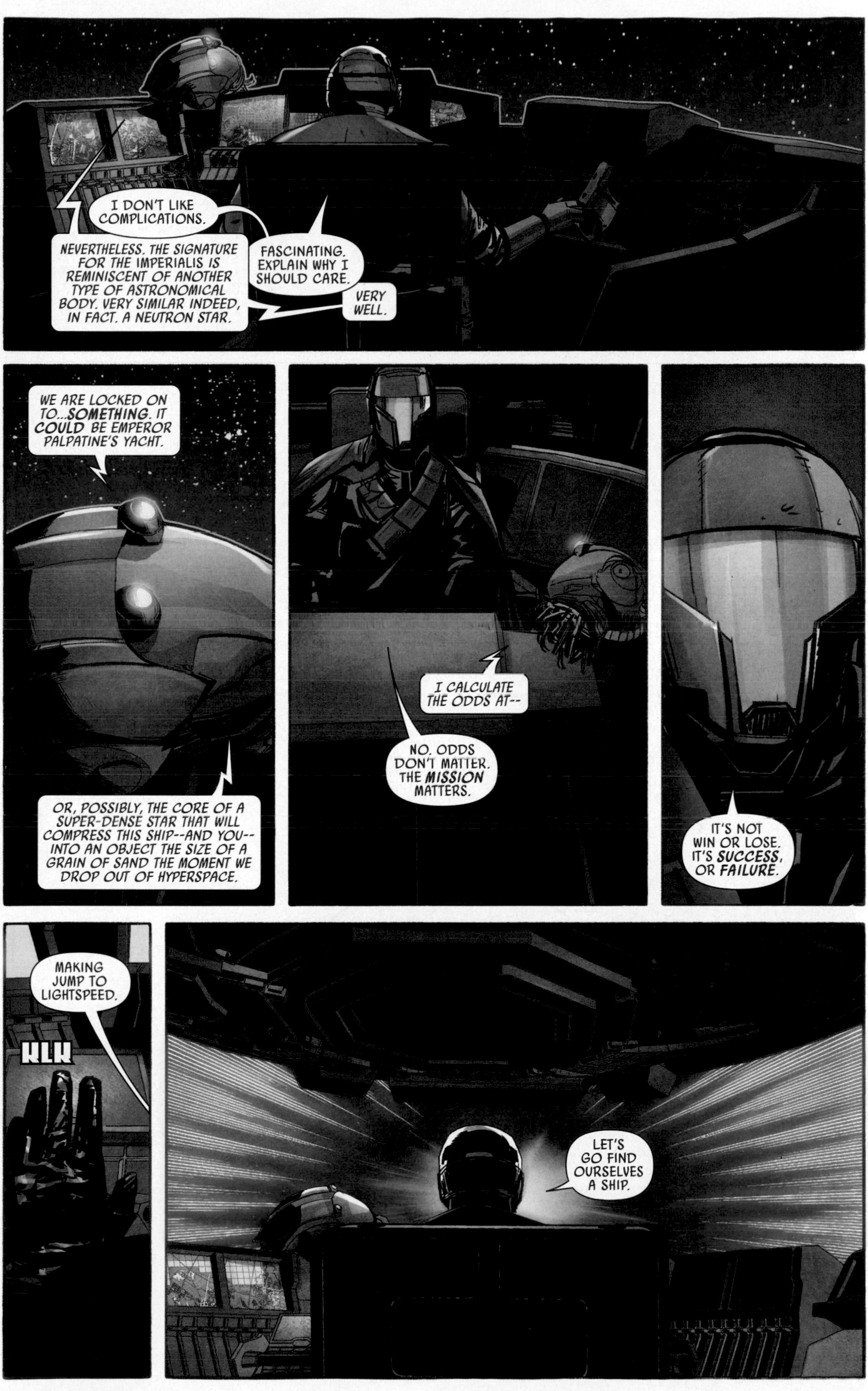
I DON'T LIKE COMPLICATIONS.
FASCINATING. EXPLAIN WHY I SHOULD CARE.
NEVERTHELESS. THE SIGNATURE FOR THE IMPERIALIS IS REMINISCENT OF ANOTHER TYPE OF ASTRONOMICAL BODY. VERY SIMILAR INDEED, IN FACT. A NEUTRON STAR.
VERY WELL.
WE ARE LOCKED ON TO...SOMETHING. IT COULD BE EMPEROR PALPATINE'S YACHT.
OR, POSSIBLY, THE CORE OF A SUPER-DENSE STAR THAT WILL COMPRESS THIS SHIP--AND YOU--INTO AN OBJECT THE SIZE OF A GRAIN OF SAND THE MOMENT WE DROP OUT OF HYPERSPACE.
I CALCULATE THE ODDS AT--
NO. ODDS DON'T MATTER. THE MISSION MATTERS.
IT'S NOT WIN OR LOSE. IT'S SUCCESS, OR FAILURE.
MAKING JUMP TO LIGHTSPEED.
KLK
LET'S GO FIND OURSELVES A SHIP.

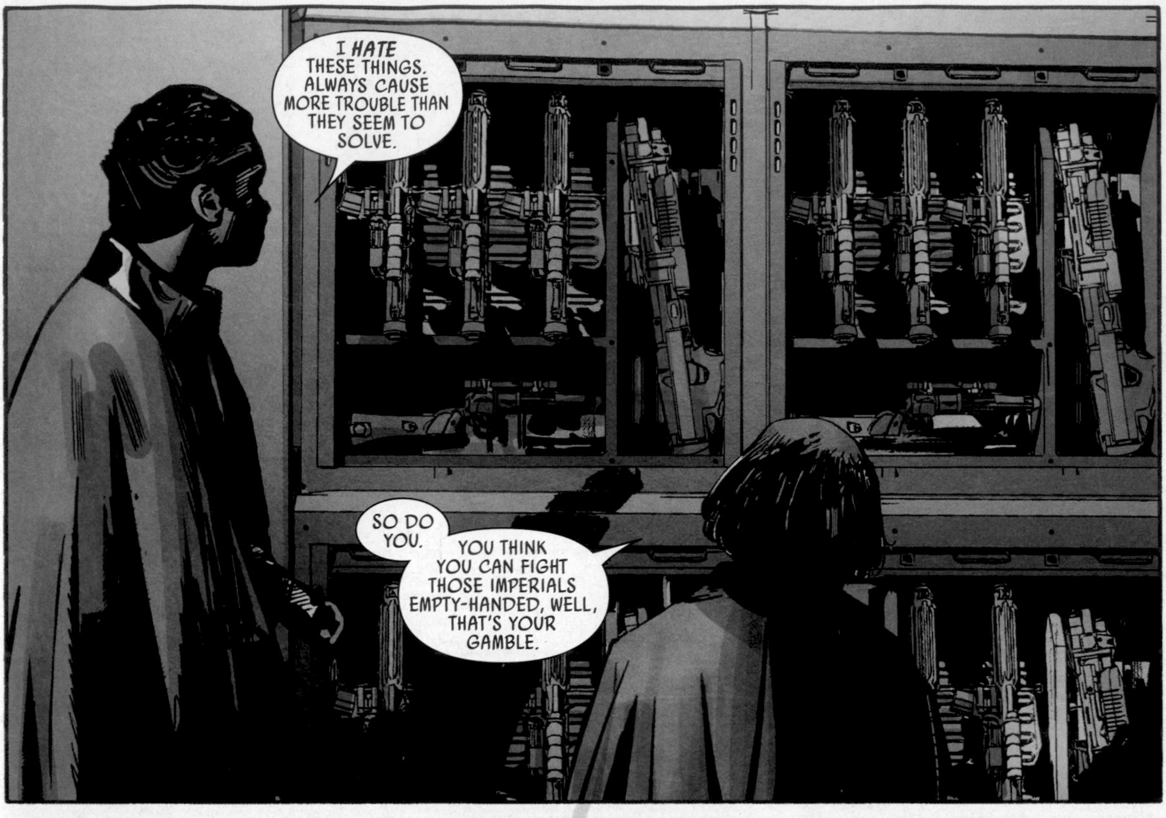
I *HATE* THESE THINGS. ALWAYS CAUSE MORE TROUBLE THAN THEY SEEM TO SOLVE.
SO DO YOU.
YOU THINK YOU CAN FIGHT THOSE IMPERIALS EMPTY-HANDED, WELL, THAT'S YOUR GAMBLE.

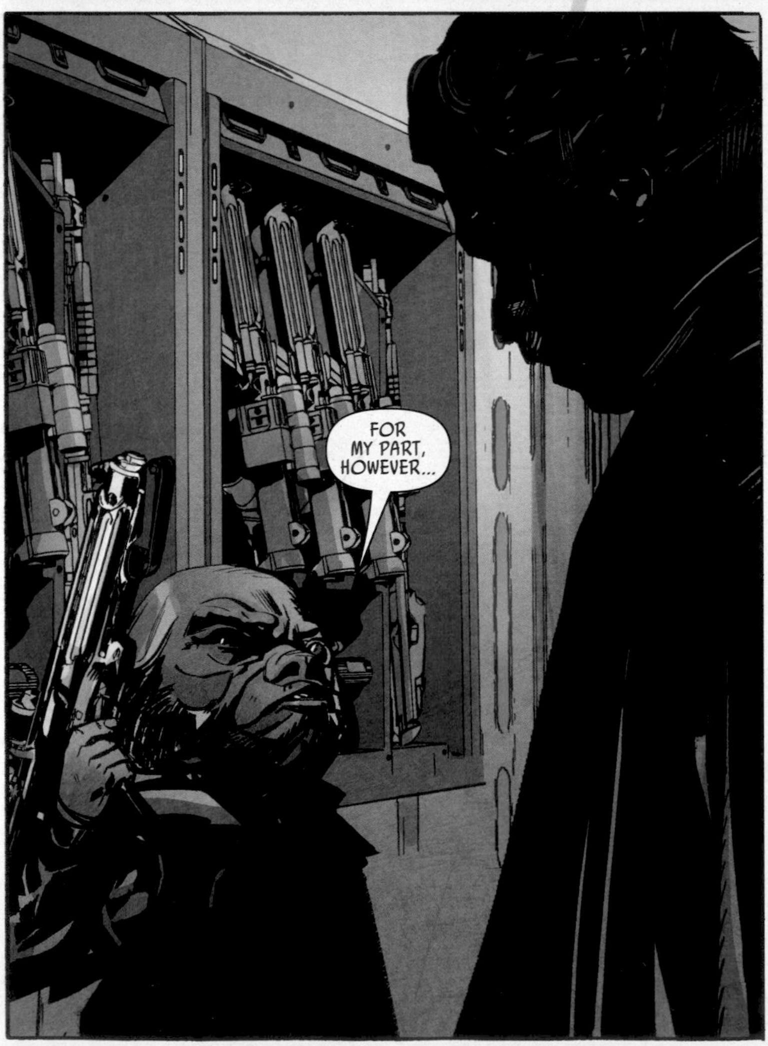
FOR MY PART, HOWEVER...

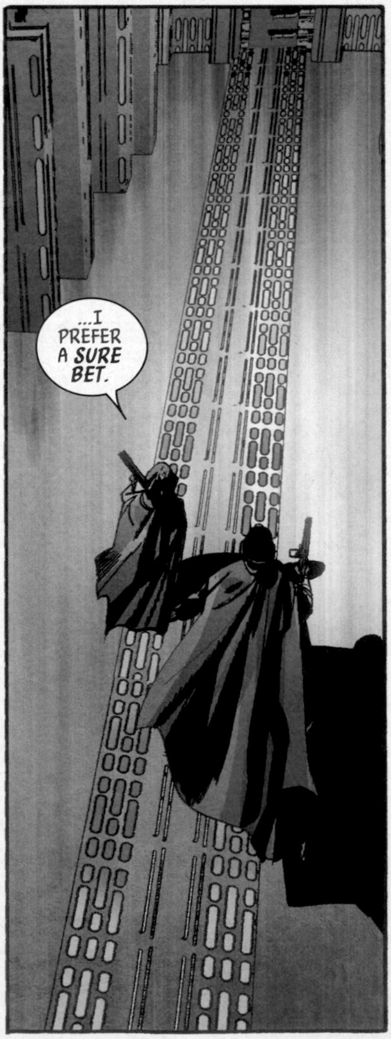
...I PREFER A *SURE BET*.

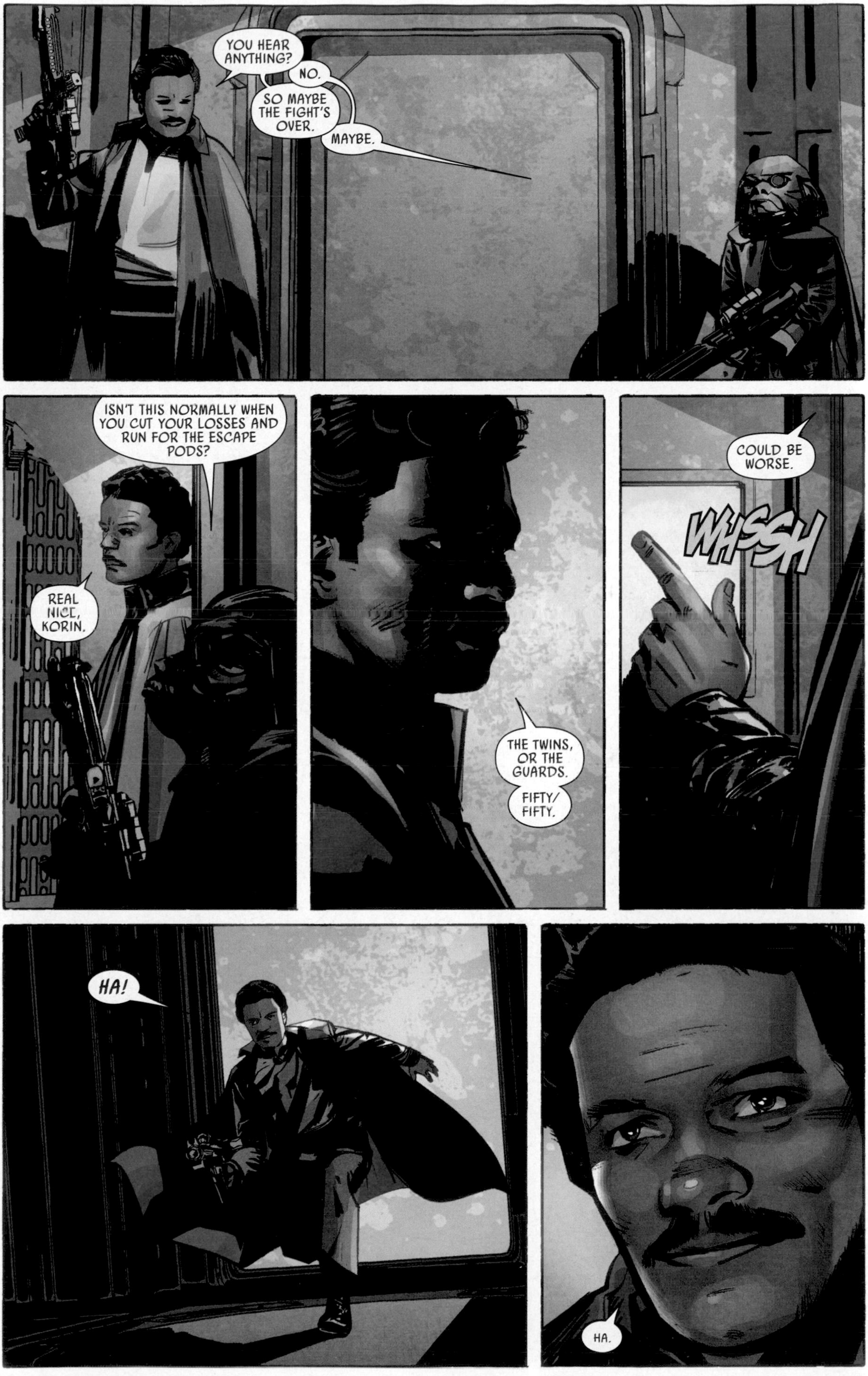
YOU HEAR ANYTHING?
NO.
SO MAYBE THE FIGHT'S OVER.
MAYBE.
ISN'T THIS NORMALLY WHEN YOU CUT YOUR LOSSES AND RUN FOR THE ESCAPE PODS?
REAL NICE, KORIN.
THE TWINS, OR THE GUARDS.
FIFTY/ FIFTY.
COULD BE WORSE.
WHSSH
HA!
HA.

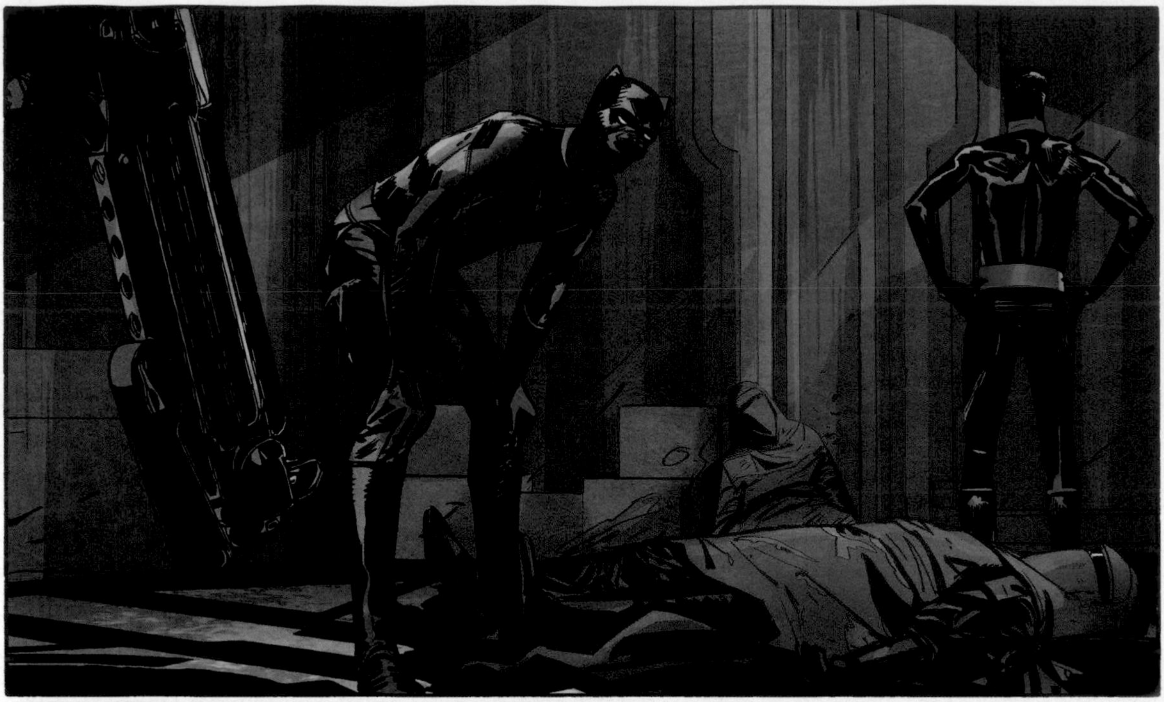

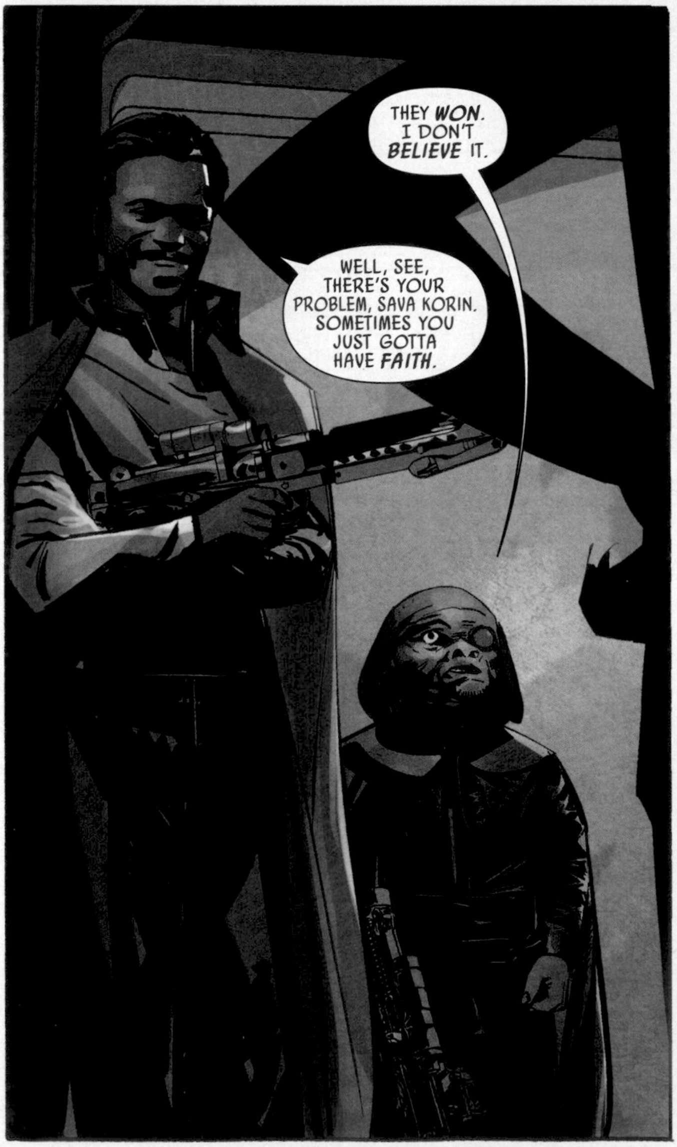
THEY WON. I DON'T BELIEVE IT.
WELL, SEE, THERE'S YOUR PROBLEM, SAVA KORIN. SOMETIMES YOU JUST GOTTA HAVE FAITH.

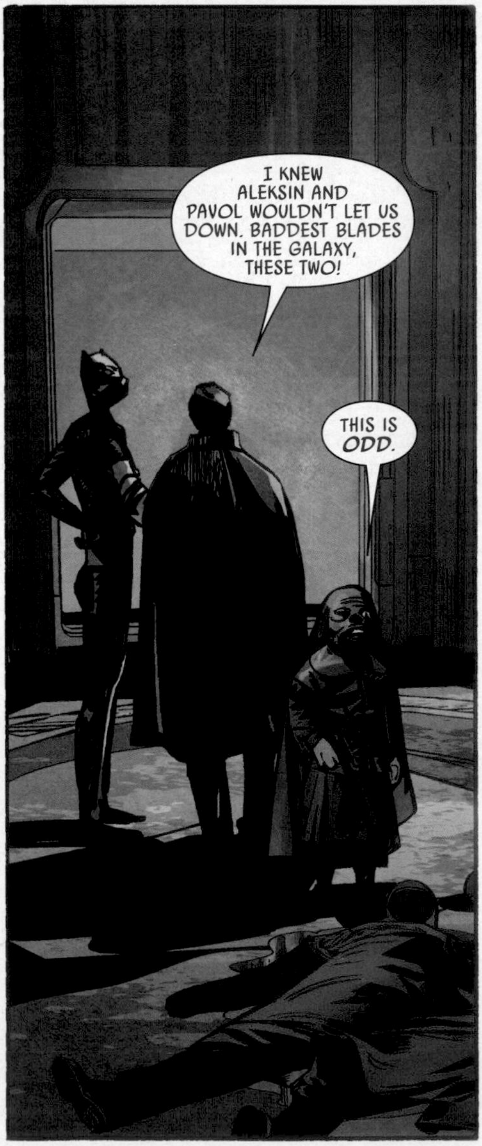
I KNEW ALEKSIN AND PAVOL WOULDN'T LET US DOWN. BADDEST BLADES IN THE GALAXY, THESE TWO!
THIS IS ODD.

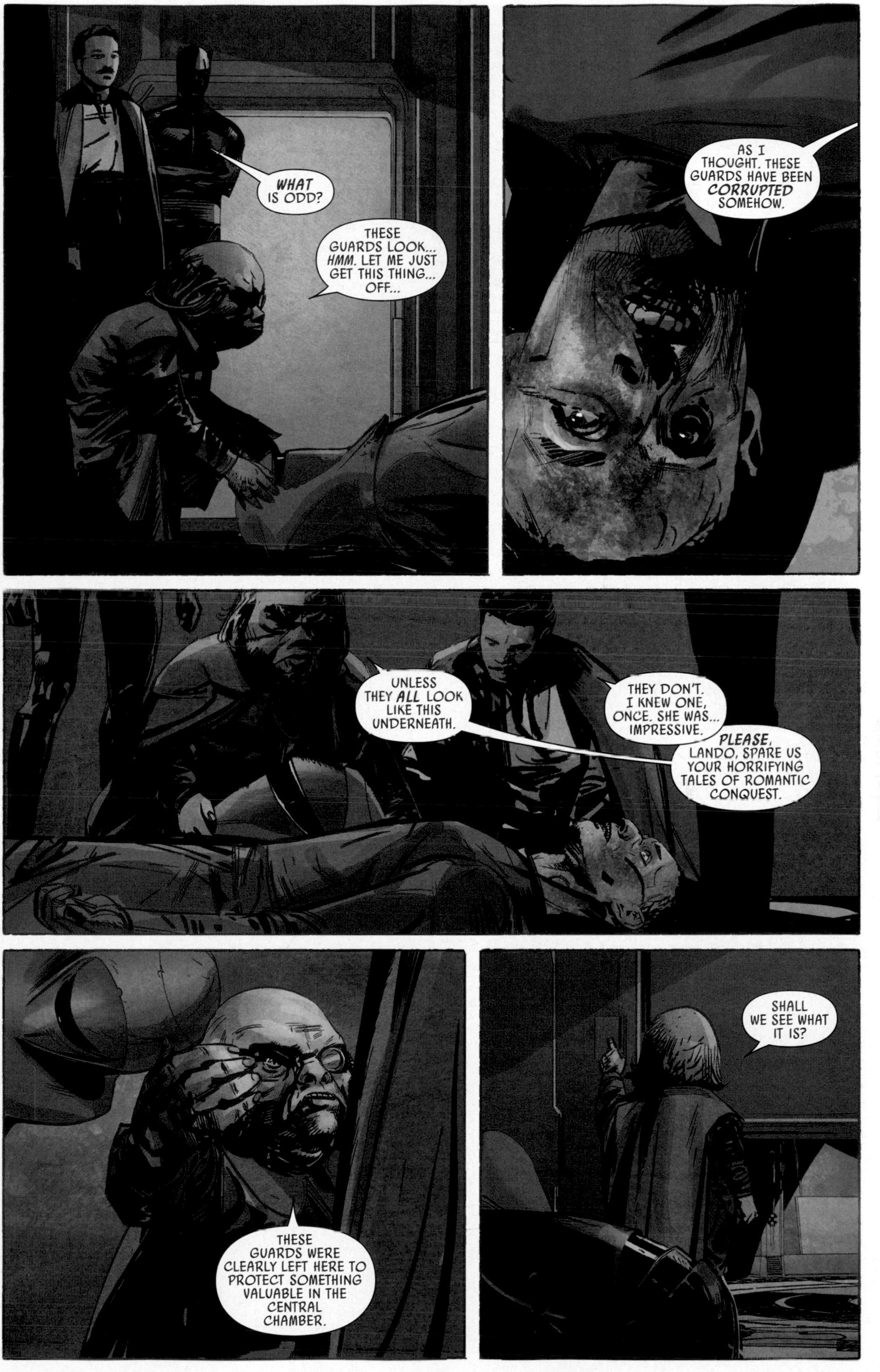
WHAT IS ODD?
THESE GUARDS LOOK... HMM. LET ME JUST GET THIS THING... OFF...
AS I THOUGHT. THESE GUARDS HAVE BEEN CORRUPTED SOMEHOW.
UNLESS THEY ALL LOOK LIKE THIS UNDERNEATH.
THEY DON'T. I KNEW ONE, ONCE. SHE WAS... IMPRESSIVE.
PLEASE, LANDO, SPARE US YOUR HORRIFYING TALES OF ROMANTIC CONQUEST.
THESE GUARDS WERE CLEARLY LEFT HERE TO PROTECT SOMETHING VALUABLE IN THE CENTRAL CHAMBER.
SHALL WE SEE WHAT IT IS?

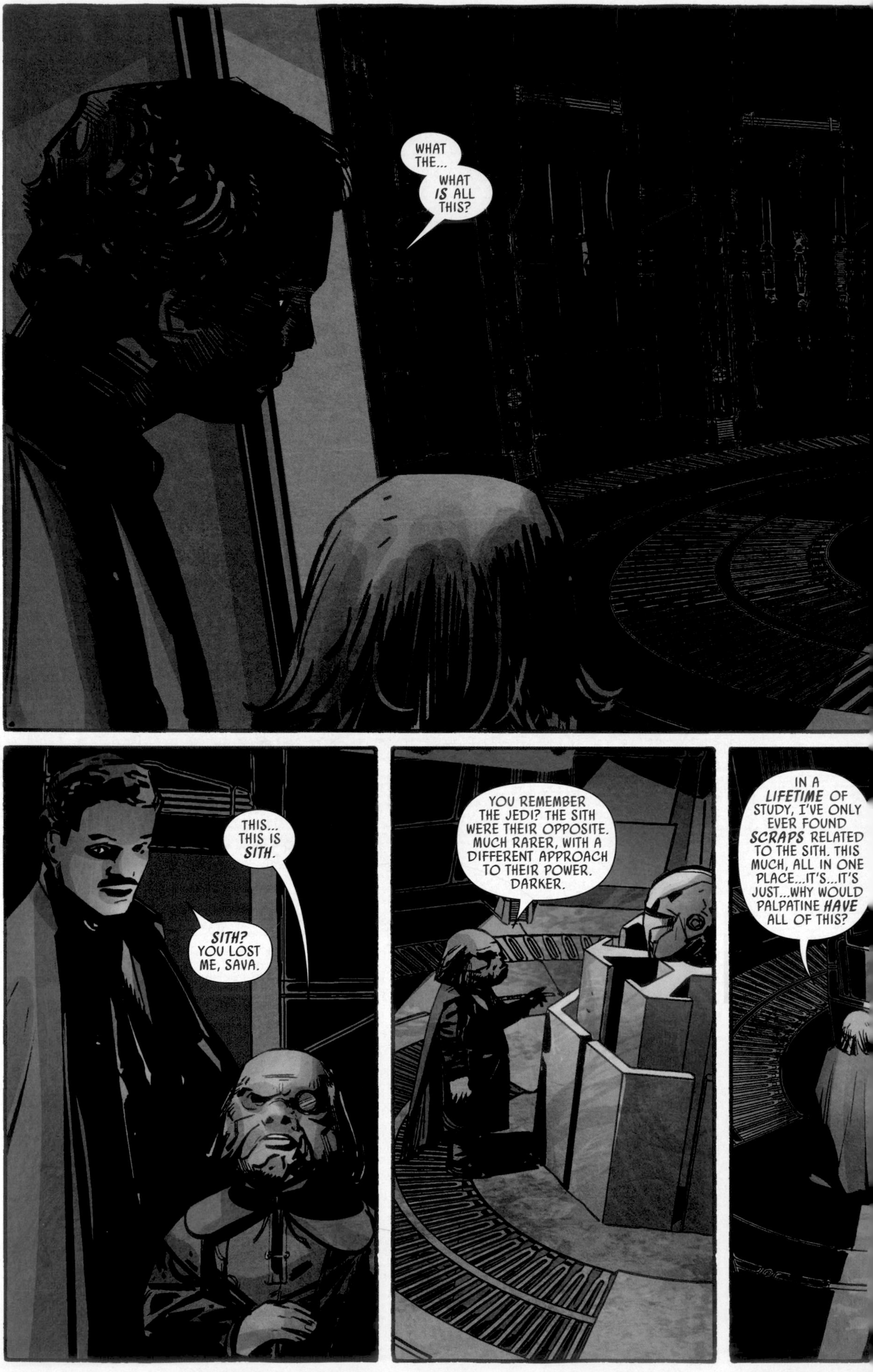
WHAT THE... WHAT IS ALL THIS?
THIS... THIS IS SITH.
SITH? YOU LOST ME, SAVA.
YOU REMEMBER THE JEDI? THE SITH WERE THEIR OPPOSITE. MUCH RARER, WITH A DIFFERENT APPROACH TO THEIR POWER. DARKER.
IN A LIFETIME OF STUDY, I'VE ONLY EVER FOUND SCRAPS RELATED TO THE SITH. THIS MUCH, ALL IN ONE PLACE...IT'S...IT'S JUST...WHY WOULD PALPATINE HAVE ALL OF THIS?

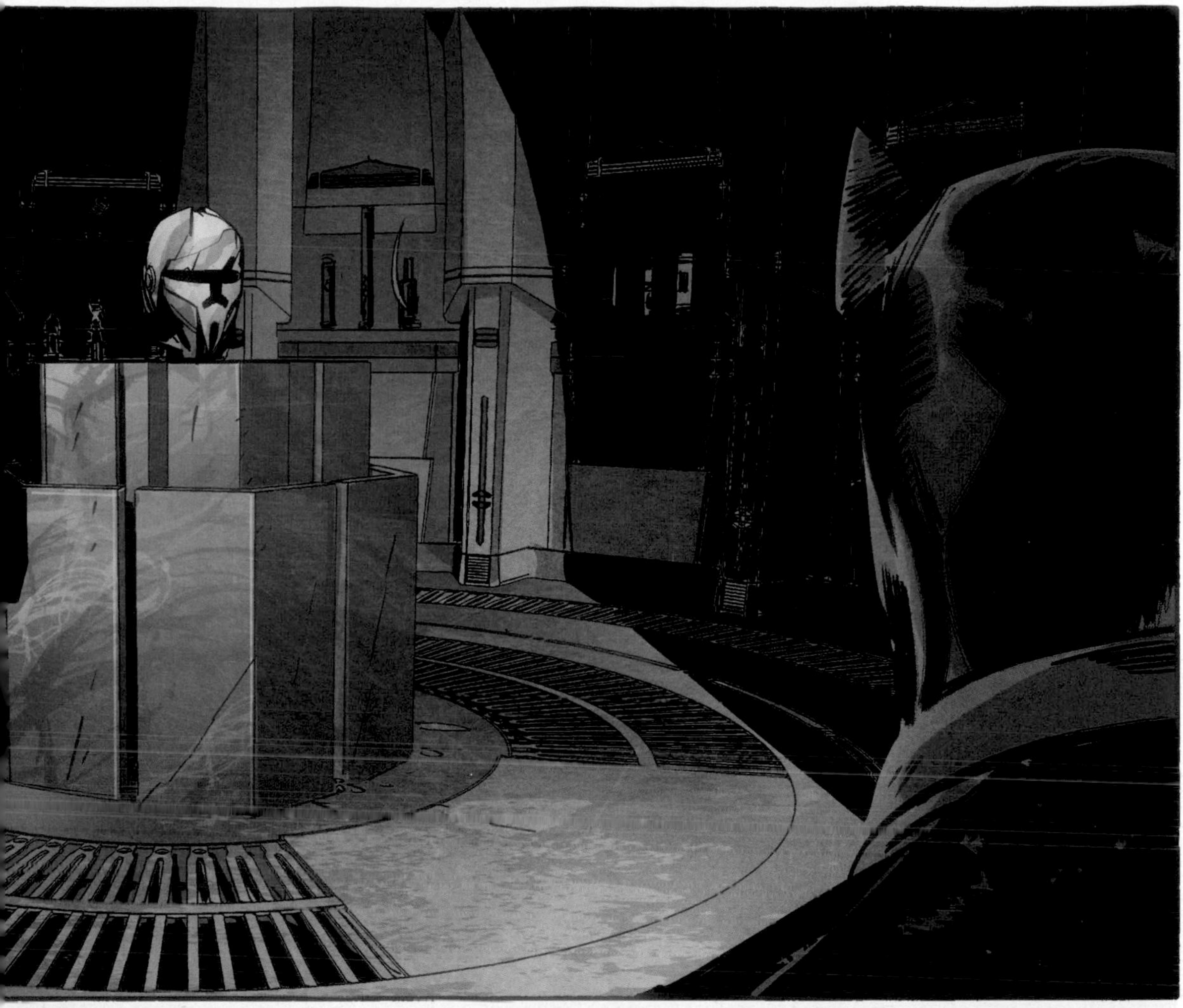

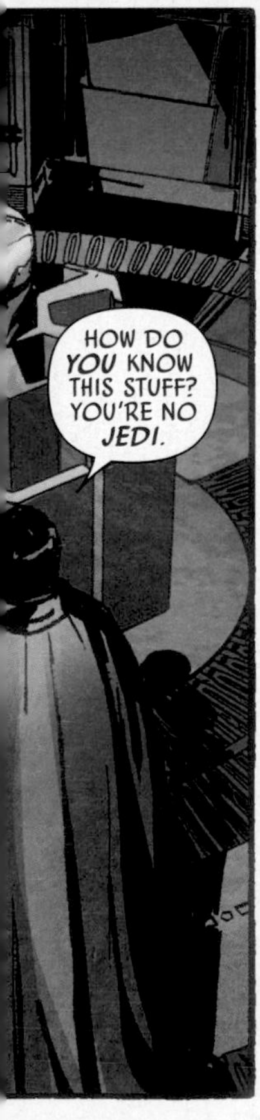
HOW DO *YOU* KNOW THIS STUFF? YOU'RE NO *JEDI*.

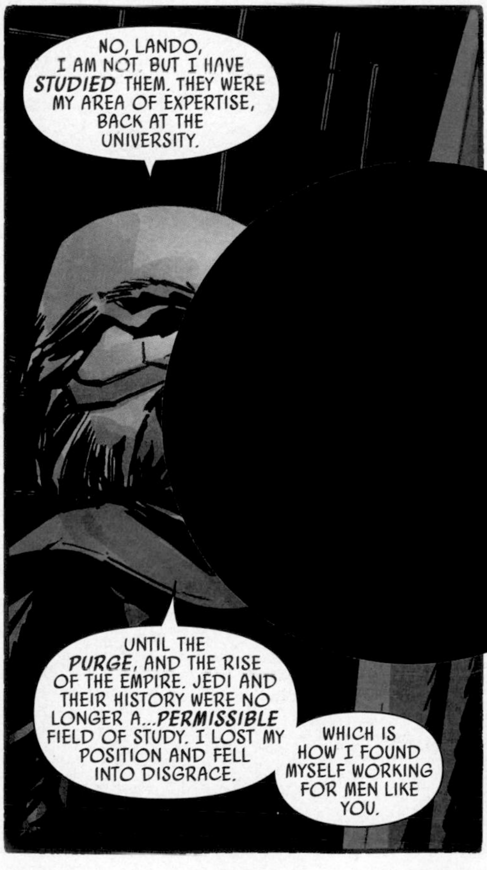
NO, LANDO, I AM NOT. BUT I HAVE *STUDIED* THEM. THEY WERE MY AREA OF EXPERTISE, BACK AT THE UNIVERSITY.
UNTIL THE *PURGE*, AND THE RISE OF THE EMPIRE. JEDI AND THEIR HISTORY WERE NO LONGER A...*PERMISSIBLE* FIELD OF STUDY. I LOST MY POSITION AND FELL INTO DISGRACE.
WHICH IS HOW I FOUND MYSELF WORKING FOR MEN LIKE YOU.

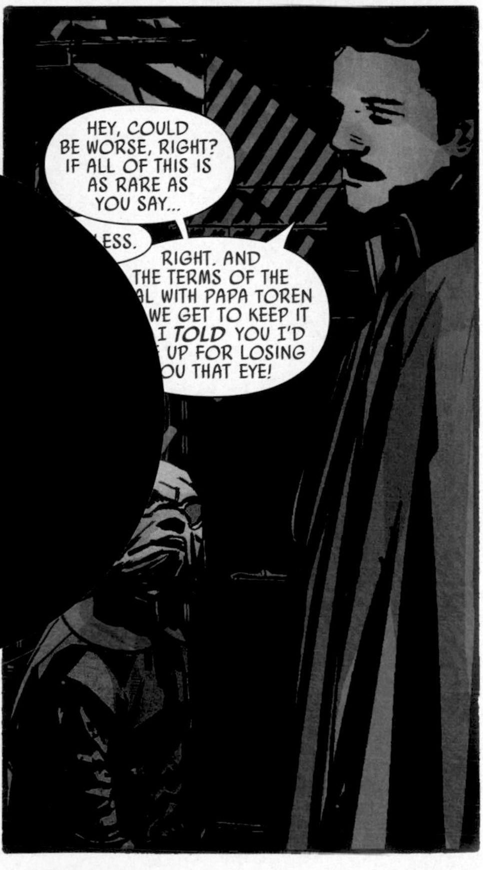
HEY, COULD BE WORSE, RIGHT? IF ALL OF THIS IS AS RARE AS YOU SAY...
[redacted]LESS.
RIGHT. AND THE TERMS OF THE [redacted]AL WITH PAPA TOREN [redacted] WE GET TO KEEP IT [redacted] I *TOLD* YOU I'D [redacted] UP FOR LOSING [redacted]OU THAT EYE!

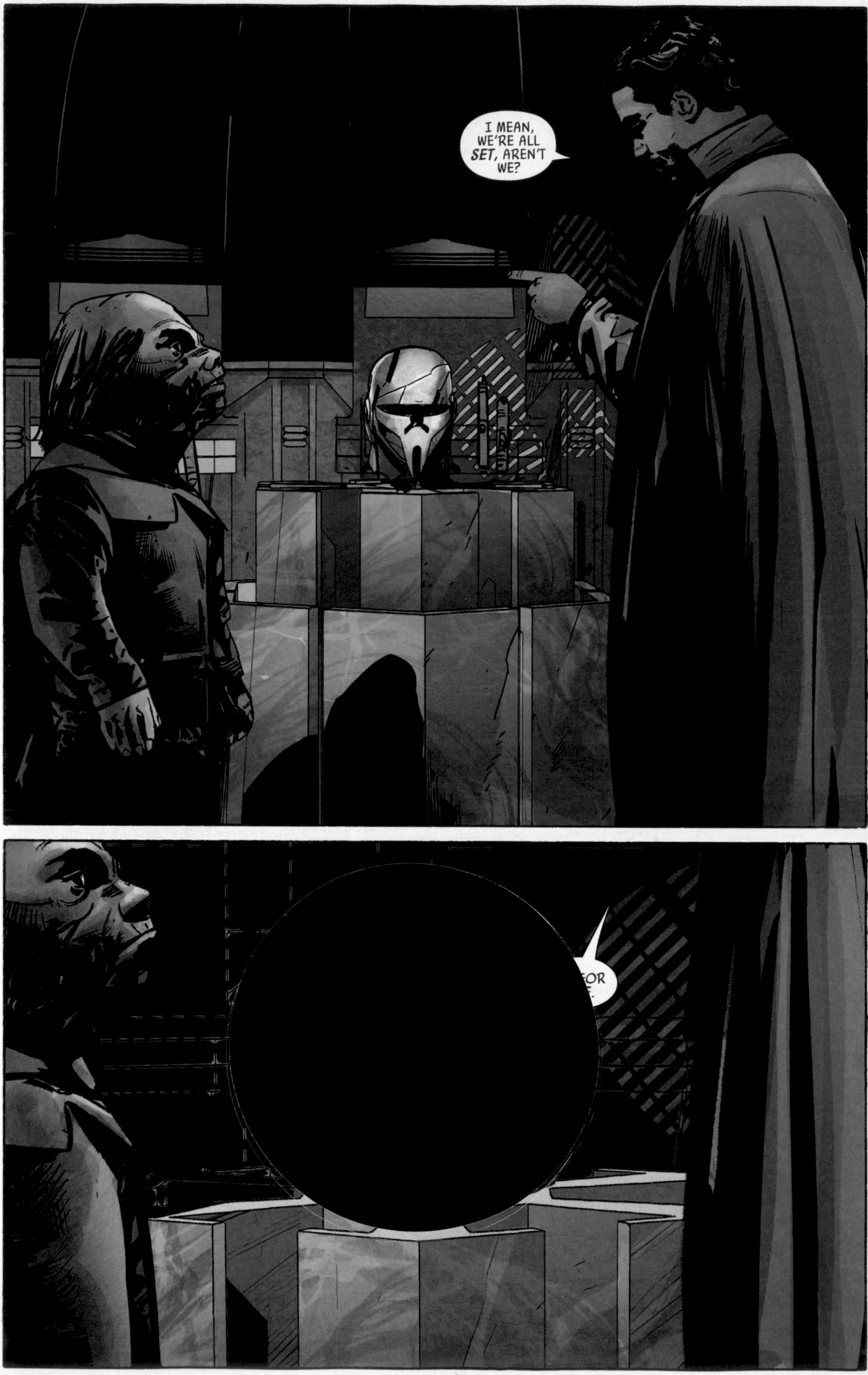
I MEAN, WE'RE ALL SET, AREN'T WE?
[redacted]

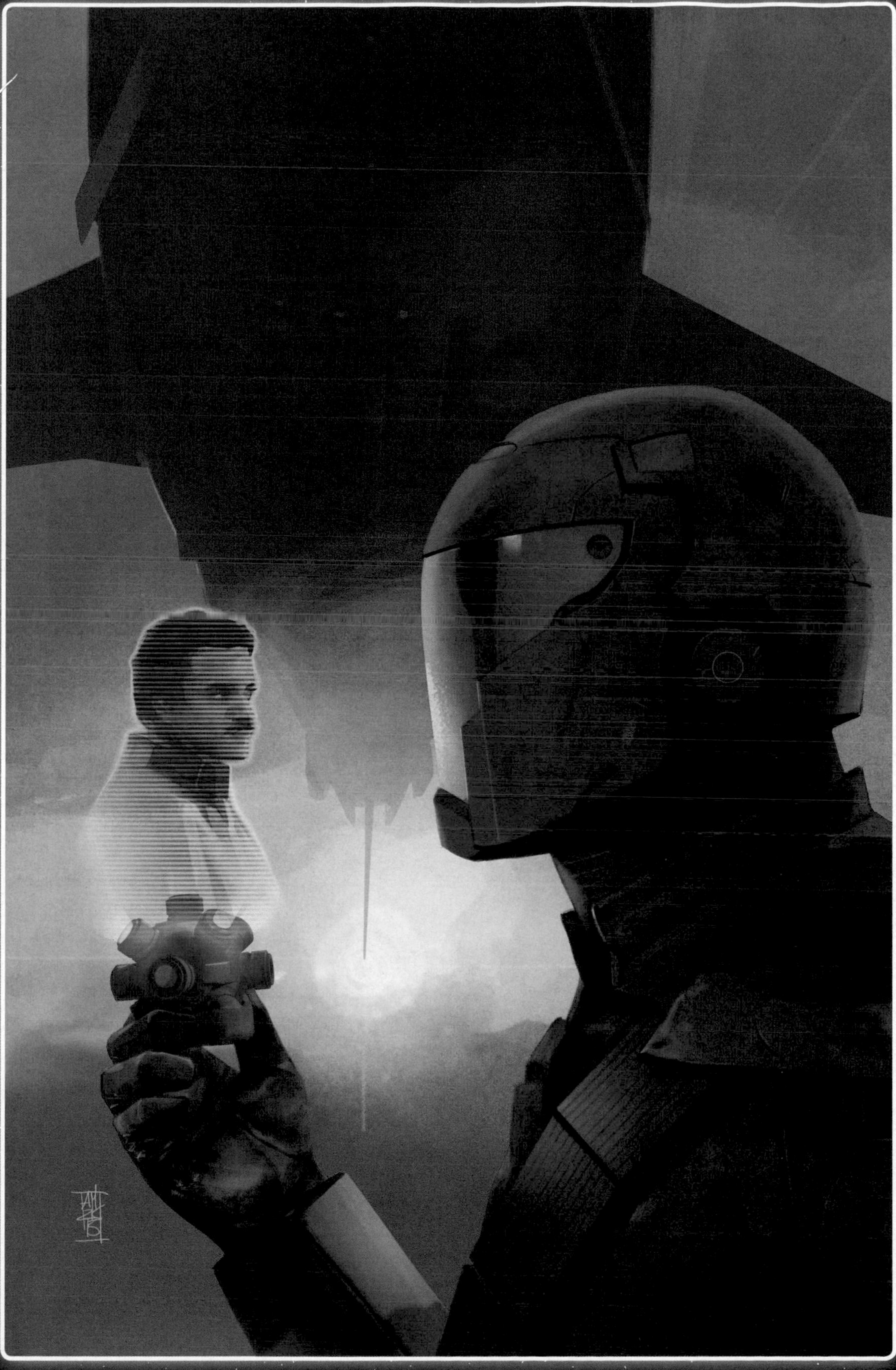

4

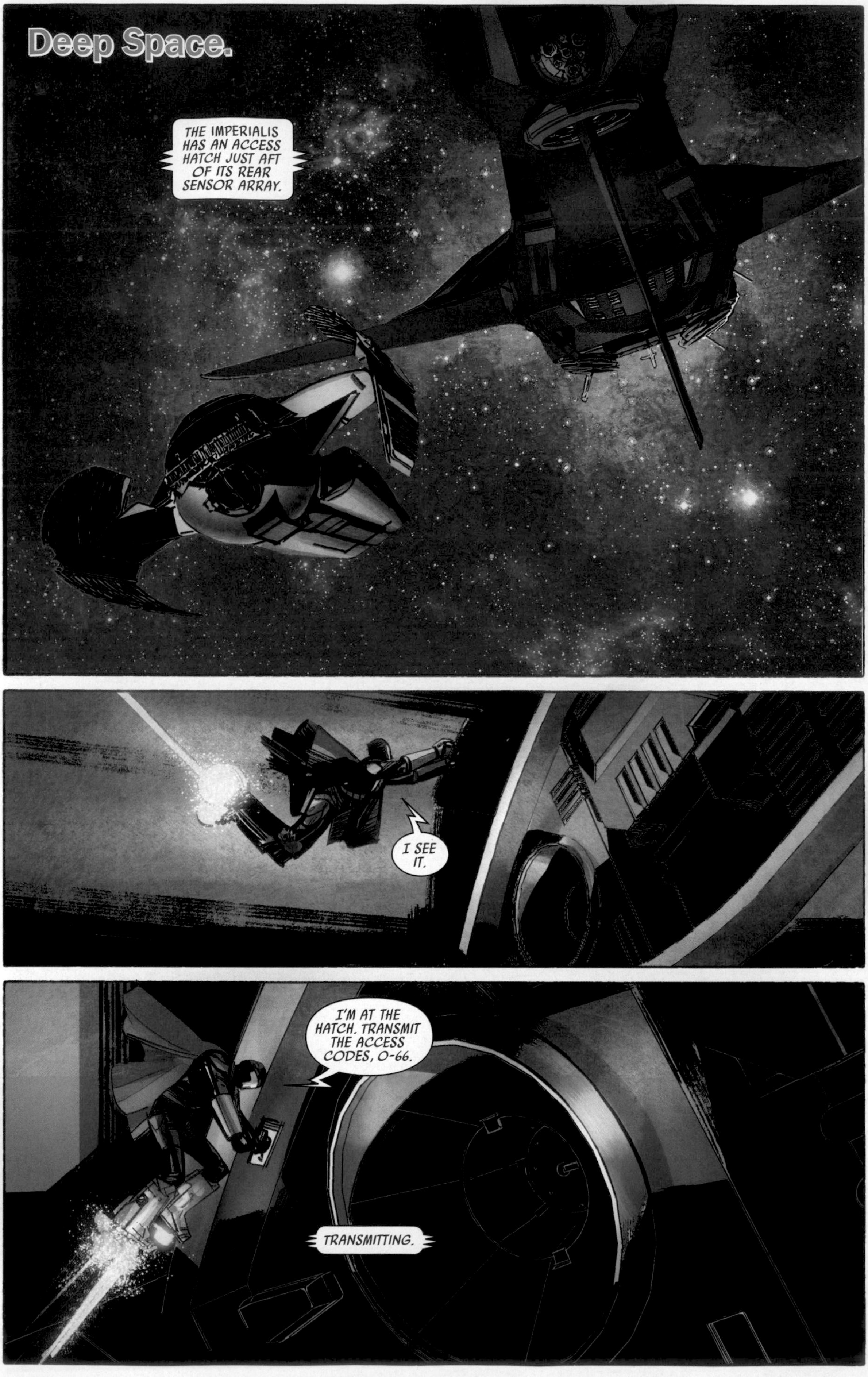
Deep Space.
THE IMPERIALIS HAS AN ACCESS HATCH JUST AFT OF ITS REAR SENSOR ARRAY.
I SEE IT.
I'M AT THE HATCH. TRANSMIT THE ACCESS CODES, 0-66.
TRANSMITTING.

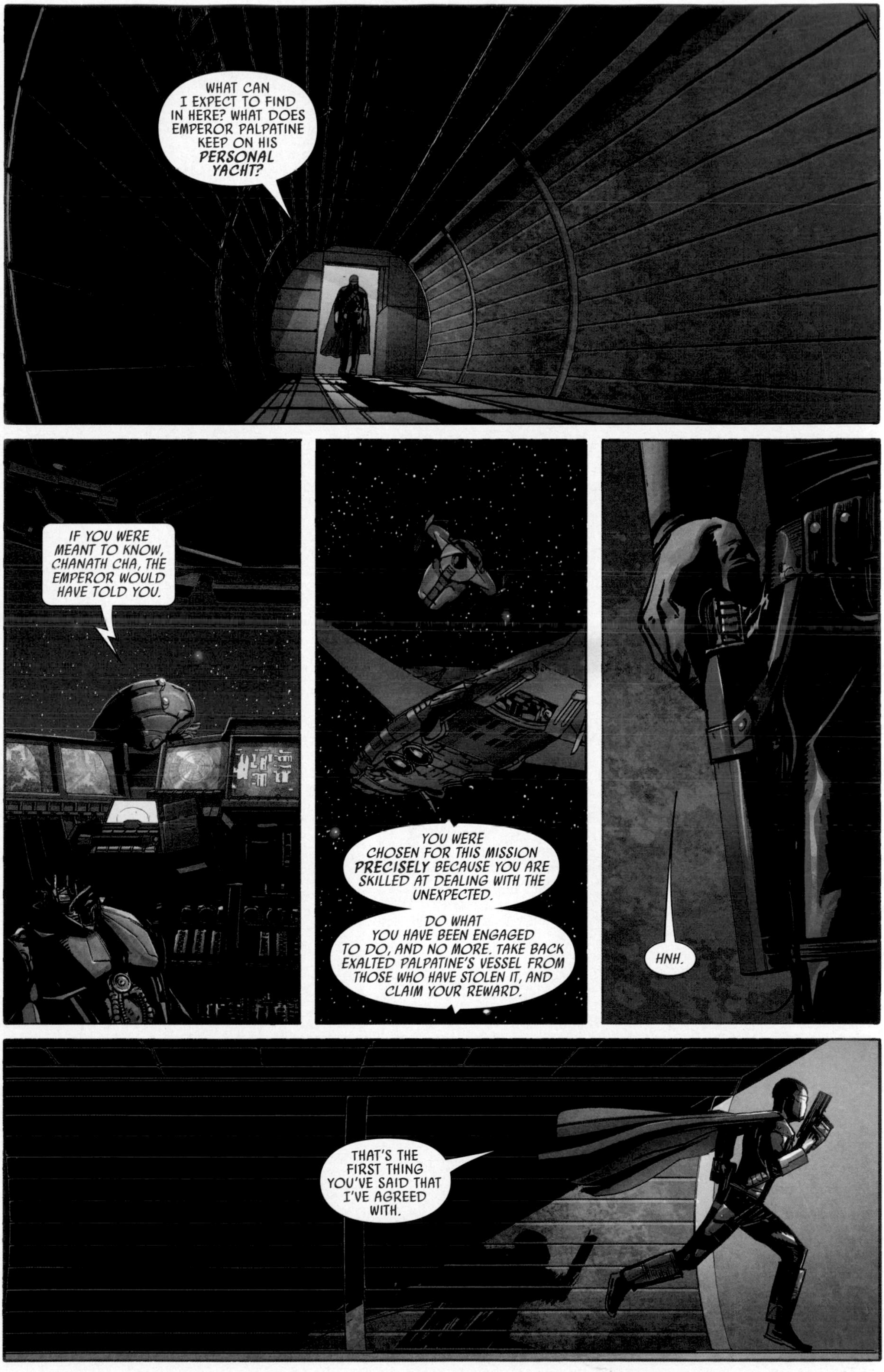
WHAT CAN I EXPECT TO FIND IN HERE? WHAT DOES EMPEROR PALPATINE KEEP ON HIS PERSONAL YACHT?
IF YOU WERE MEANT TO KNOW, CHANATH CHA, THE EMPEROR WOULD HAVE TOLD YOU.
YOU WERE CHOSEN FOR THIS MISSION PRECISELY BECAUSE YOU ARE SKILLED AT DEALING WITH THE UNEXPECTED.
DO WHAT YOU HAVE BEEN ENGAGED TO DO, AND NO MORE. TAKE BACK EXALTED PALPATINE'S VESSEL FROM THOSE WHO HAVE STOLEN IT, AND CLAIM YOUR REWARD.
HNH.
THAT'S THE FIRST THING YOU'VE SAID THAT I'VE AGREED WITH.

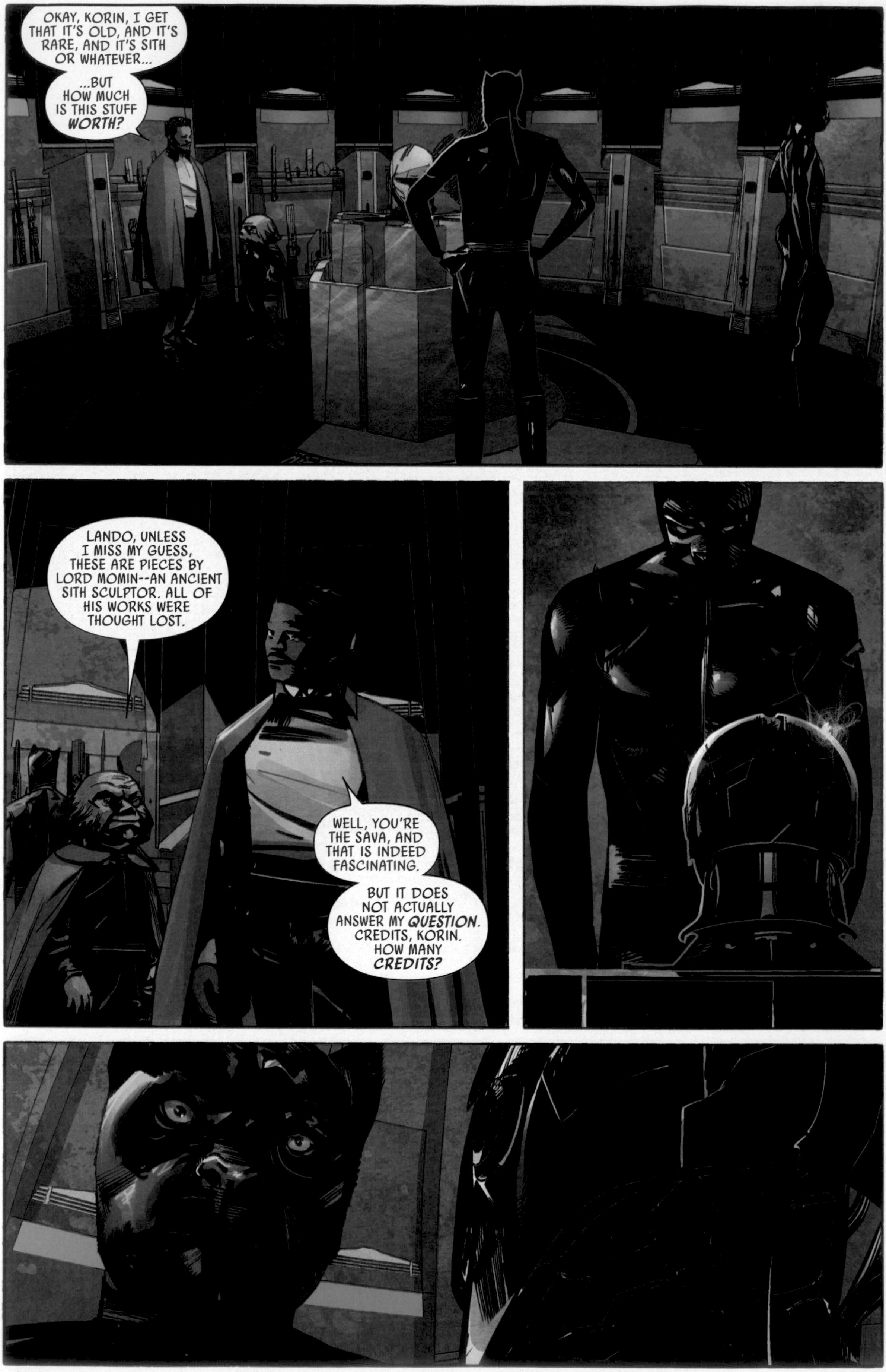
OKAY, KORIN, I GET THAT IT'S OLD, AND IT'S RARE, AND IT'S SITH OR WHATEVER...
...BUT HOW MUCH IS THIS STUFF WORTH?
LANDO, UNLESS I MISS MY GUESS, THESE ARE PIECES BY LORD MOMIN--AN ANCIENT SITH SCULPTOR. ALL OF HIS WORKS WERE THOUGHT LOST.
WELL, YOU'RE THE SAVA, AND THAT IS INDEED FASCINATING.
BUT IT DOES NOT ACTUALLY ANSWER MY QUESTION. CREDITS, KORIN. HOW MANY CREDITS?

THERE AREN'T MANY BUYERS FOR ANTIQUITIES OF THIS TYPE, BUT THE ONES OUT THERE ARE *VERY* WILLING TO SPEND IF AND WHEN NEW ITEMS APPEAR ON THE MARKET.

IF WE CAN FIND ONE OF *THOSE* INDIVIDUALS, THIS COLLECTION COULD GET US EACH ENOUGH CREDITS FOR...OH...

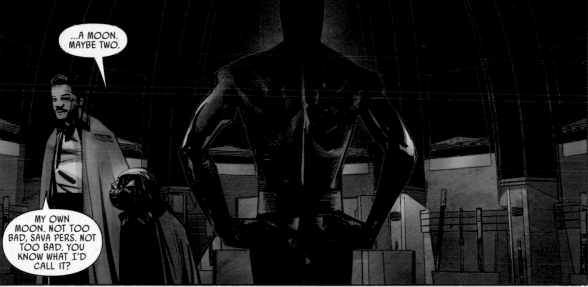

...A MOON. MAYBE TWO.

MY OWN MOON. NOT TOO BAD, SAVA PERS. NOT TOO BAD. YOU KNOW WHAT I'D CALL IT?

DO TELL.

I'D CALL IT LANDO LAND. GALAXY *NEEDS* A LANDO LAND.

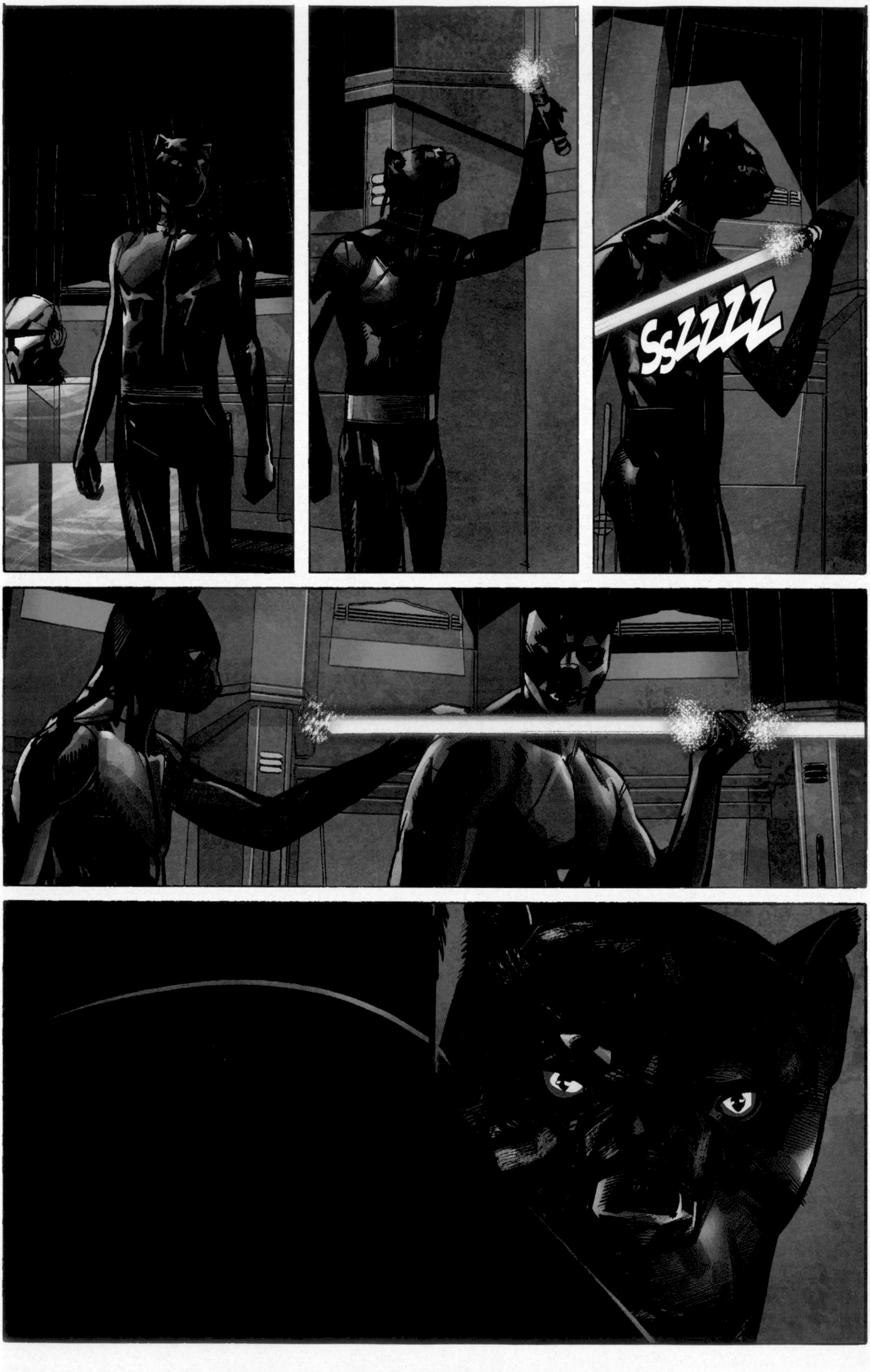
SsZZZZ

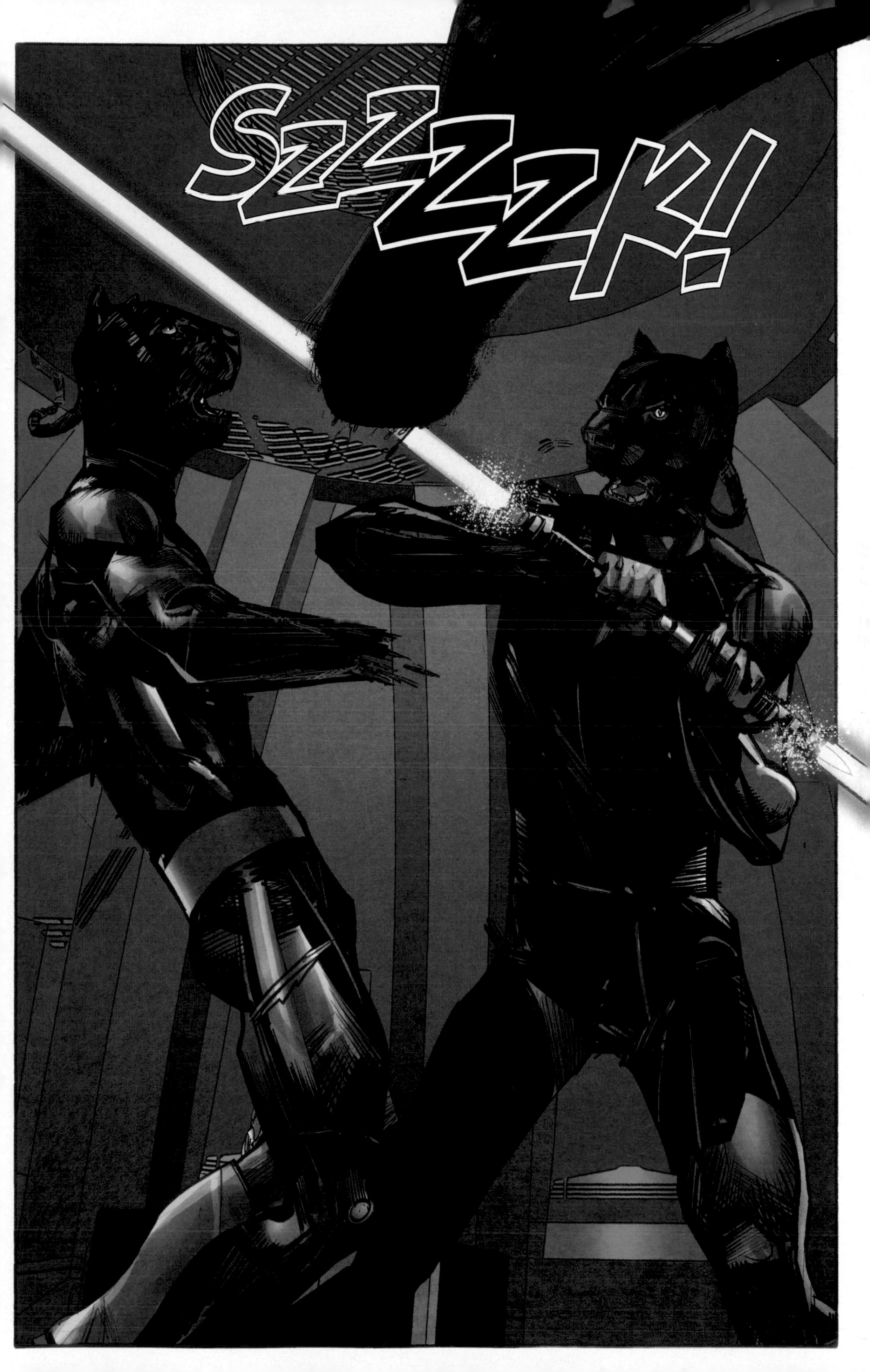
SZZZZK!

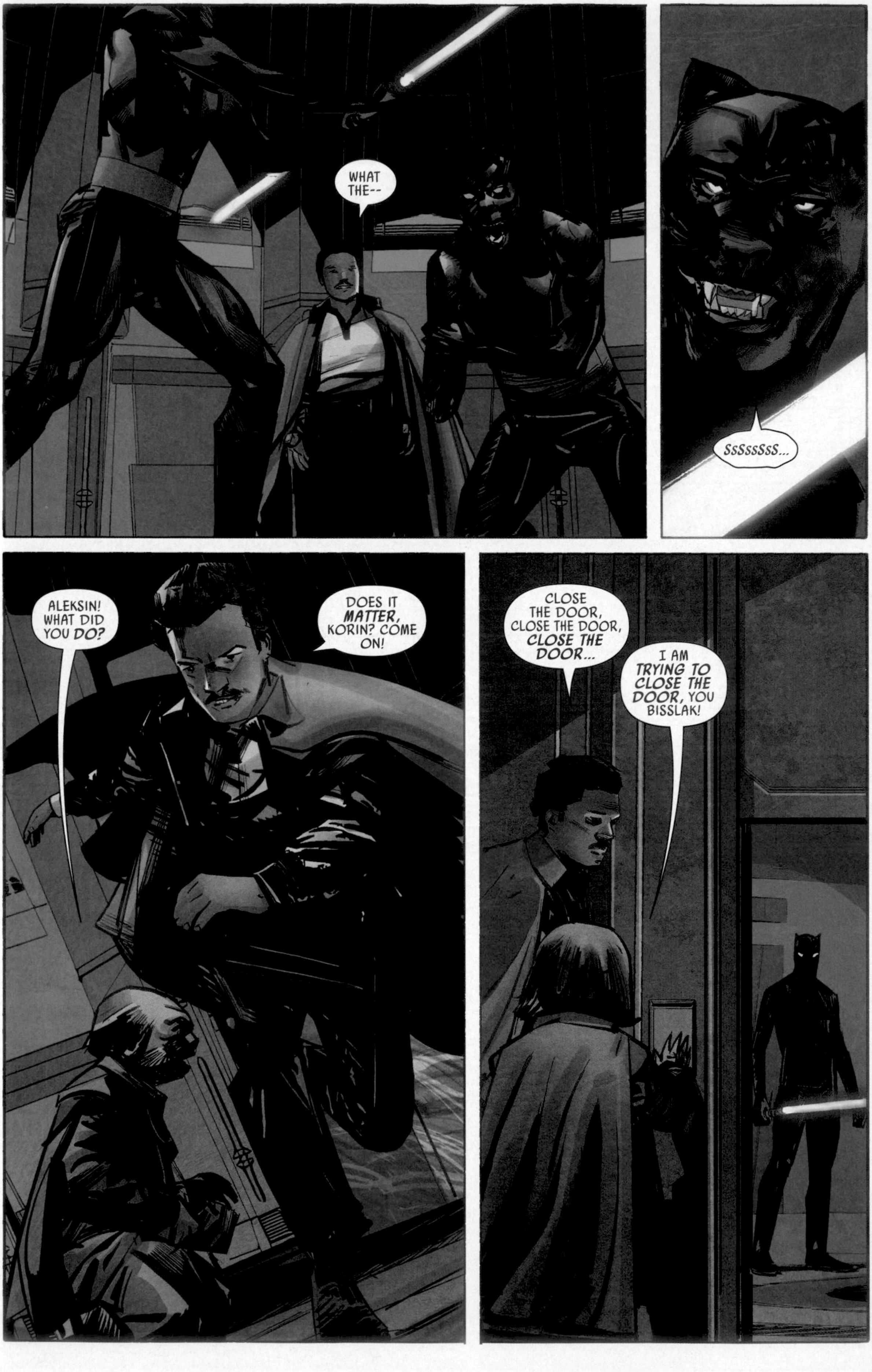

WHAT THE--
SSSSSSSS...
ALEKSIN! WHAT DID YOU *DO*?
DOES IT *MATTER*, KORIN? COME ON!
CLOSE THE DOOR, CLOSE THE DOOR, *CLOSE THE DOOR...*
I AM *TRYING TO CLOSE THE DOOR*, YOU BISSLAK!

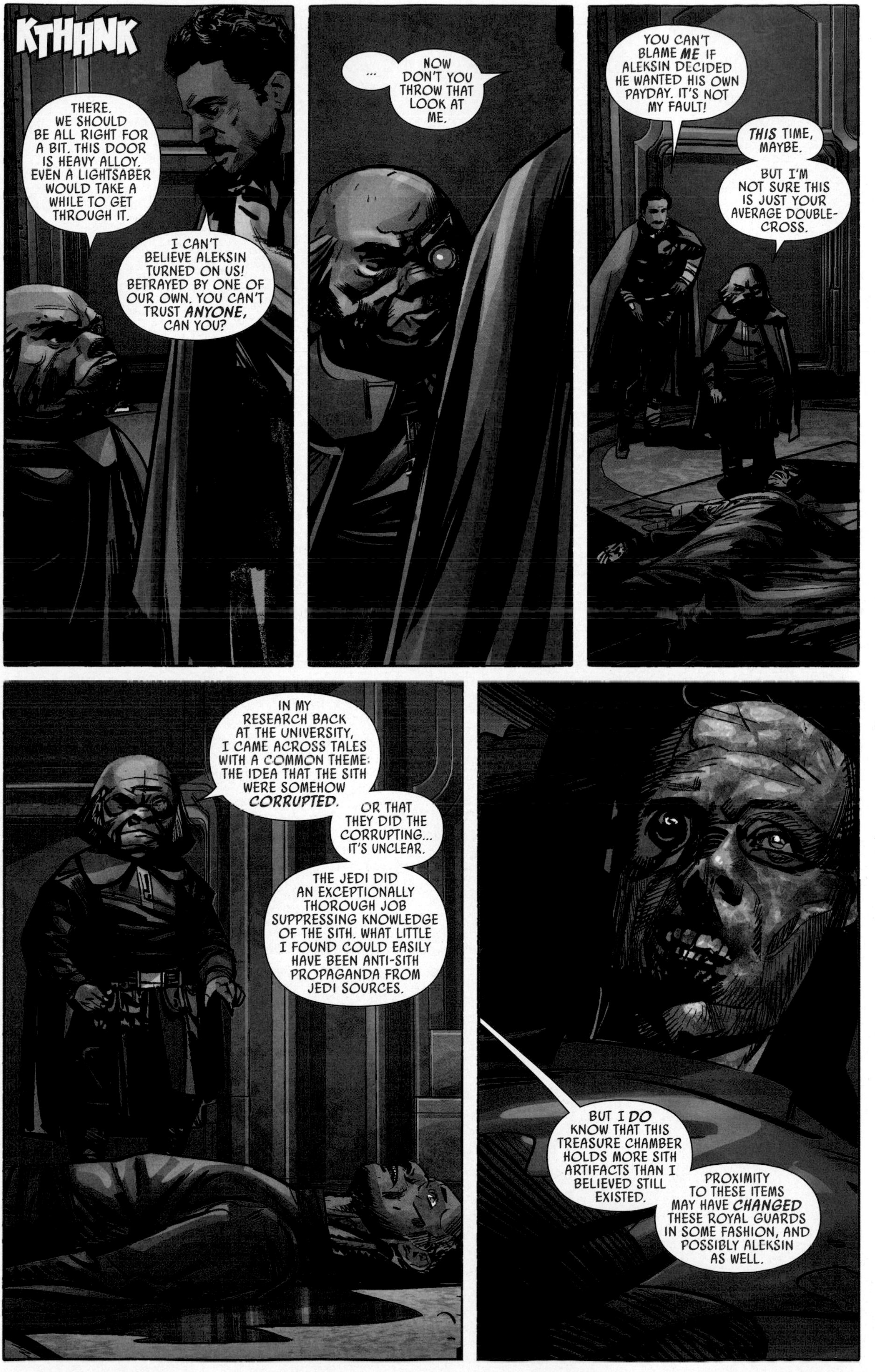
KTHHNK
THERE. WE SHOULD BE ALL RIGHT FOR A BIT. THIS DOOR IS HEAVY ALLOY. EVEN A LIGHTSABER WOULD TAKE A WHILE TO GET THROUGH IT.
I CAN'T BELIEVE ALEKSIN TURNED ON US! BETRAYED BY ONE OF OUR OWN. YOU CAN'T TRUST ANYONE, CAN YOU?
...
NOW DON'T YOU THROW THAT LOOK AT ME.
YOU CAN'T BLAME ME IF ALEKSIN DECIDED HE WANTED HIS OWN PAYDAY. IT'S NOT MY FAULT!
THIS TIME, MAYBE.
BUT I'M NOT SURE THIS IS JUST YOUR AVERAGE DOUBLE-CROSS.
IN MY RESEARCH BACK AT THE UNIVERSITY, I CAME ACROSS TALES WITH A COMMON THEME: THE IDEA THAT THE SITH WERE SOMEHOW CORRUPTED.
OR THAT THEY DID THE CORRUPTING... IT'S UNCLEAR.
THE JEDI DID AN EXCEPTIONALLY THOROUGH JOB SUPPRESSING KNOWLEDGE OF THE SITH. WHAT LITTLE I FOUND COULD EASILY HAVE BEEN ANTI-SITH PROPAGANDA FROM JEDI SOURCES.
BUT I DO KNOW THAT THIS TREASURE CHAMBER HOLDS MORE SITH ARTIFACTS THAN I BELIEVED STILL EXISTED.
PROXIMITY TO THESE ITEMS MAY HAVE CHANGED THESE ROYAL GUARDS IN SOME FASHION, AND POSSIBLY ALEKSIN AS WELL.

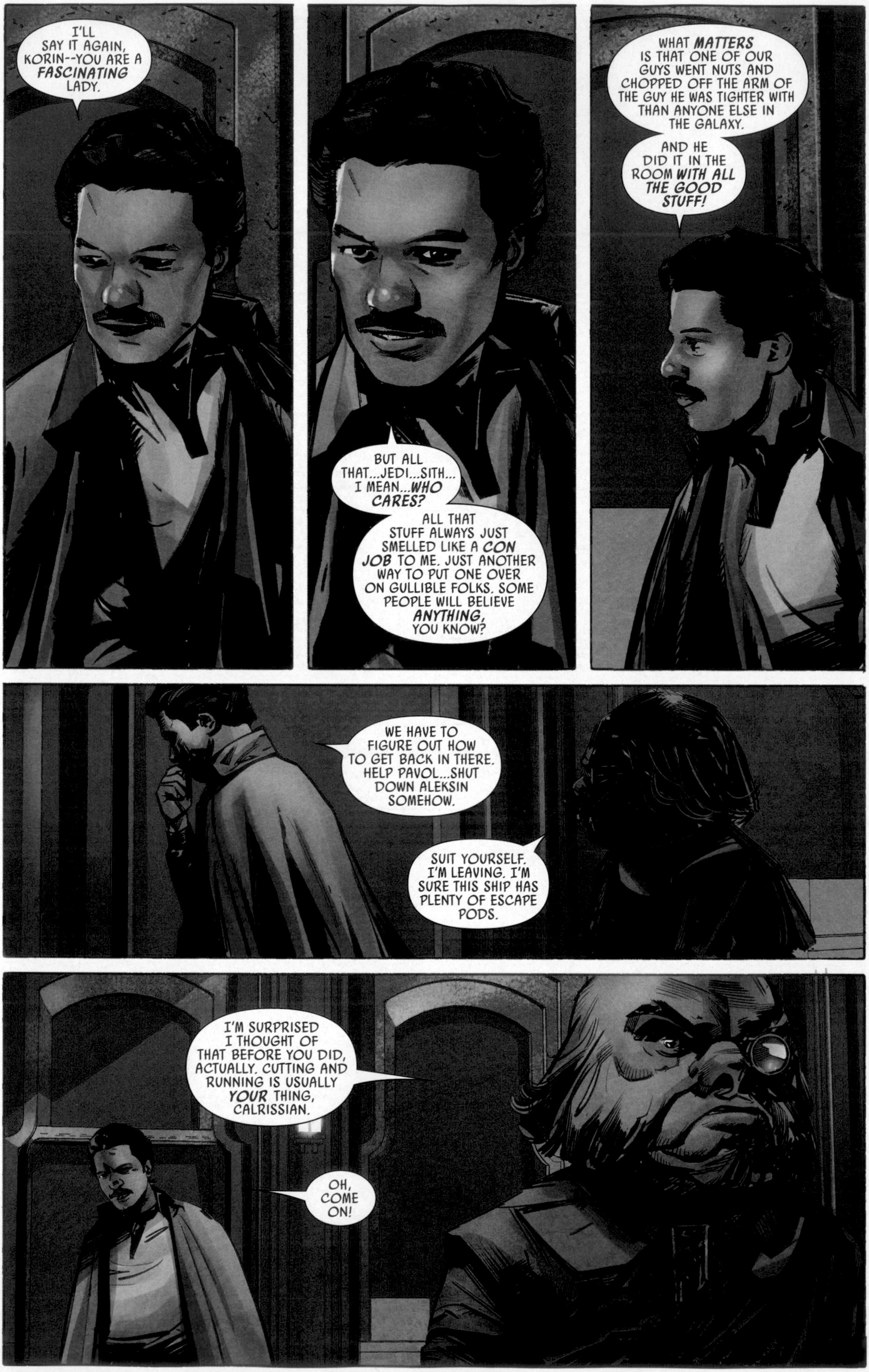
I'LL SAY IT AGAIN, KORIN--YOU ARE A FASCINATING LADY.
BUT ALL THAT...JEDI...SITH... I MEAN...WHO CARES?
ALL THAT STUFF ALWAYS JUST SMELLED LIKE A CON JOB TO ME. JUST ANOTHER WAY TO PUT ONE OVER ON GULLIBLE FOLKS. SOME PEOPLE WILL BELIEVE ANYTHING, YOU KNOW?
WHAT MATTERS IS THAT ONE OF OUR GUYS WENT NUTS AND CHOPPED OFF THE ARM OF THE GUY HE WAS TIGHTER WITH THAN ANYONE ELSE IN THE GALAXY.
AND HE DID IT IN THE ROOM WITH ALL THE GOOD STUFF!
WE HAVE TO FIGURE OUT HOW TO GET BACK IN THERE. HELP PAVOL...SHUT DOWN ALEKSIN SOMEHOW.
SUIT YOURSELF. I'M LEAVING. I'M SURE THIS SHIP HAS PLENTY OF ESCAPE PODS.
I'M SURPRISED I THOUGHT OF THAT BEFORE YOU DID, ACTUALLY. CUTTING AND RUNNING IS USUALLY YOUR THING, CALRISSIAN.
OH, COME ON!

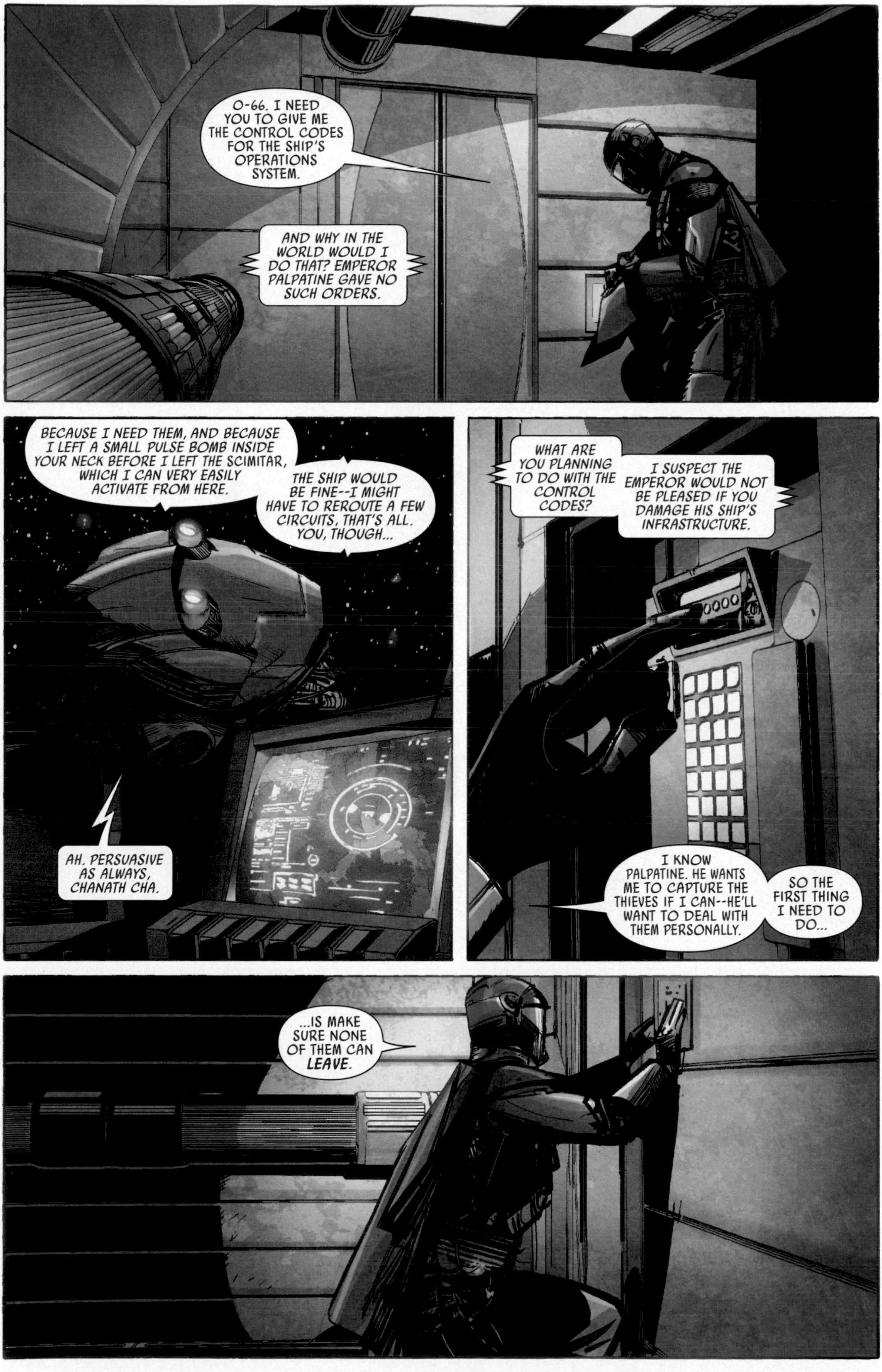
O-66. I NEED YOU TO GIVE ME THE CONTROL CODES FOR THE SHIP'S OPERATIONS SYSTEM.
AND WHY IN THE WORLD WOULD I DO THAT? EMPEROR PALPATINE GAVE NO SUCH ORDERS.
BECAUSE I NEED THEM, AND BECAUSE I LEFT A SMALL PULSE BOMB INSIDE YOUR NECK BEFORE I LEFT THE SCIMITAR, WHICH I CAN VERY EASILY ACTIVATE FROM HERE.
THE SHIP WOULD BE FINE--I MIGHT HAVE TO REROUTE A FEW CIRCUITS, THAT'S ALL. YOU, THOUGH...
AH. PERSUASIVE AS ALWAYS, CHANATH CHA.
WHAT ARE YOU PLANNING TO DO WITH THE CONTROL CODES?
I SUSPECT THE EMPEROR WOULD NOT BE PLEASED IF YOU DAMAGE HIS SHIP'S INFRASTRUCTURE.
I KNOW PALPATINE. HE WANTS ME TO CAPTURE THE THIEVES IF I CAN--HE'LL WANT TO DEAL WITH THEM PERSONALLY.
SO THE FIRST THING I NEED TO DO...
...IS MAKE SURE NONE OF THEM CAN LEAVE.

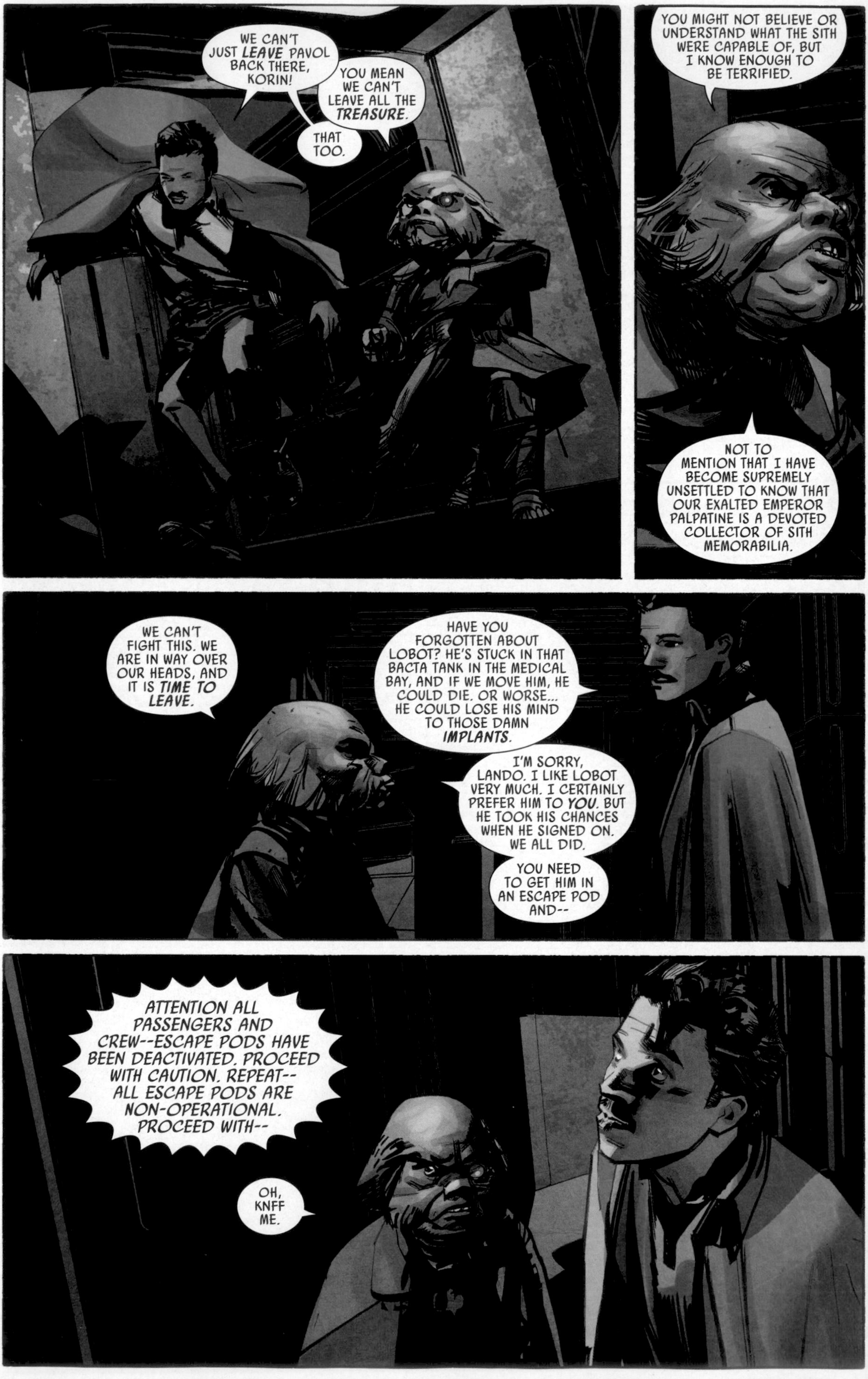
WE CAN'T JUST LEAVE PAVOL BACK THERE, KORIN!
YOU MEAN WE CAN'T LEAVE ALL THE TREASURE.
THAT TOO.
YOU MIGHT NOT BELIEVE OR UNDERSTAND WHAT THE SITH WERE CAPABLE OF, BUT I KNOW ENOUGH TO BE TERRIFIED.
NOT TO MENTION THAT I HAVE BECOME SUPREMELY UNSETTLED TO KNOW THAT OUR EXALTED EMPEROR PALPATINE IS A DEVOTED COLLECTOR OF SITH MEMORABILIA.
WE CAN'T FIGHT THIS. WE ARE IN WAY OVER OUR HEADS, AND IT IS TIME TO LEAVE.
HAVE YOU FORGOTTEN ABOUT LOBOT? HE'S STUCK IN THAT BACTA TANK IN THE MEDICAL BAY, AND IF WE MOVE HIM, HE COULD DIE. OR WORSE... HE COULD LOSE HIS MIND TO THOSE DAMN IMPLANTS.
I'M SORRY, LANDO. I LIKE LOBOT VERY MUCH. I CERTAINLY PREFER HIM TO YOU. BUT HE TOOK HIS CHANCES WHEN HE SIGNED ON. WE ALL DID.
YOU NEED TO GET HIM IN AN ESCAPE POD AND--
ATTENTION ALL PASSENGERS AND CREW--ESCAPE PODS HAVE BEEN DEACTIVATED. PROCEED WITH CAUTION. REPEAT--ALL ESCAPE PODS ARE NON-OPERATIONAL. PROCEED WITH--
OH, KNFF ME.

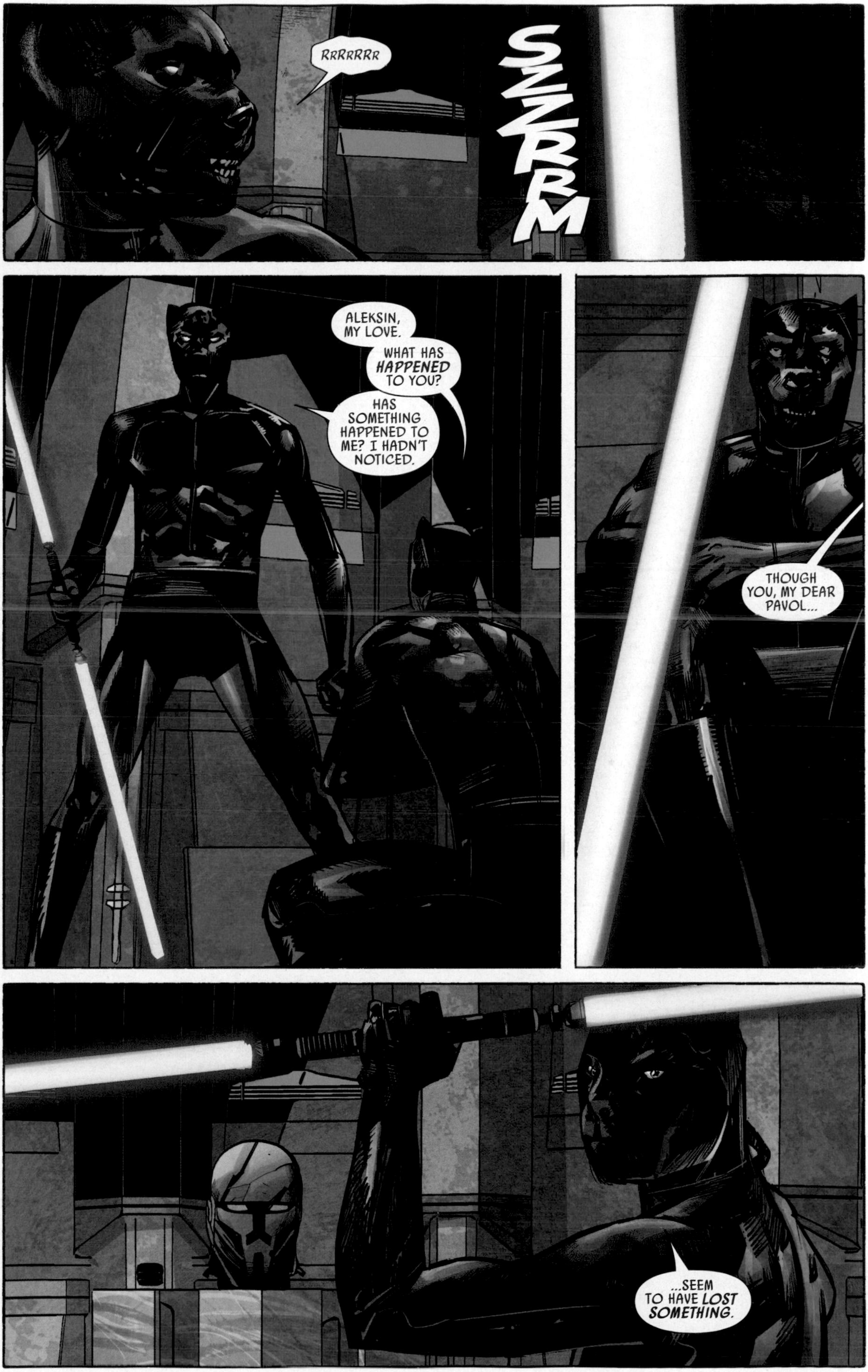
RRRRRRR
SZZRRM
ALEKSIN, MY LOVE.
WHAT HAS HAPPENED TO YOU?
HAS SOMETHING HAPPENED TO ME? I HADN'T NOTICED.
THOUGH YOU, MY DEAR PAVOL...
...SEEM TO HAVE LOST SOMETHING.

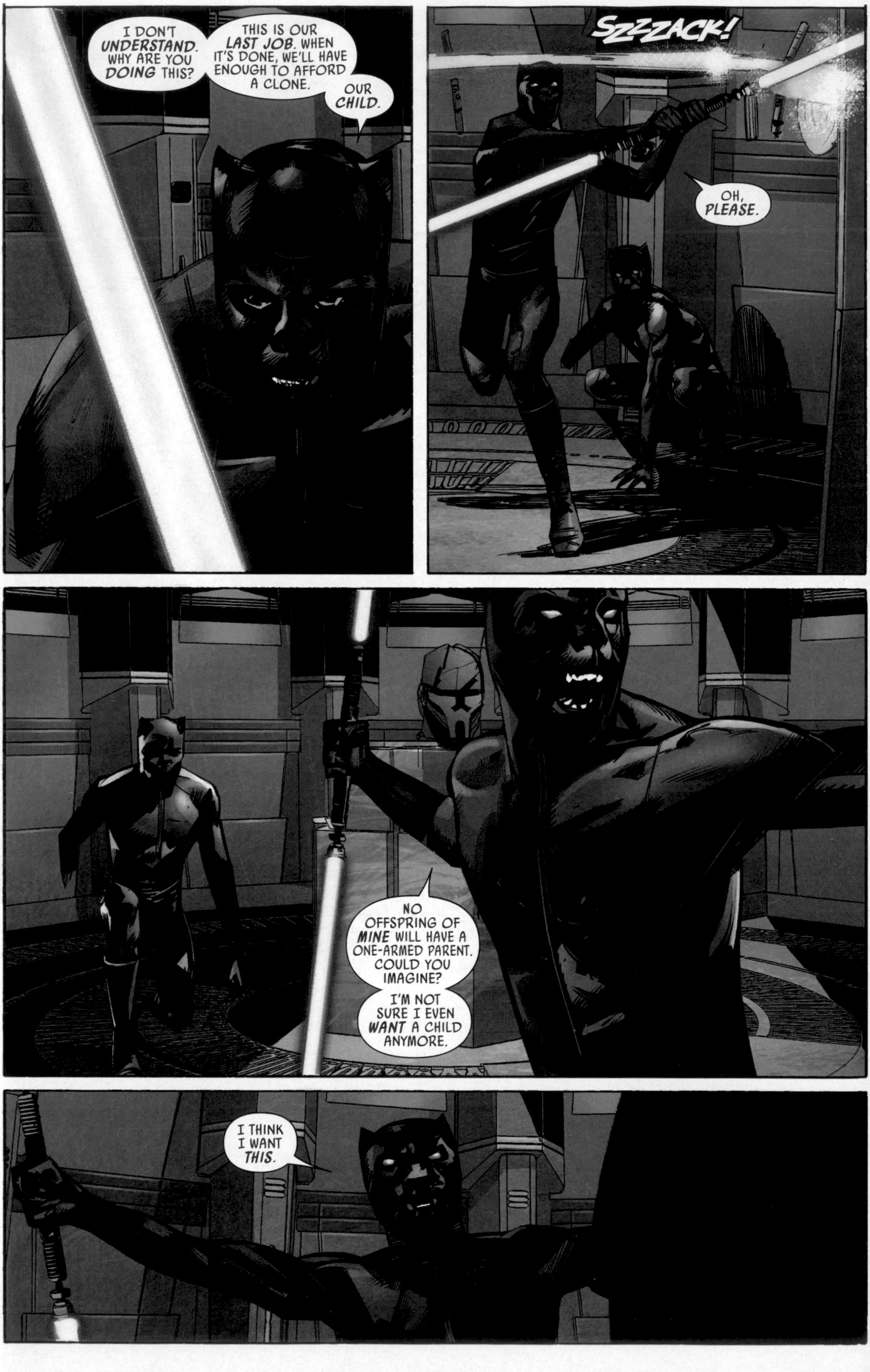
I DON'T UNDERSTAND. WHY ARE YOU DOING THIS?
THIS IS OUR LAST JOB. WHEN IT'S DONE, WE'LL HAVE ENOUGH TO AFFORD A CLONE.
OUR CHILD.
SZZZZACK!
OH, PLEASE.
NO OFFSPRING OF MINE WILL HAVE A ONE-ARMED PARENT. COULD YOU IMAGINE?
I'M NOT SURE I EVEN WANT A CHILD ANYMORE.
I THINK I WANT THIS.

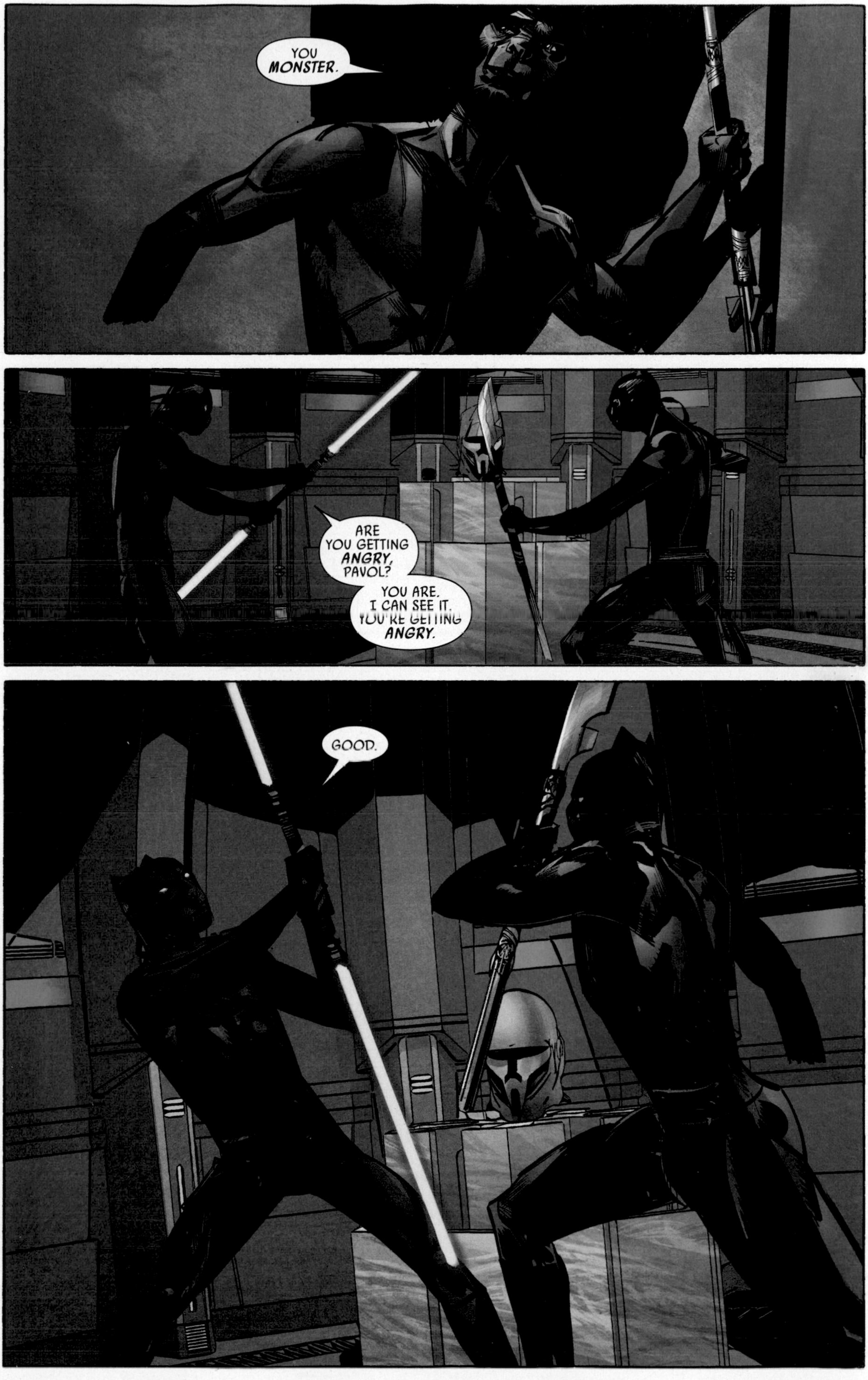
YOU MONSTER.
ARE YOU GETTING ANGRY, PAVOL?
YOU ARE. I CAN SEE IT. YOU'RE GETTING ANGRY.
GOOD.

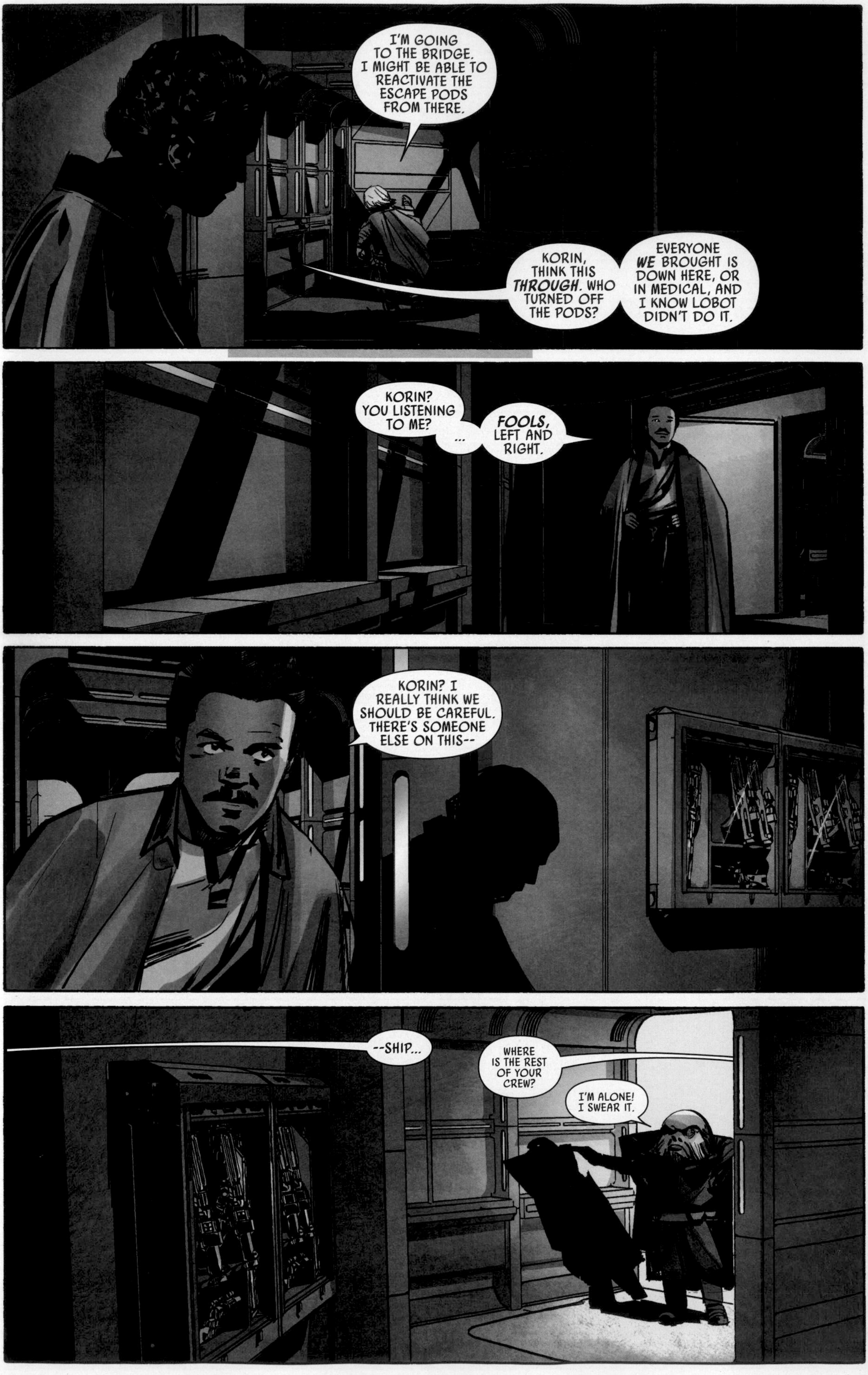
I'M GOING TO THE BRIDGE. I MIGHT BE ABLE TO REACTIVATE THE ESCAPE PODS FROM THERE.
KORIN, THINK THIS THROUGH. WHO TURNED OFF THE PODS?
EVERYONE WE BROUGHT IS DOWN HERE, OR IN MEDICAL, AND I KNOW LOBOT DIDN'T DO IT.
KORIN? YOU LISTENING TO ME?
...
FOOLS, LEFT AND RIGHT.
KORIN? I REALLY THINK WE SHOULD BE CAREFUL. THERE'S SOMEONE ELSE ON THIS--
--SHIP...
WHERE IS THE REST OF YOUR CREW?
I'M ALONE! I SWEAR IT.

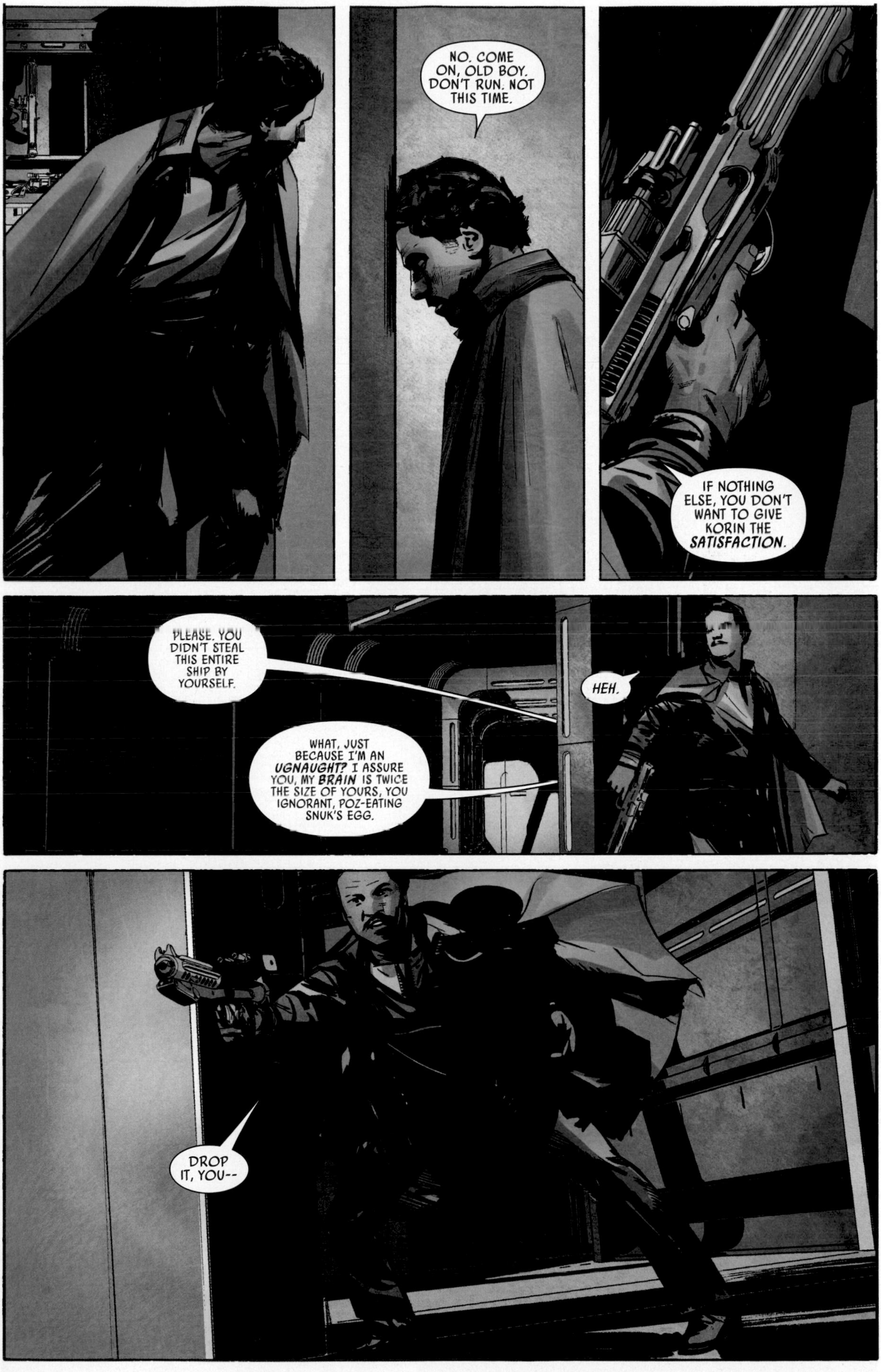
NO. COME ON, OLD BOY. DON'T RUN. NOT THIS TIME.
IF NOTHING ELSE, YOU DON'T WANT TO GIVE KORIN THE SATISFACTION.
PLEASE. YOU DIDN'T STEAL THIS ENTIRE SHIP BY YOURSELF.
HEH.
WHAT, JUST BECAUSE I'M AN UGNAUGHT? I ASSURE YOU, MY BRAIN IS TWICE THE SIZE OF YOURS, YOU IGNORANT, POZ-EATING SNUK'S EGG.
DROP IT, YOU--

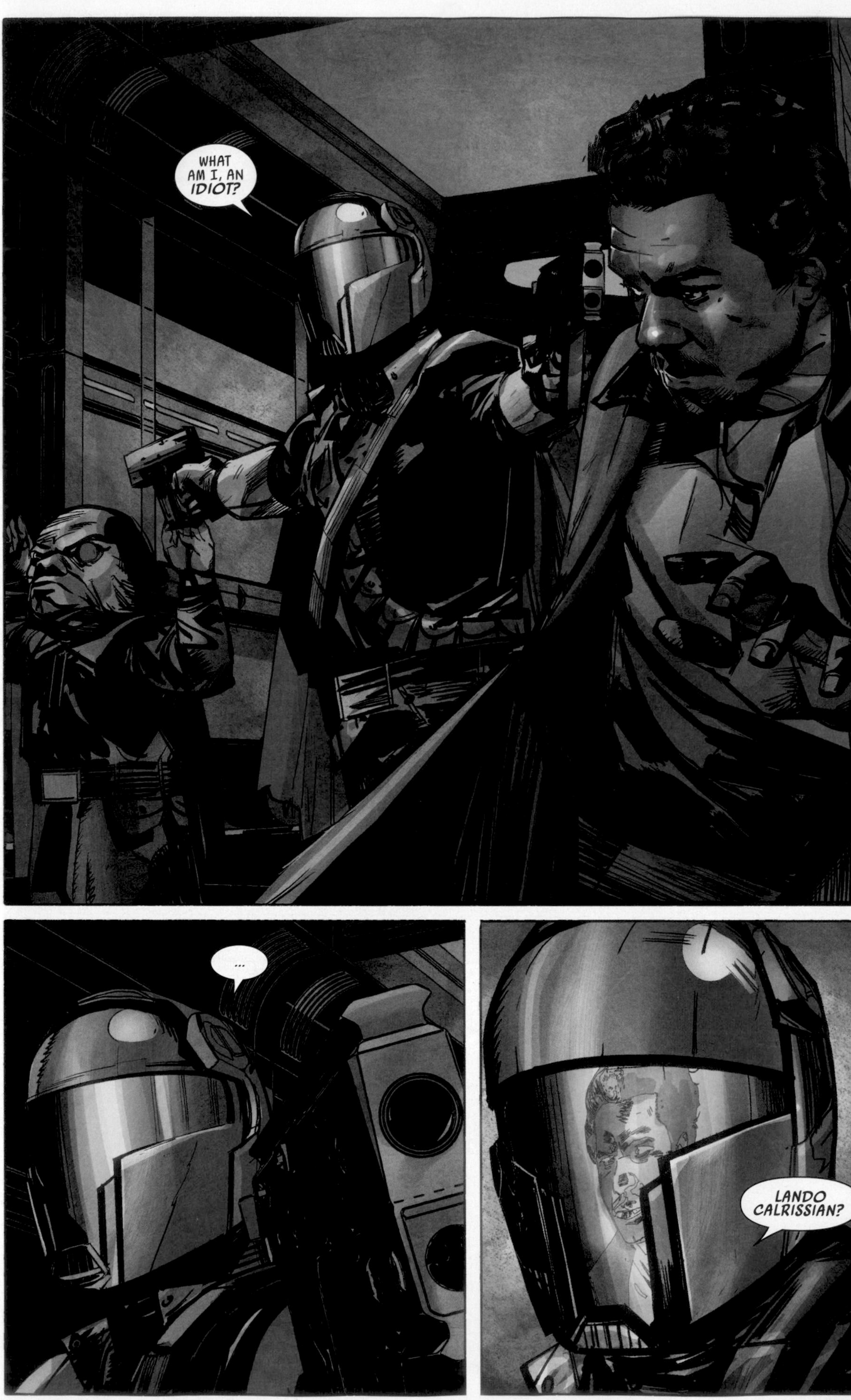
WHAT AM I, AN IDIOT?
...
LANDO CALRISSIAN?

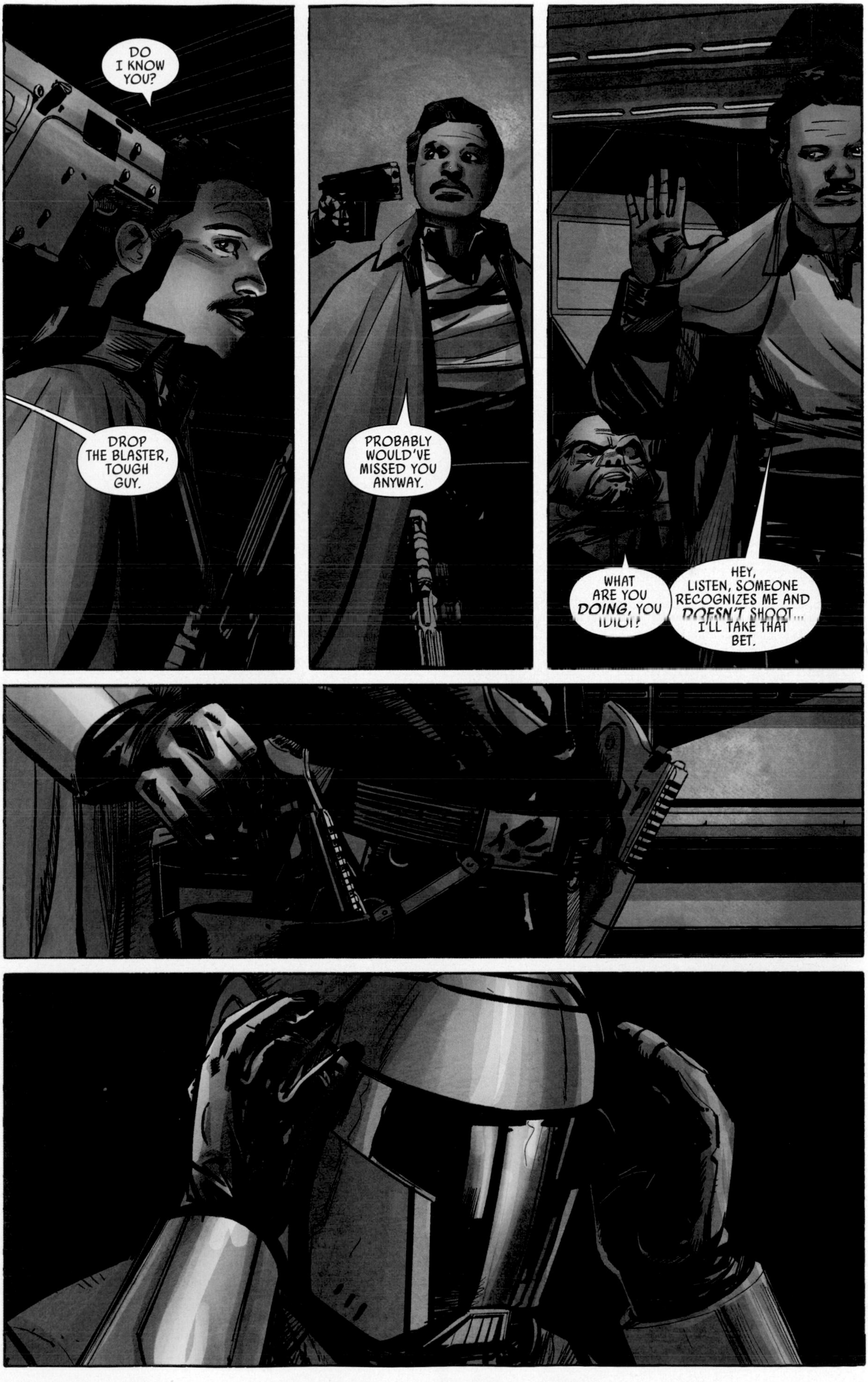
DO I KNOW YOU?
DROP THE BLASTER, TOUGH GUY.
PROBABLY WOULD'VE MISSED YOU ANYWAY.
HEY, LISTEN, SOMEONE RECOGNIZES ME AND *DOESN'T* SHOOT... I'LL TAKE THAT BET.
WHAT ARE YOU *DOING*, YOU IDIOT?

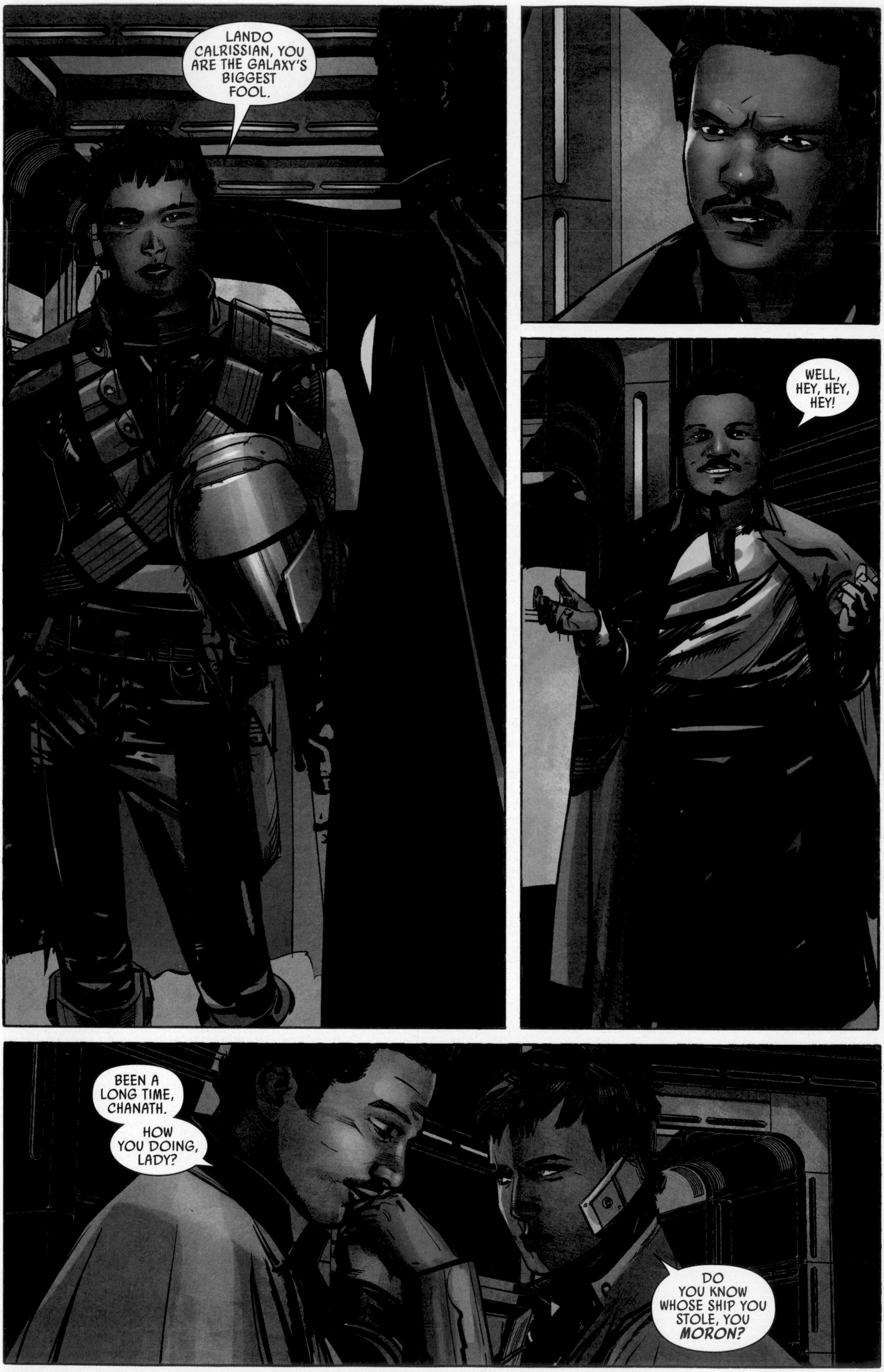
LANDO CALRISSIAN, YOU ARE THE GALAXY'S BIGGEST FOOL.
WELL, HEY, HEY, HEY!
BEEN A LONG TIME, CHANATH.
HOW YOU DOING, LADY?
DO YOU KNOW WHOSE SHIP YOU STOLE, YOU MORON?

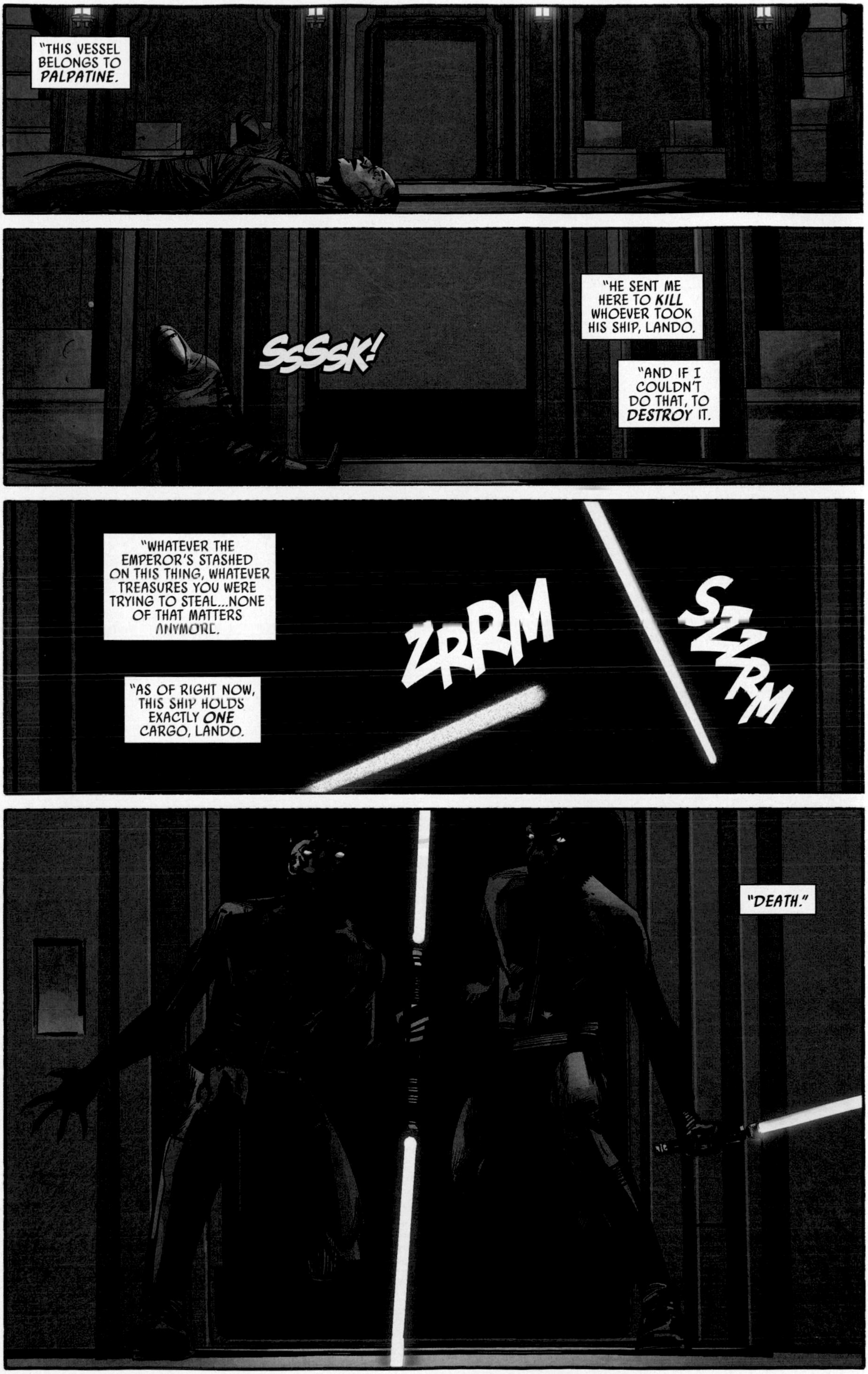
"THIS VESSEL BELONGS TO PALPATINE.
"HE SENT ME HERE TO KILL WHOEVER TOOK HIS SHIP, LANDO.
SSSSK!
"AND IF I COULDN'T DO THAT, TO DESTROY IT.
"WHATEVER THE EMPEROR'S STASHED ON THIS THING, WHATEVER TREASURES YOU WERE TRYING TO STEAL...NONE OF THAT MATTERS ANYMORE.
"AS OF RIGHT NOW, THIS SHIP HOLDS EXACTLY ONE CARGO, LANDO.
ZRRM
SZZRM
"DEATH."

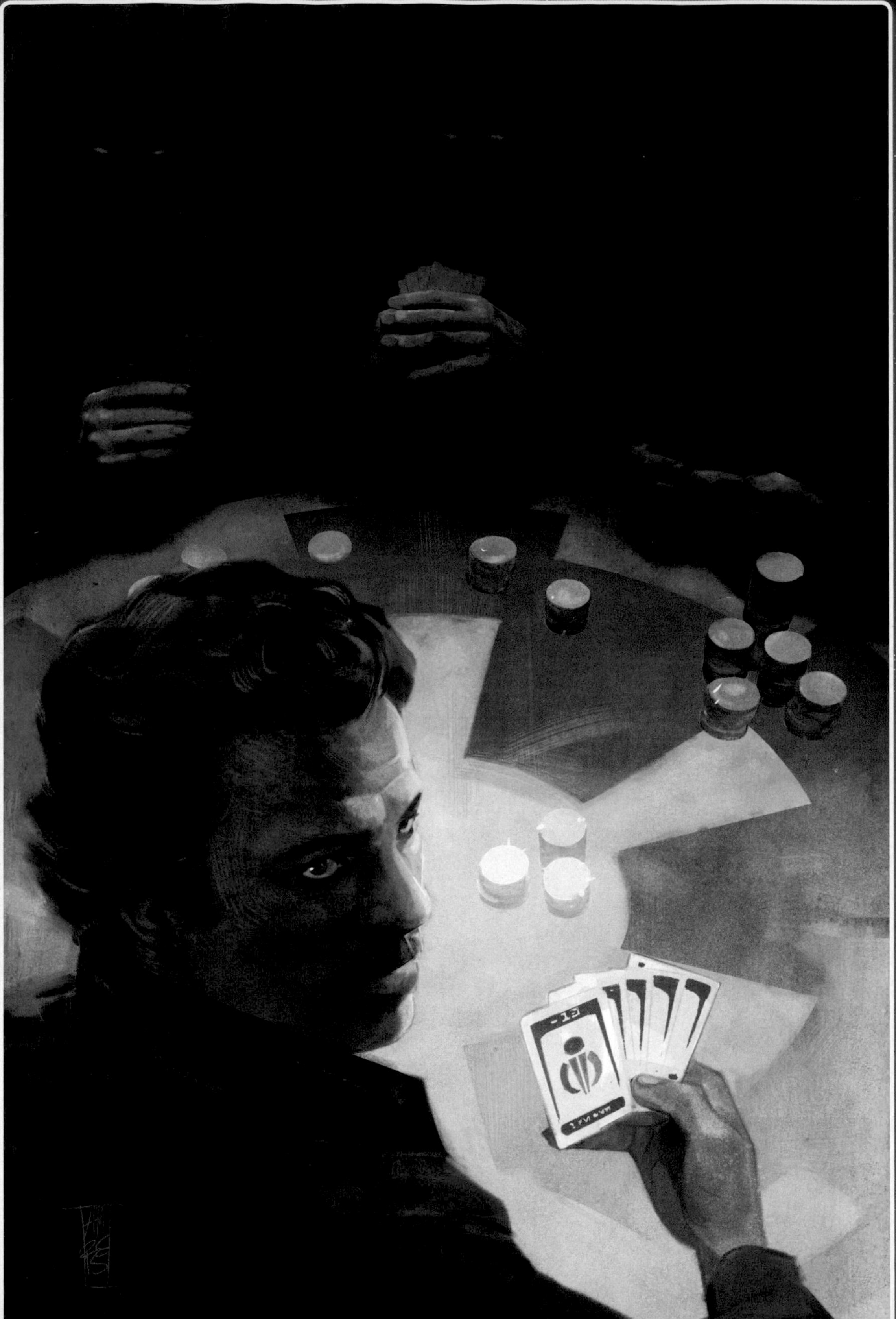

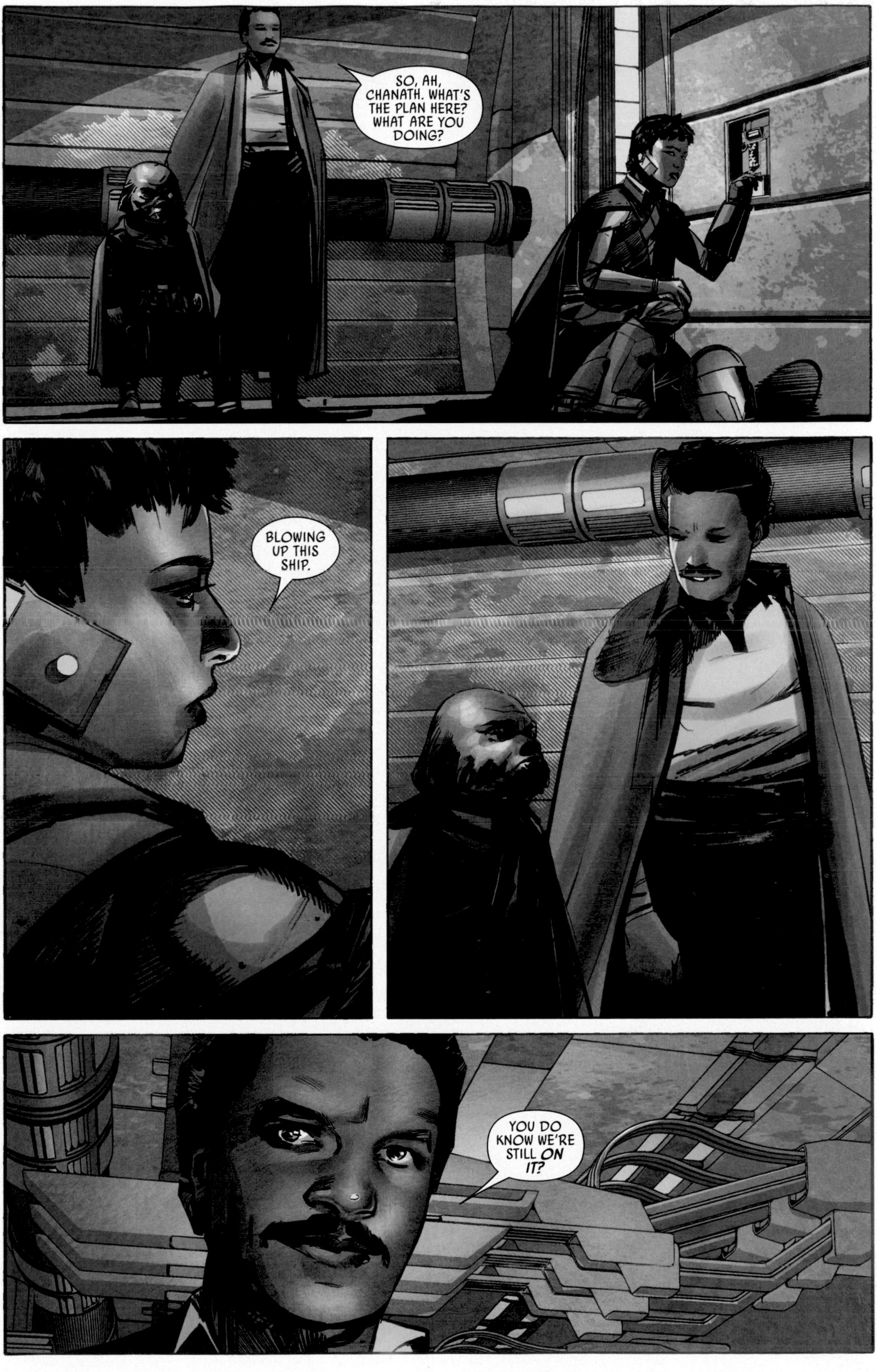
SO, AH, CHANATH. WHAT'S THE PLAN HERE? WHAT ARE YOU DOING?
BLOWING UP THIS SHIP.
YOU DO KNOW WE'RE STILL *ON* IT?

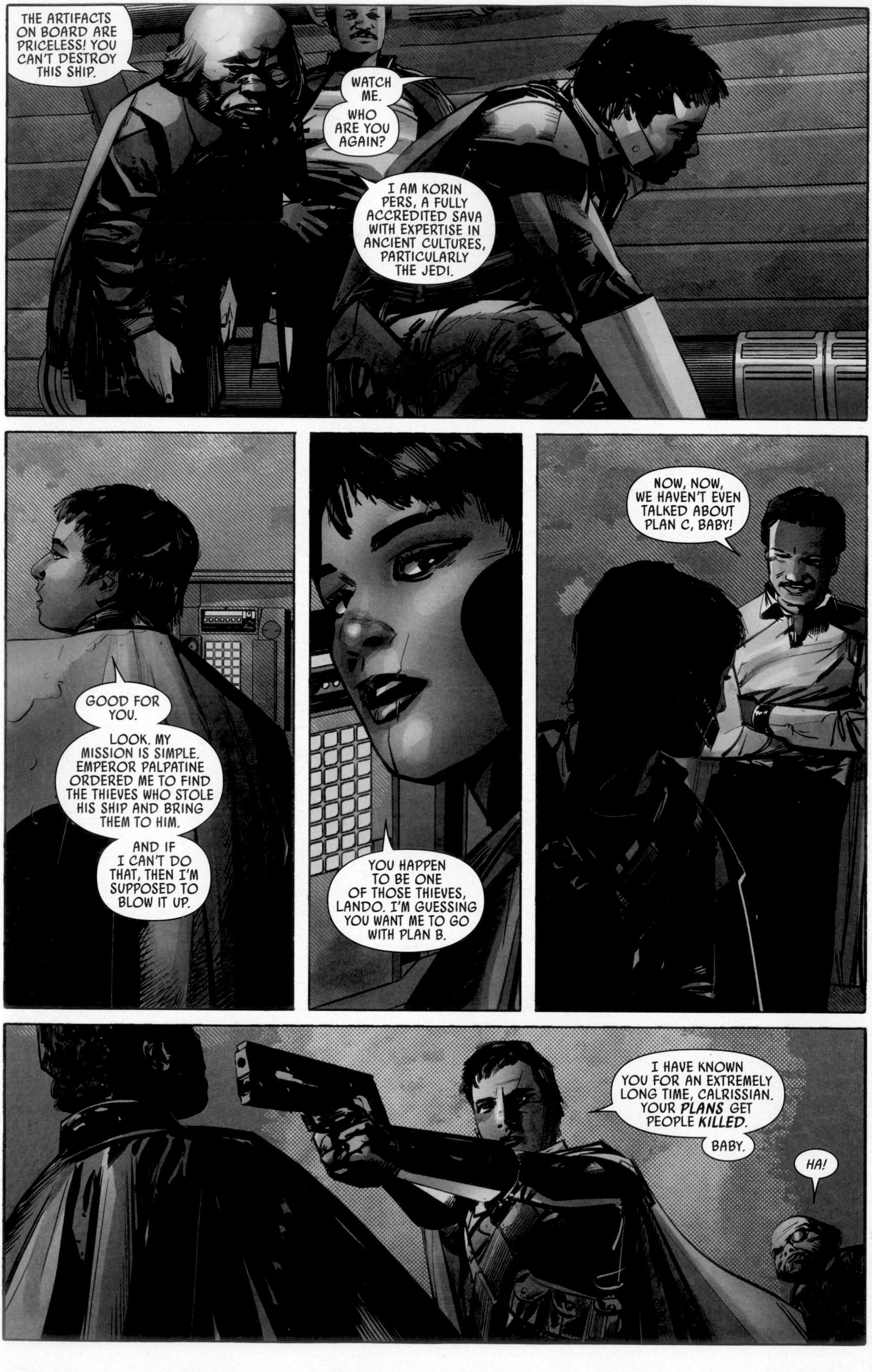
THE ARTIFACTS ON BOARD ARE PRICELESS! YOU CAN'T DESTROY THIS SHIP.
WATCH ME.
WHO ARE YOU AGAIN?
I AM KORIN PERS, A FULLY ACCREDITED SAVA WITH EXPERTISE IN ANCIENT CULTURES, PARTICULARLY THE JEDI.
GOOD FOR YOU.
LOOK. MY MISSION IS SIMPLE. EMPEROR PALPATINE ORDERED ME TO FIND THE THIEVES WHO STOLE HIS SHIP AND BRING THEM TO HIM.
AND IF I CAN'T DO THAT, THEN I'M SUPPOSED TO BLOW IT UP.
YOU HAPPEN TO BE ONE OF THOSE THIEVES, LANDO. I'M GUESSING YOU WANT ME TO GO WITH PLAN B.
NOW, NOW, WE HAVEN'T EVEN TALKED ABOUT PLAN C, BABY!
I HAVE KNOWN YOU FOR AN EXTREMELY LONG TIME, CALRISSIAN. YOUR PLANS GET PEOPLE KILLED.
BABY.
HA!

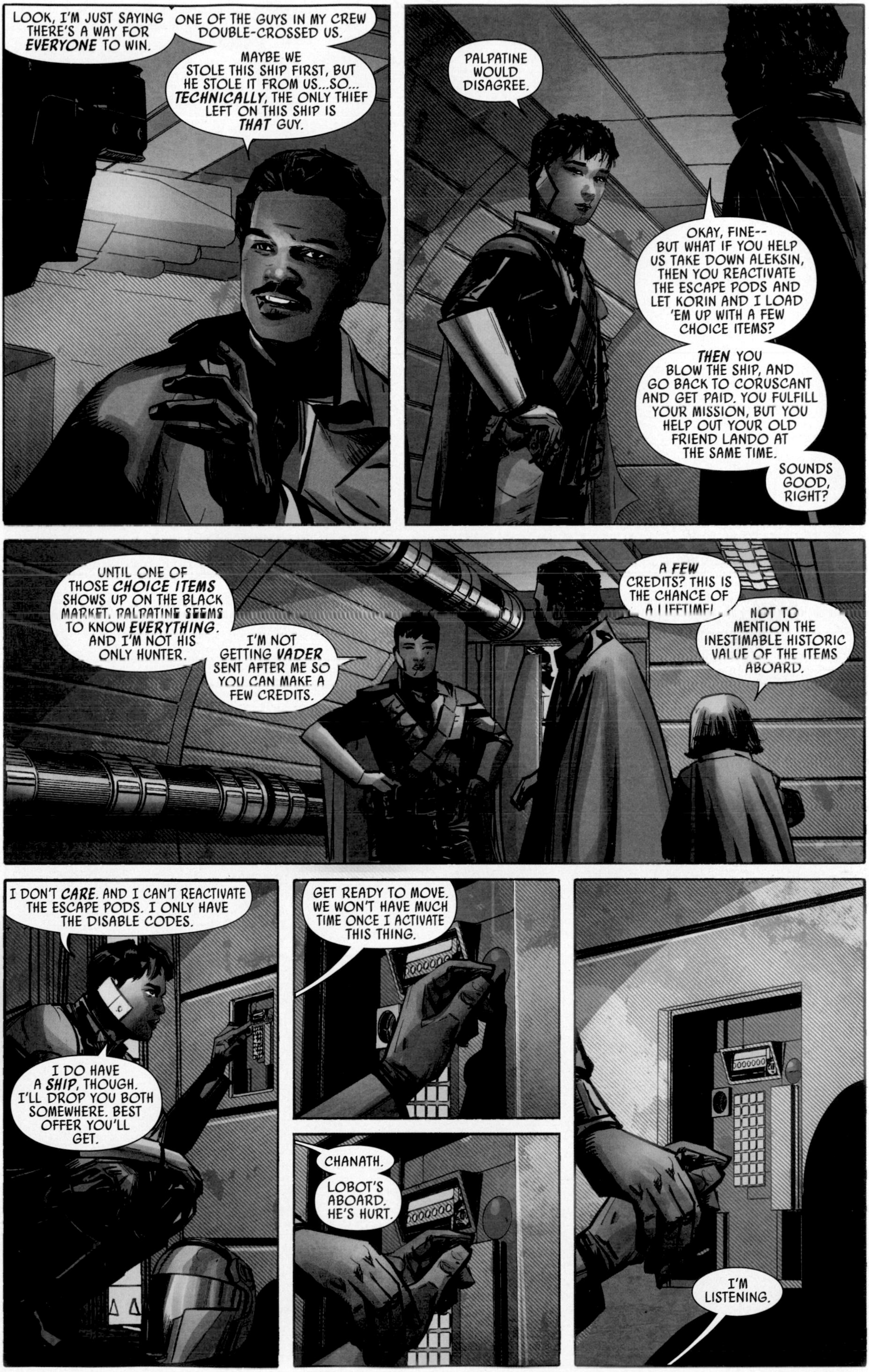

LOOK, I'M JUST SAYING THERE'S A WAY FOR EVERYONE TO WIN.
ONE OF THE GUYS IN MY CREW DOUBLE-CROSSED US.
MAYBE WE STOLE THIS SHIP FIRST, BUT HE STOLE IT FROM US...SO... TECHNICALLY, THE ONLY THIEF LEFT ON THIS SHIP IS THAT GUY.
PALPATINE WOULD DISAGREE.
OKAY, FINE-- BUT WHAT IF YOU HELP US TAKE DOWN ALEKSIN, THEN YOU REACTIVATE THE ESCAPE PODS AND LET KORIN AND I LOAD 'EM UP WITH A FEW CHOICE ITEMS?
THEN YOU BLOW THE SHIP, AND GO BACK TO CORUSCANT AND GET PAID. YOU FULFILL YOUR MISSION, BUT YOU HELP OUT YOUR OLD FRIEND LANDO AT THE SAME TIME.
SOUNDS GOOD, RIGHT?
UNTIL ONE OF THOSE CHOICE ITEMS SHOWS UP ON THE BLACK MARKET. PALPATINE SEEMS TO KNOW EVERYTHING. AND I'M NOT HIS ONLY HUNTER.
I'M NOT GETTING VADER SENT AFTER ME SO YOU CAN MAKE A FEW CREDITS.
A FEW CREDITS? THIS IS THE CHANCE OF A LIFETIME!
NOT TO MENTION THE INESTIMABLE HISTORIC VALUE OF THE ITEMS ABOARD.
I DON'T CARE. AND I CAN'T REACTIVATE THE ESCAPE PODS. I ONLY HAVE THE DISABLE CODES.
I DO HAVE A SHIP, THOUGH. I'LL DROP YOU BOTH SOMEWHERE. BEST OFFER YOU'LL GET.
GET READY TO MOVE. WE WON'T HAVE MUCH TIME ONCE I ACTIVATE THIS THING.
CHANATH.
LOBOT'S ABOARD. HE'S HURT.
I'M LISTENING.

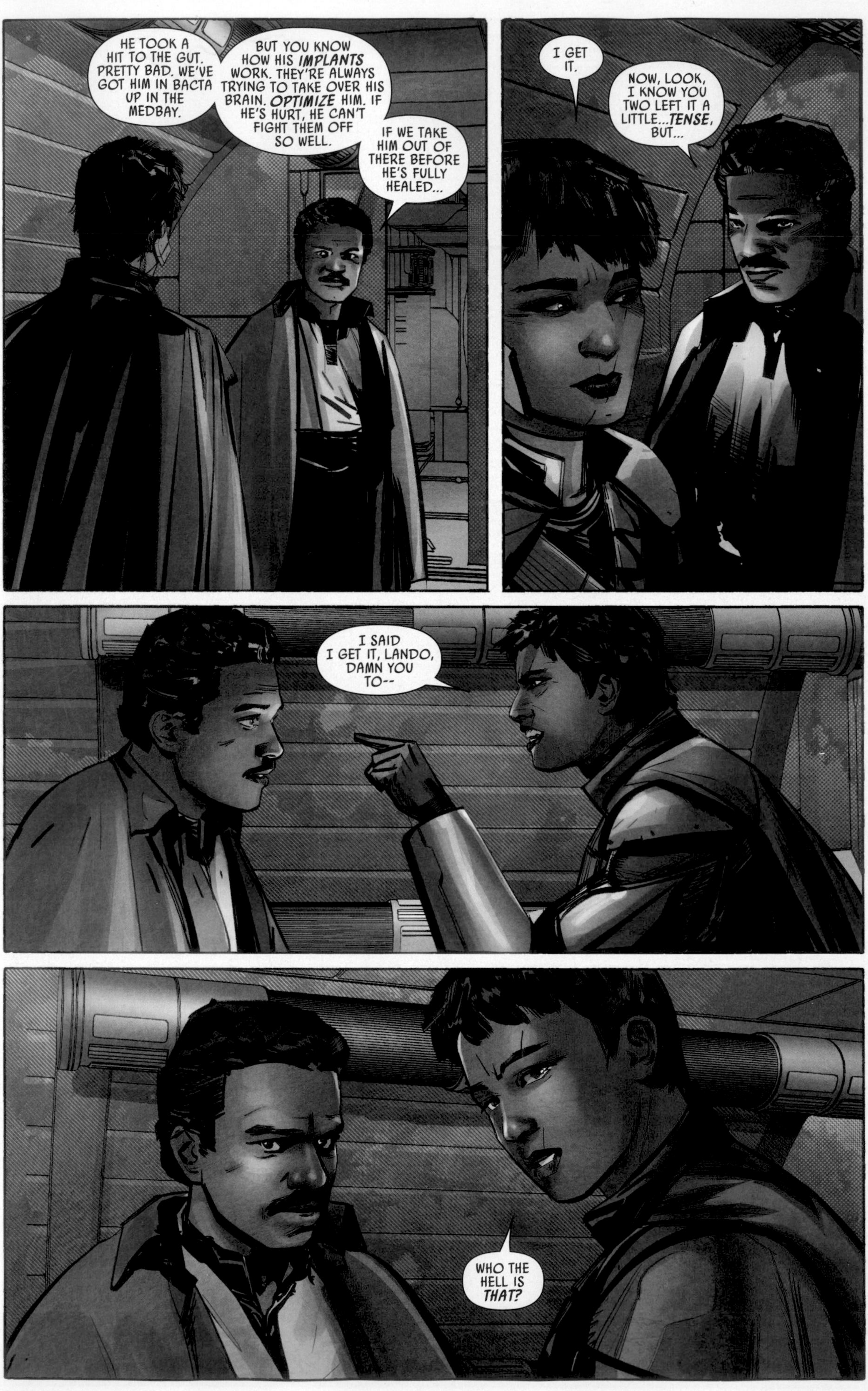
HE TOOK A HIT TO THE GUT. PRETTY BAD. WE'VE GOT HIM IN BACTA UP IN THE MEDBAY.
BUT YOU KNOW HOW HIS IMPLANTS WORK. THEY'RE ALWAYS TRYING TO TAKE OVER HIS BRAIN. OPTIMIZE HIM. IF HE'S HURT, HE CAN'T FIGHT THEM OFF SO WELL.
IF WE TAKE HIM OUT OF THERE BEFORE HE'S FULLY HEALED...
I GET IT.
NOW, LOOK, I KNOW YOU TWO LEFT IT A LITTLE...TENSE, BUT...
I SAID I GET IT, LANDO, DAMN YOU TO--
WHO THE HELL IS THAT?

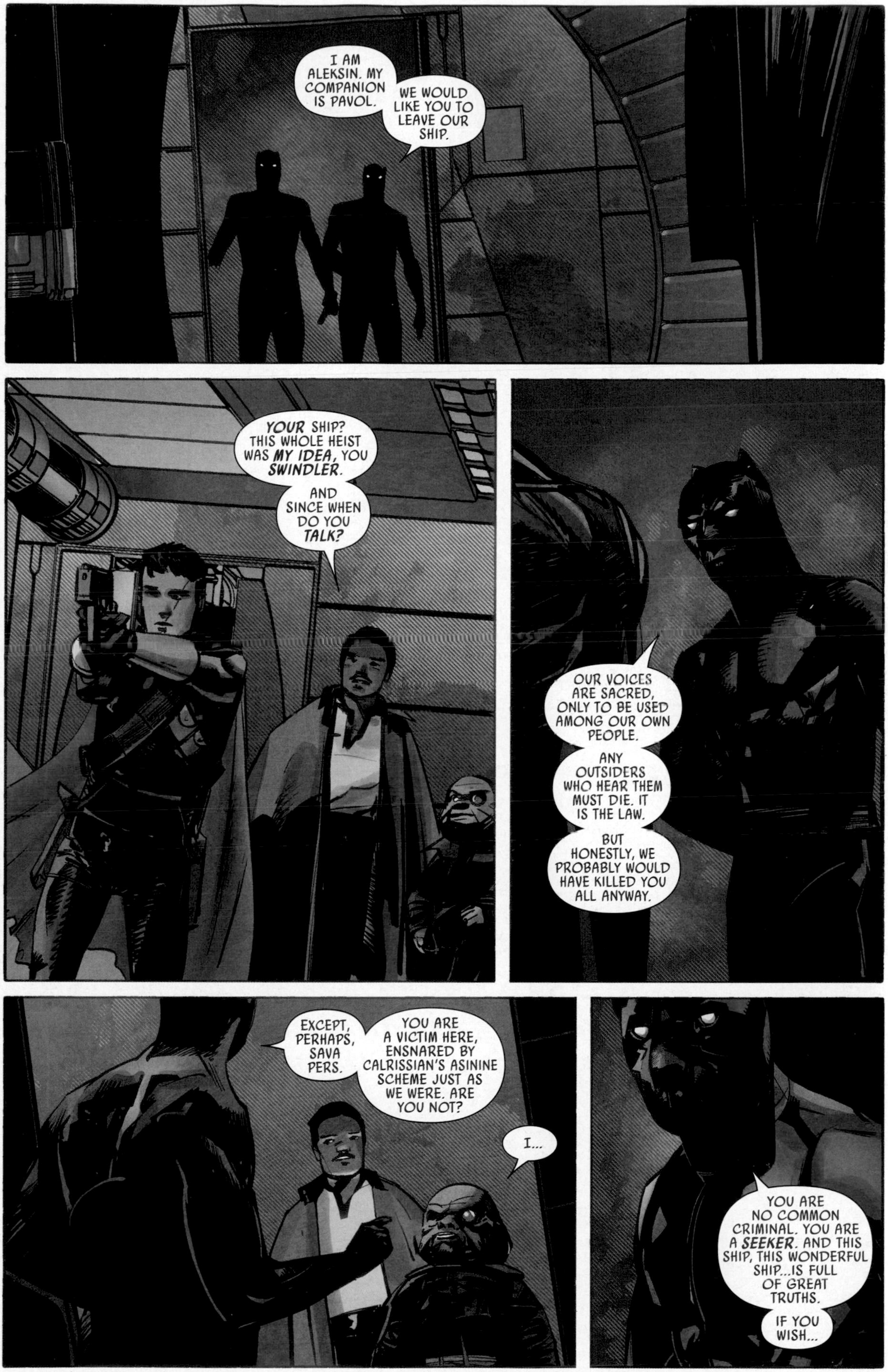

I AM ALEKSIN. MY COMPANION IS PAVOL.
WE WOULD LIKE YOU TO LEAVE OUR SHIP.
YOUR SHIP? THIS WHOLE HEIST WAS MY IDEA, YOU SWINDLER.
AND SINCE WHEN DO YOU TALK?
OUR VOICES ARE SACRED, ONLY TO BE USED AMONG OUR OWN PEOPLE.
ANY OUTSIDERS WHO HEAR THEM MUST DIE. IT IS THE LAW.
BUT HONESTLY, WE PROBABLY WOULD HAVE KILLED YOU ALL ANYWAY.
EXCEPT, PERHAPS, SAVA PERS.
YOU ARE A VICTIM HERE, ENSNARED BY CALRISSIAN'S ASININE SCHEME JUST AS WE WERE. ARE YOU NOT?
I...
YOU ARE NO COMMON CRIMINAL. YOU ARE A SEEKER. AND THIS SHIP, THIS WONDERFUL SHIP...IS FULL OF GREAT TRUTHS.
IF YOU WISH...

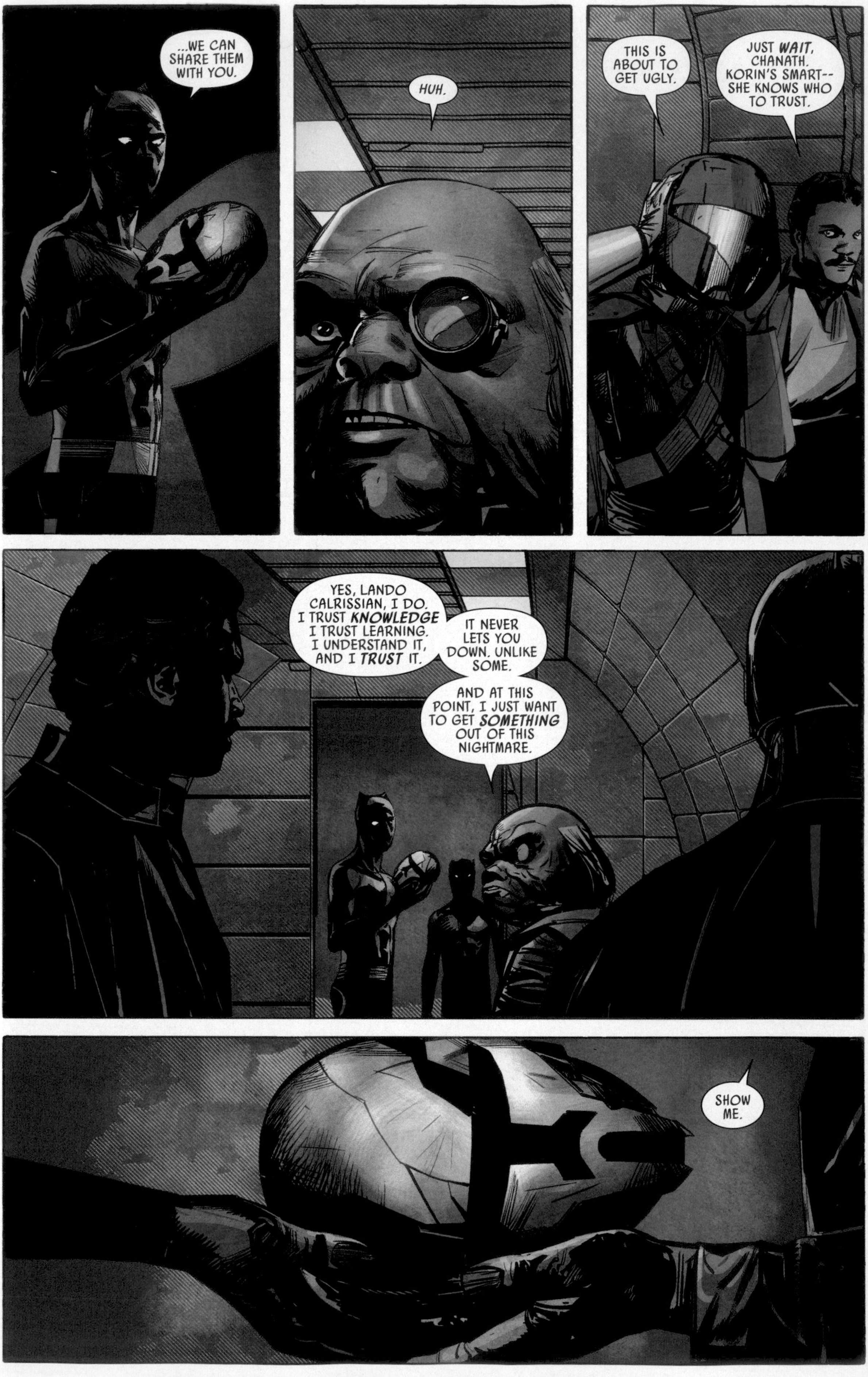
...WE CAN SHARE THEM WITH YOU.
HUH.
THIS IS ABOUT TO GET UGLY.
JUST WAIT, CHANATH. KORIN'S SMART-- SHE KNOWS WHO TO TRUST.
YES, LANDO CALRISSIAN, I DO. I TRUST KNOWLEDGE I TRUST LEARNING. I UNDERSTAND IT, AND I TRUST IT.
IT NEVER LETS YOU DOWN. UNLIKE SOME.
AND AT THIS POINT, I JUST WANT TO GET SOMETHING OUT OF THIS NIGHTMARE.
SHOW ME.

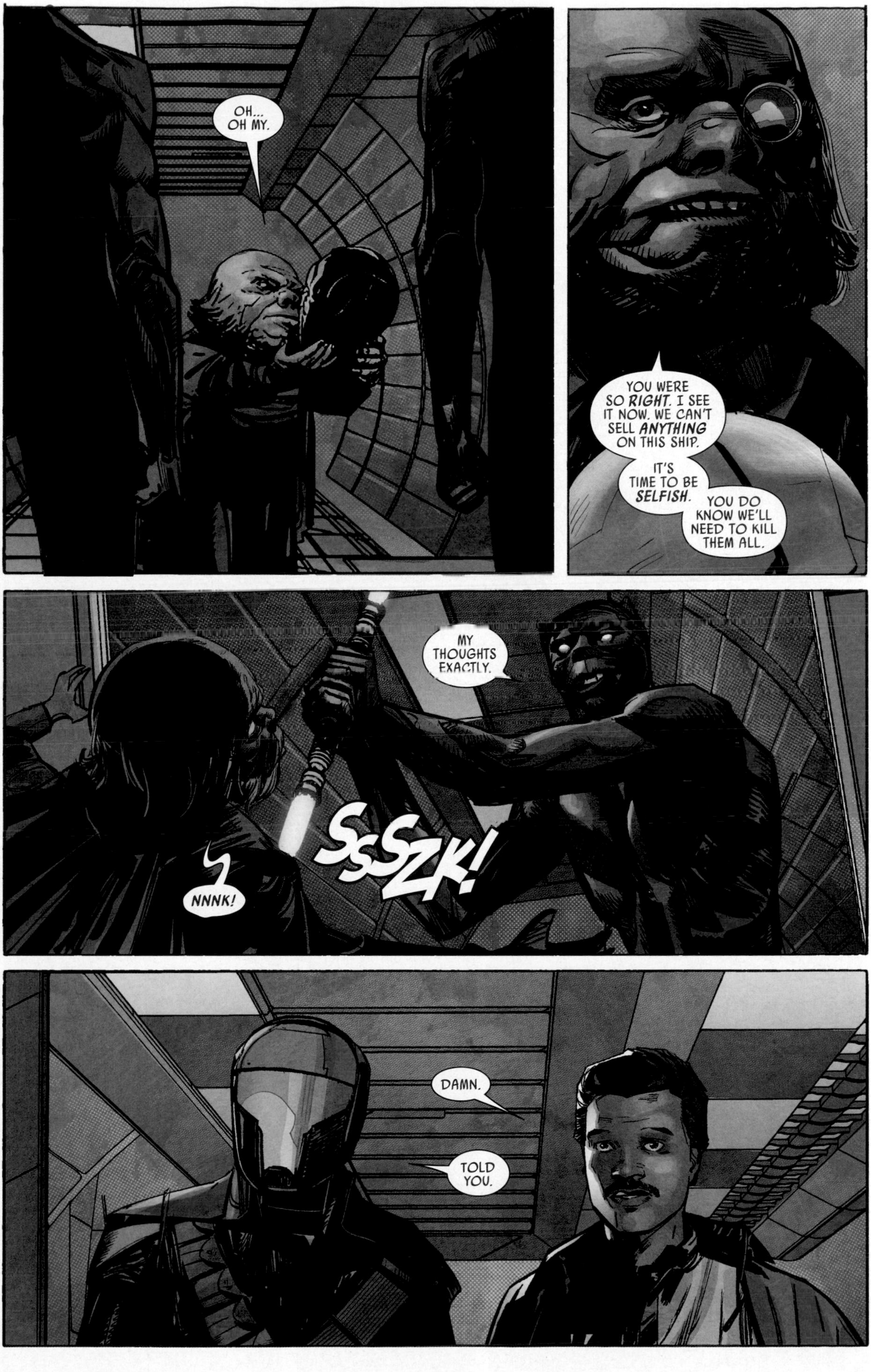
OH... OH MY.
YOU WERE SO RIGHT. I SEE IT NOW. WE CAN'T SELL ANYTHING ON THIS SHIP.
IT'S TIME TO BE SELFISH.
YOU DO KNOW WE'LL NEED TO KILL THEM ALL.
MY THOUGHTS EXACTLY.
NNNK!
SSSZK!
DAMN.
TOLD YOU.

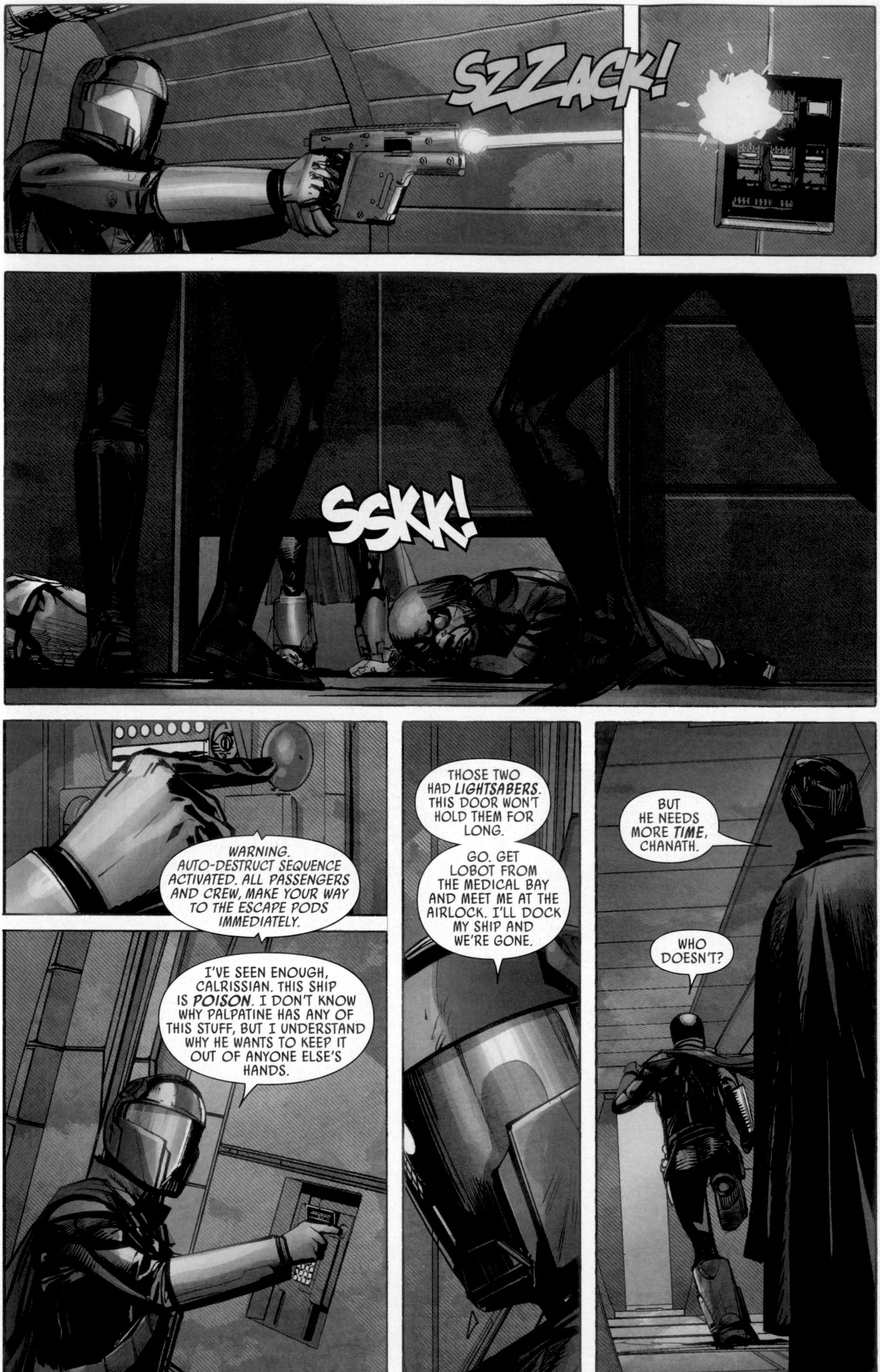

SZZACK!
SSKK!
WARNING. AUTO-DESTRUCT SEQUENCE ACTIVATED. ALL PASSENGERS AND CREW, MAKE YOUR WAY TO THE ESCAPE PODS IMMEDIATELY.
I'VE SEEN ENOUGH, CALRISSIAN. THIS SHIP IS POISON. I DON'T KNOW WHY PALPATINE HAS ANY OF THIS STUFF, BUT I UNDERSTAND WHY HE WANTS TO KEEP IT OUT OF ANYONE ELSE'S HANDS.
THOSE TWO HAD LIGHTSABERS. THIS DOOR WON'T HOLD THEM FOR LONG.
GO. GET LOBOT FROM THE MEDICAL BAY AND MEET ME AT THE AIRLOCK. I'LL DOCK MY SHIP AND WE'RE GONE.
BUT HE NEEDS MORE TIME, CHANATH.
WHO DOESN'T?

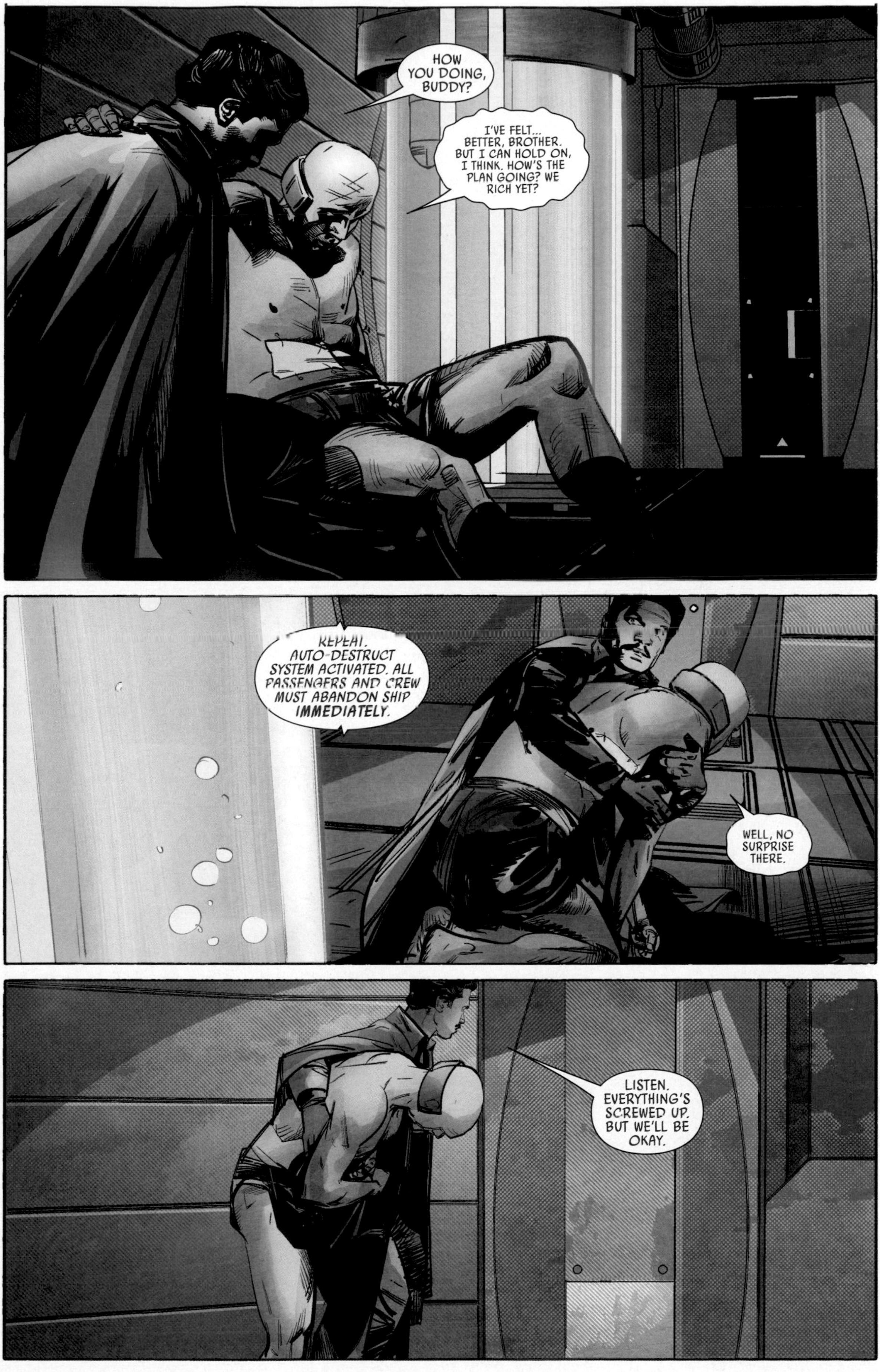
HOW YOU DOING, BUDDY?
I'VE FELT... BETTER, BROTHER. BUT I CAN HOLD ON, I THINK. HOW'S THE PLAN GOING? WE RICH YET?
REPEAT. AUTO-DESTRUCT SYSTEM ACTIVATED. ALL PASSENGERS AND CREW MUST ABANDON SHIP IMMEDIATELY.
WELL, NO SURPRISE THERE.
LISTEN. EVERYTHING'S SCREWED UP. BUT WE'LL BE OKAY.

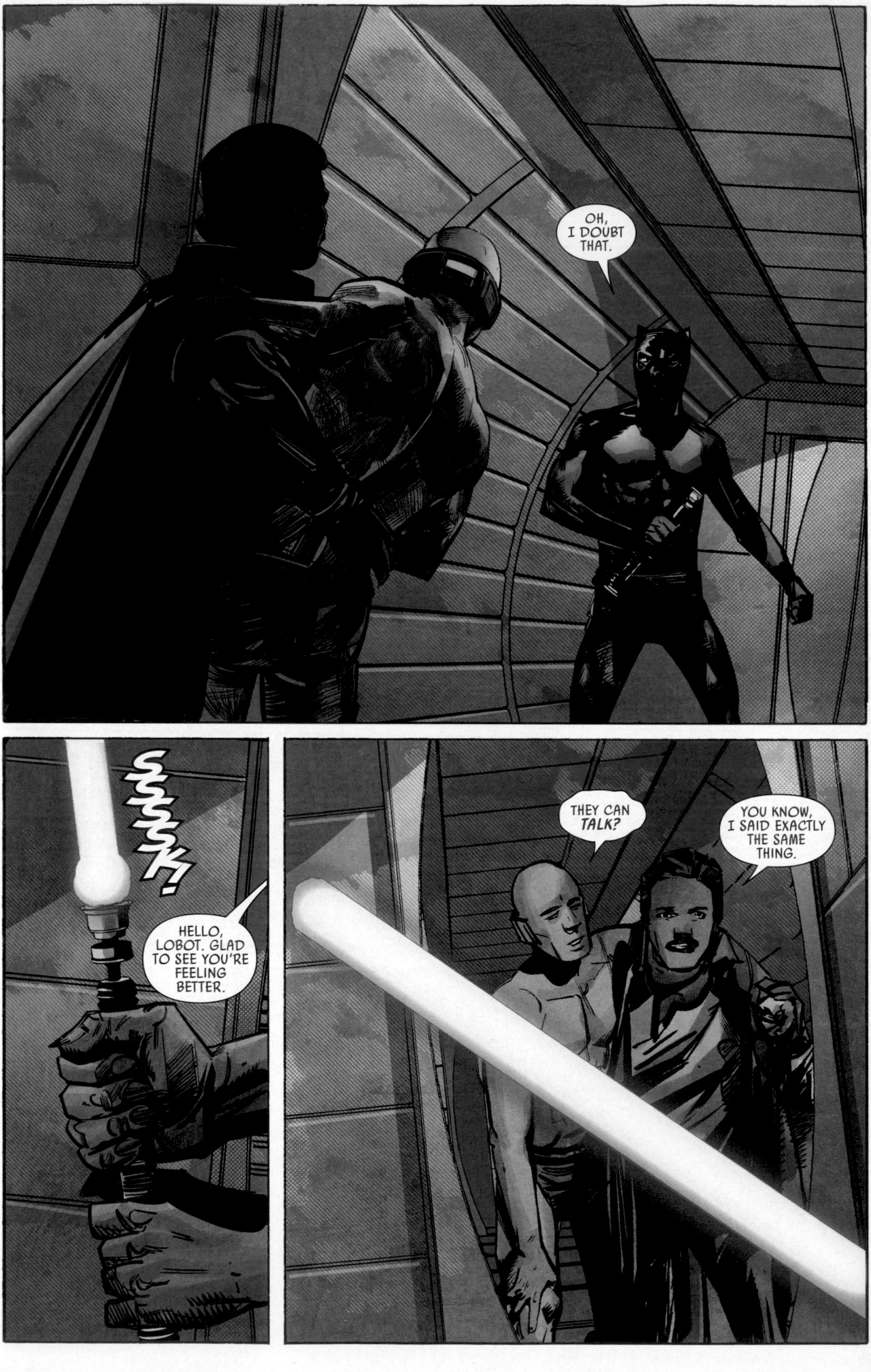
OH, I DOUBT THAT.
SSSSK!
HELLO, LOBOT. GLAD TO SEE YOU'RE FEELING BETTER.
THEY CAN *TALK?*
YOU KNOW, I SAID EXACTLY THE SAME THING.

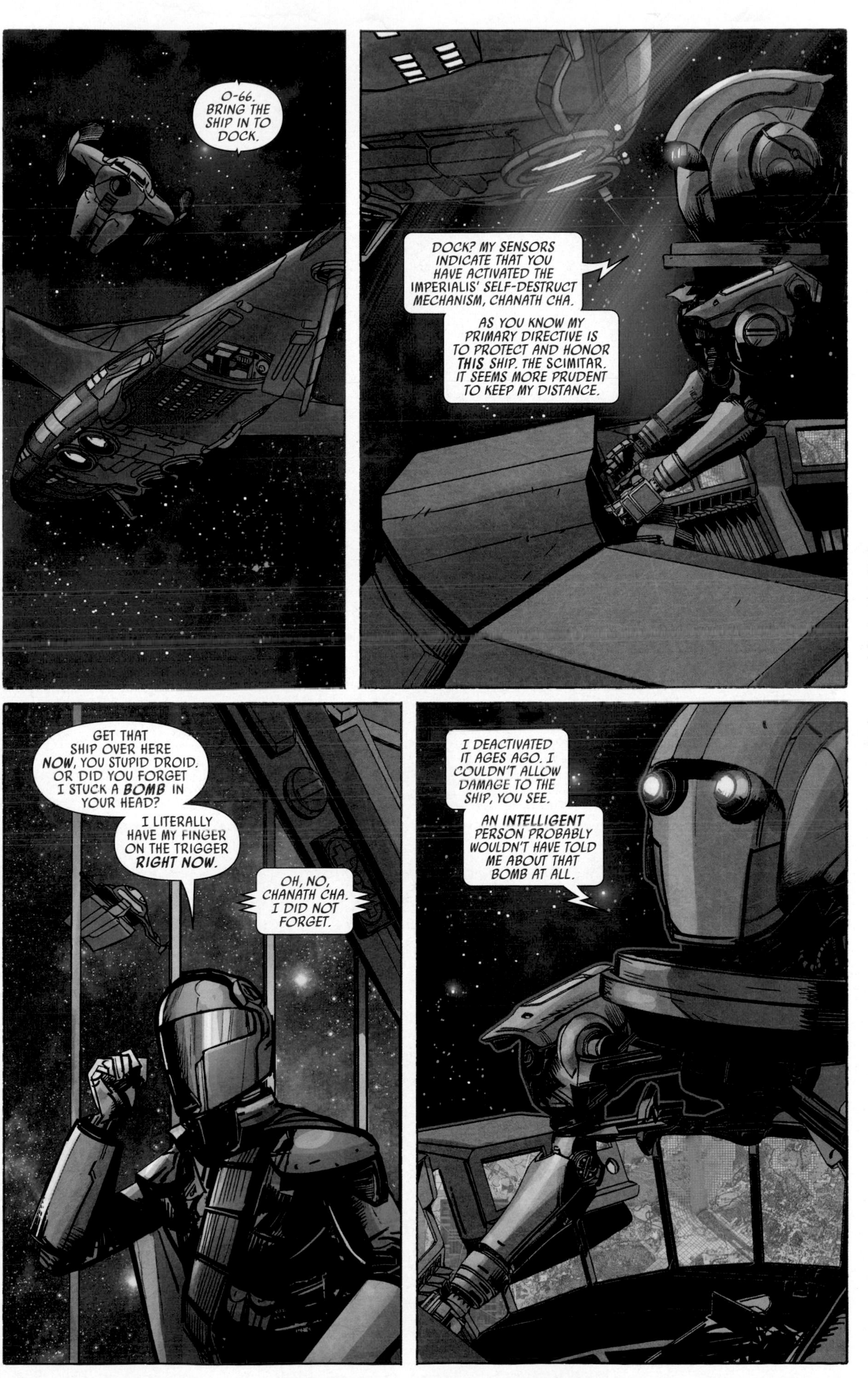
O-66. BRING THE SHIP IN TO DOCK.
DOCK? MY SENSORS INDICATE THAT YOU HAVE ACTIVATED THE IMPERIALIS' SELF-DESTRUCT MECHANISM, CHANATH CHA.
AS YOU KNOW MY PRIMARY DIRECTIVE IS TO PROTECT AND HONOR THIS SHIP. THE SCIMITAR. IT SEEMS MORE PRUDENT TO KEEP MY DISTANCE.
GET THAT SHIP OVER HERE NOW, YOU STUPID DROID. OR DID YOU FORGET I STUCK A BOMB IN YOUR HEAD?
I LITERALLY HAVE MY FINGER ON THE TRIGGER RIGHT NOW.
OH, NO, CHANATH CHA. I DID NOT FORGET.
I DEACTIVATED IT AGES AGO. I COULDN'T ALLOW DAMAGE TO THE SHIP, YOU SEE.
AN INTELLIGENT PERSON PROBABLY WOULDN'T HAVE TOLD ME ABOUT THAT BOMB AT ALL.

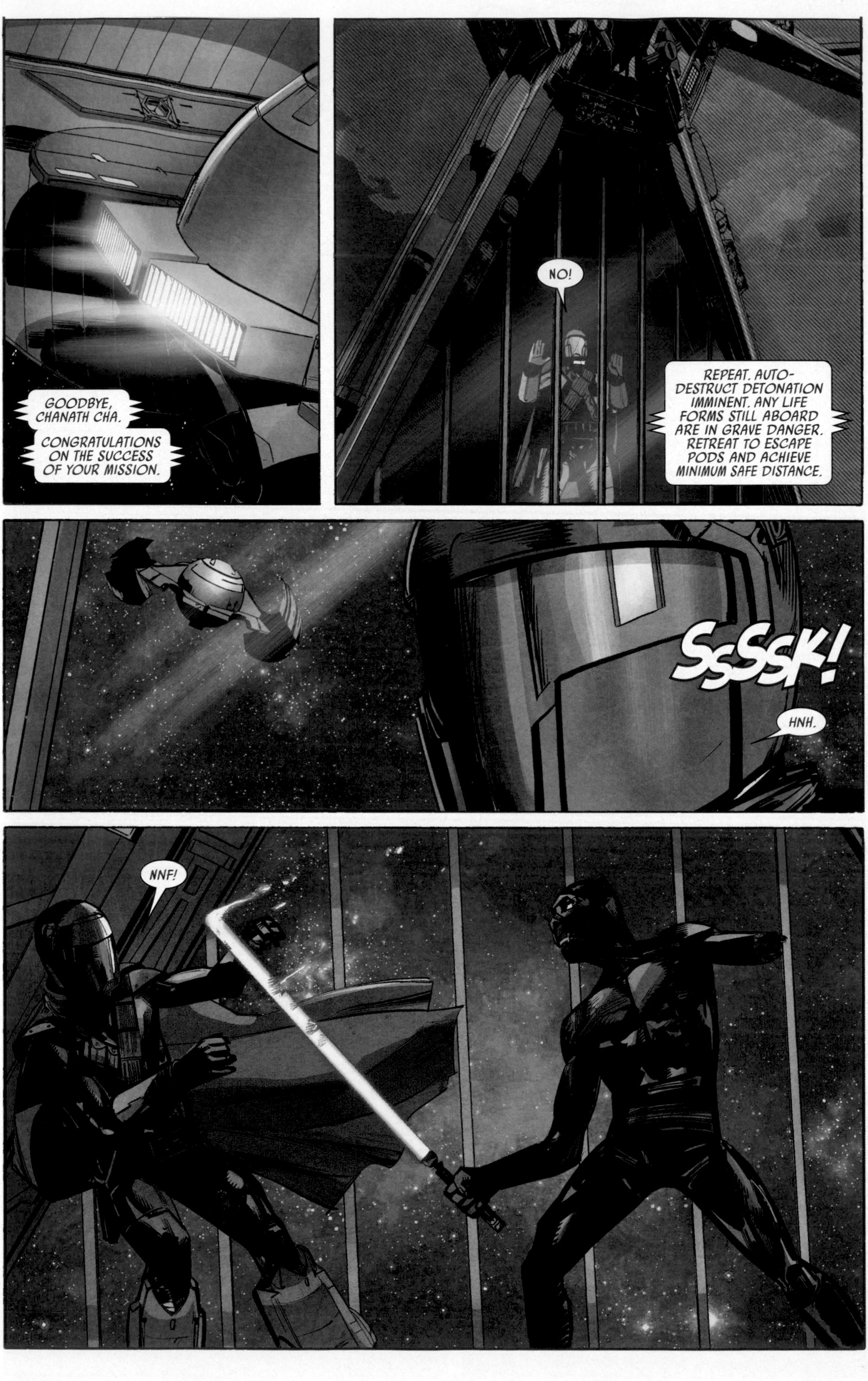
GOODBYE, CHANATH CHA.
CONGRATULATIONS ON THE SUCCESS OF YOUR MISSION.
NO!
REPEAT. AUTO-DESTRUCT DETONATION IMMINENT. ANY LIFE FORMS STILL ABOARD ARE IN GRAVE DANGER. RETREAT TO ESCAPE PODS AND ACHIEVE MINIMUM SAFE DISTANCE.
SsSSK!
HNH.
NNF!

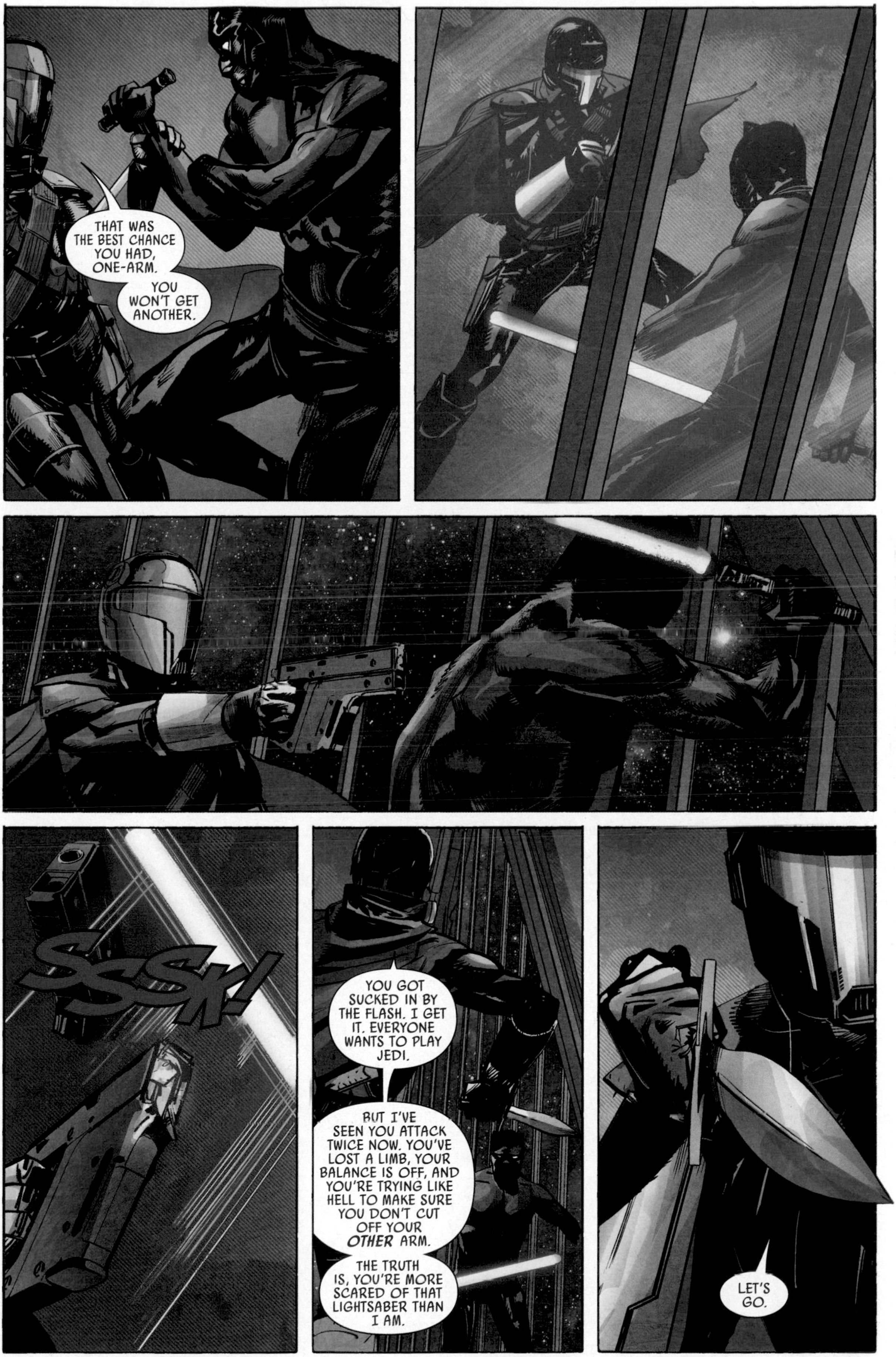
THAT WAS THE BEST CHANCE YOU HAD, ONE-ARM.
YOU WON'T GET ANOTHER.
SSSK!
YOU GOT SUCKED IN BY THE FLASH. I GET IT. EVERYONE WANTS TO PLAY JEDI.
BUT I'VE SEEN YOU ATTACK TWICE NOW. YOU'VE LOST A LIMB, YOUR BALANCE IS OFF, AND YOU'RE TRYING LIKE HELL TO MAKE SURE YOU DON'T CUT OFF YOUR OTHER ARM.
THE TRUTH IS, YOU'RE MORE SCARED OF THAT LIGHTSABER THAN I AM.
LET'S GO.

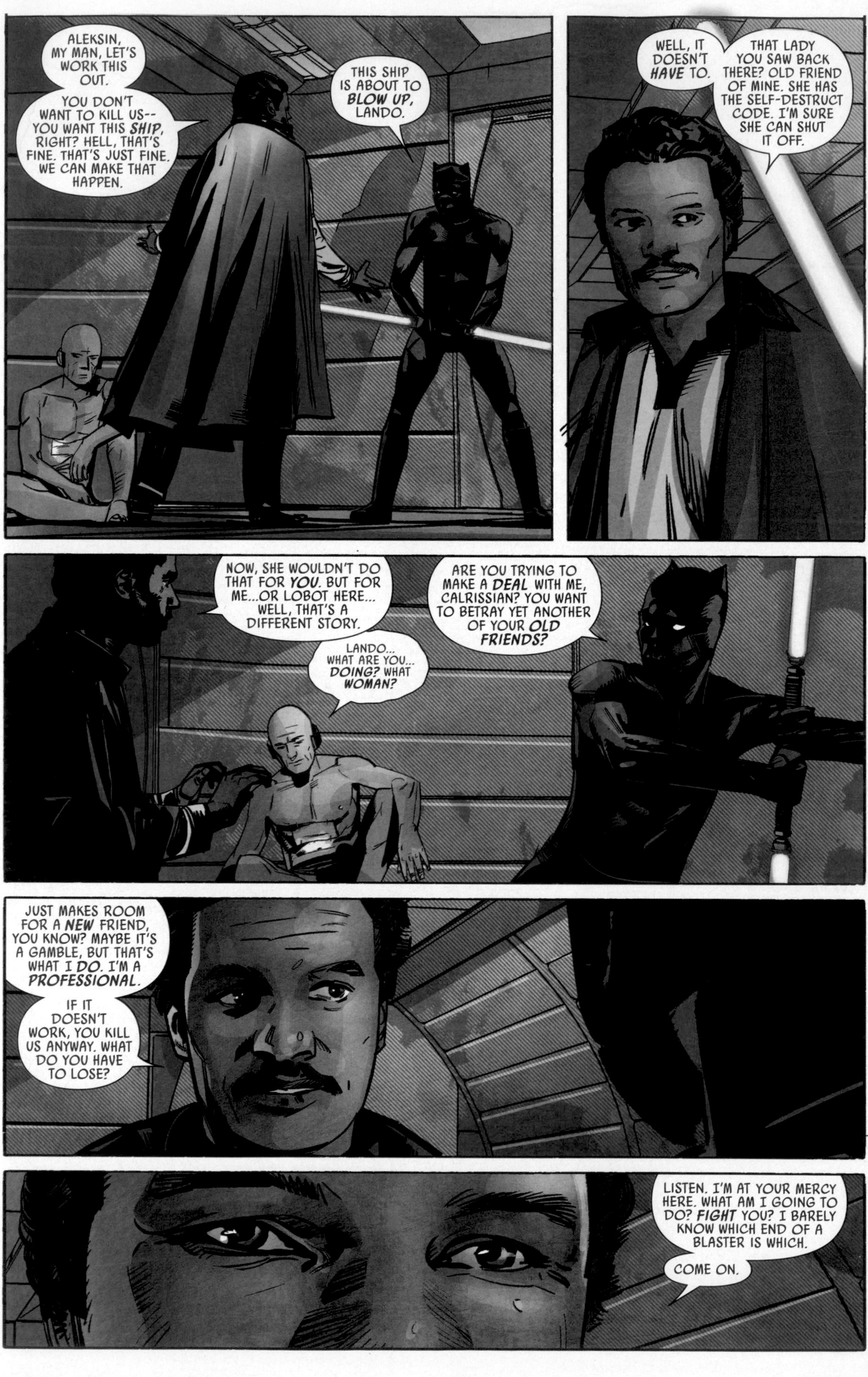
ALEKSIN, MY MAN, LET'S WORK THIS OUT.
YOU DON'T WANT TO KILL US-- YOU WANT THIS SHIP, RIGHT? HELL, THAT'S FINE. THAT'S JUST FINE. WE CAN MAKE THAT HAPPEN.
THIS SHIP IS ABOUT TO BLOW UP, LANDO.
WELL, IT DOESN'T HAVE TO.
THAT LADY YOU SAW BACK THERE? OLD FRIEND OF MINE. SHE HAS THE SELF-DESTRUCT CODE. I'M SURE SHE CAN SHUT IT OFF.
NOW, SHE WOULDN'T DO THAT FOR YOU. BUT FOR ME...OR LOBOT HERE... WELL, THAT'S A DIFFERENT STORY.
LANDO... WHAT ARE YOU... DOING? WHAT WOMAN?
ARE YOU TRYING TO MAKE A DEAL WITH ME, CALRISSIAN? YOU WANT TO BETRAY YET ANOTHER OF YOUR OLD FRIENDS?
JUST MAKES ROOM FOR A NEW FRIEND, YOU KNOW? MAYBE IT'S A GAMBLE, BUT THAT'S WHAT I DO. I'M A PROFESSIONAL.
IF IT DOESN'T WORK, YOU KILL US ANYWAY. WHAT DO YOU HAVE TO LOSE?
LISTEN. I'M AT YOUR MERCY HERE. WHAT AM I GOING TO DO? FIGHT YOU? I BARELY KNOW WHICH END OF A BLASTER IS WHICH.
COME ON.

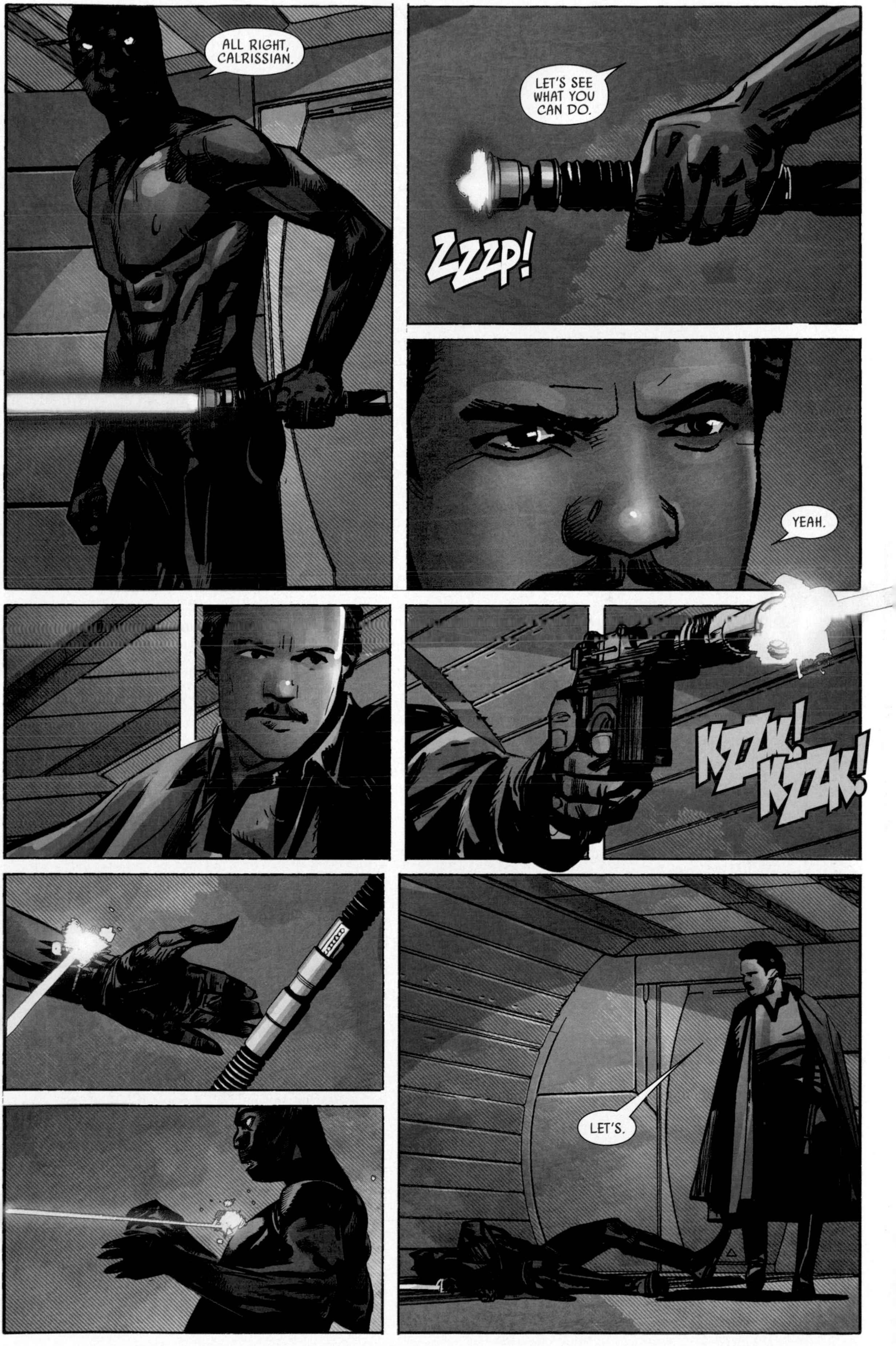
ALL RIGHT, CALRISSIAN.
LET'S SEE WHAT YOU CAN DO.
ZZZP!
YEAH.
KZZK! KZZK!
LET'S.

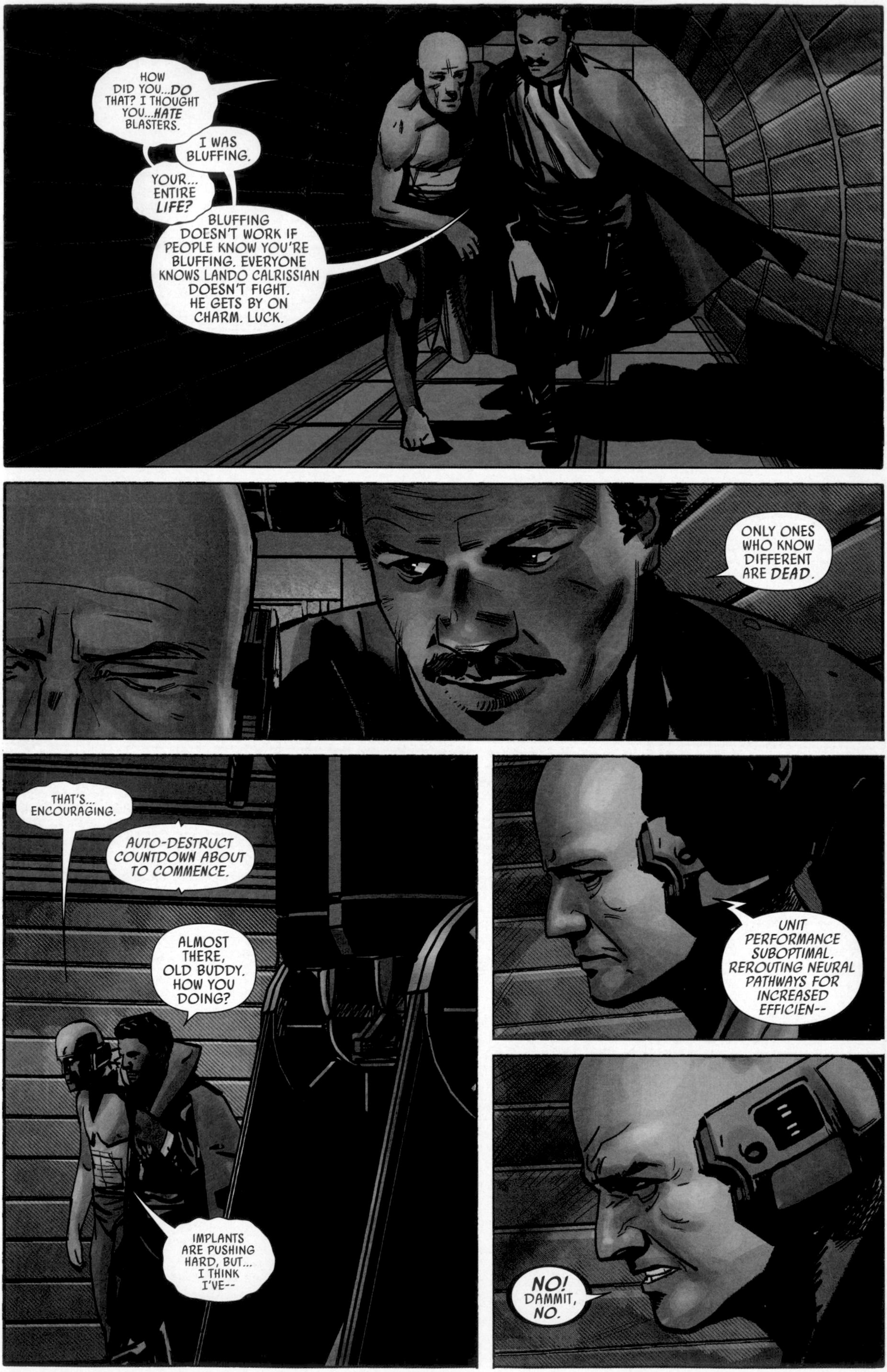
HOW DID YOU...DO THAT? I THOUGHT YOU...HATE BLASTERS.
I WAS BLUFFING.
YOUR... ENTIRE LIFE?
BLUFFING DOESN'T WORK IF PEOPLE KNOW YOU'RE BLUFFING. EVERYONE KNOWS LANDO CALRISSIAN DOESN'T FIGHT. HE GETS BY ON CHARM. LUCK.
ONLY ONES WHO KNOW DIFFERENT ARE DEAD.
THAT'S... ENCOURAGING.
AUTO-DESTRUCT COUNTDOWN ABOUT TO COMMENCE.
ALMOST THERE, OLD BUDDY. HOW YOU DOING?
IMPLANTS ARE PUSHING HARD, BUT... I THINK I'VE--
UNIT PERFORMANCE SUBOPTIMAL. REROUTING NEURAL PATHWAYS FOR INCREASED EFFICIEN--
NO! DAMMIT, NO.

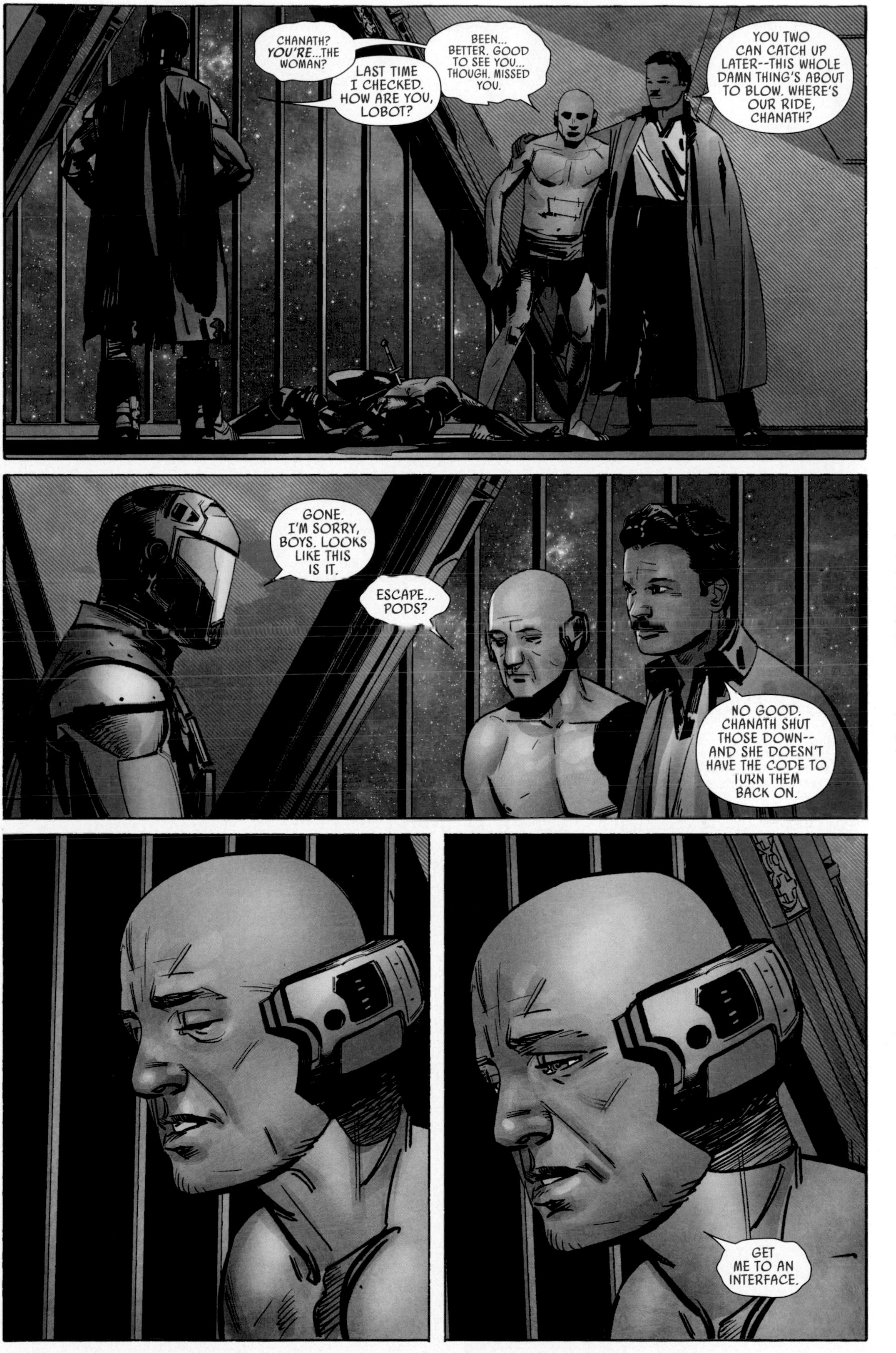
CHANATH? *YOU'RE*...THE WOMAN?
LAST TIME I CHECKED. HOW ARE YOU, LOBOT?
BEEN... BETTER. GOOD TO SEE YOU... THOUGH. MISSED YOU.
YOU TWO CAN CATCH UP LATER--THIS WHOLE DAMN THING'S ABOUT TO BLOW. WHERE'S OUR RIDE, CHANATH?
GONE. I'M SORRY, BOYS. LOOKS LIKE THIS IS IT.
ESCAPE... PODS?
NO GOOD. CHANATH SHUT THOSE DOWN--AND SHE DOESN'T HAVE THE CODE TO TURN THEM BACK ON.
GET ME TO AN INTERFACE.

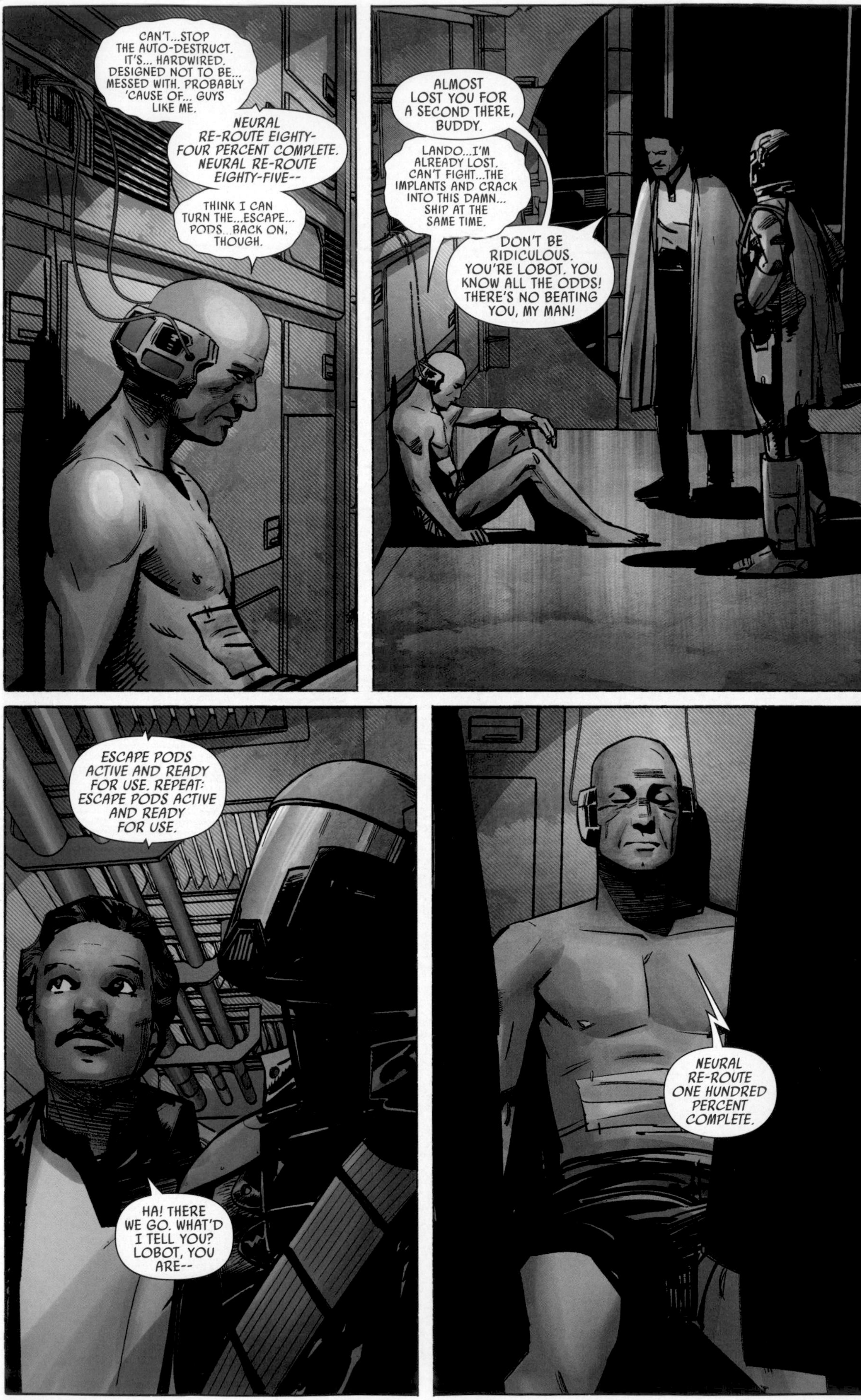
CAN'T...STOP THE AUTO-DESTRUCT. IT'S... HARDWIRED. DESIGNED NOT TO BE... MESSED WITH. PROBABLY 'CAUSE OF... GUYS LIKE ME.
NEURAL RE-ROUTE EIGHTY-FOUR PERCENT COMPLETE. NEURAL RE-ROUTE EIGHTY-FIVE--
THINK I CAN TURN THE...ESCAPE... PODS...BACK ON, THOUGH.
ALMOST LOST YOU FOR A SECOND THERE, BUDDY.
LANDO...I'M ALREADY LOST. CAN'T FIGHT...THE IMPLANTS AND CRACK INTO THIS DAMN... SHIP AT THE SAME TIME.
DON'T BE RIDICULOUS. YOU'RE LOBOT. YOU KNOW ALL THE ODDS! THERE'S NO BEATING YOU, MY MAN!
ESCAPE PODS ACTIVE AND READY FOR USE. REPEAT: ESCAPE PODS ACTIVE AND READY FOR USE.
HA! THERE WE GO. WHAT'D I TELL YOU? LOBOT, YOU ARE--
NEURAL RE-ROUTE ONE HUNDRED PERCENT COMPLETE.

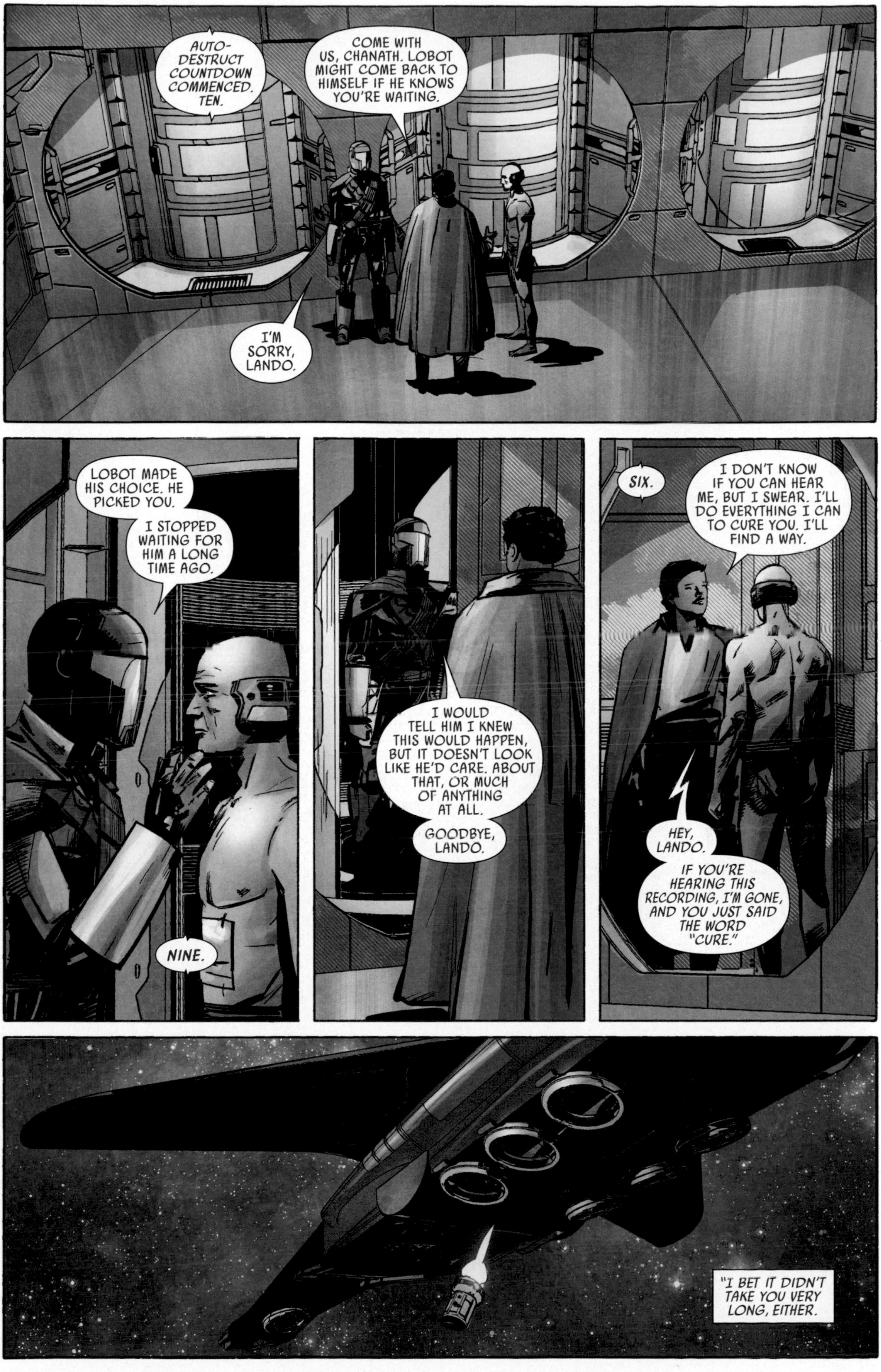
AUTO-DESTRUCT COUNTDOWN COMMENCED. TEN.
COME WITH US, CHANATH. LOBOT MIGHT COME BACK TO HIMSELF IF HE KNOWS YOU'RE WAITING.
I'M SORRY, LANDO.
LOBOT MADE HIS CHOICE. HE PICKED YOU.
I STOPPED WAITING FOR HIM A LONG TIME AGO.
NINE.
I WOULD TELL HIM I KNEW THIS WOULD HAPPEN, BUT IT DOESN'T LOOK LIKE HE'D CARE. ABOUT THAT, OR MUCH OF ANYTHING AT ALL.
GOODBYE, LANDO.
SIX.
I DON'T KNOW IF YOU CAN HEAR ME, BUT I SWEAR. I'LL DO EVERYTHING I CAN TO CURE YOU. I'LL FIND A WAY.
HEY, LANDO.
IF YOU'RE HEARING THIS RECORDING, I'M GONE, AND YOU JUST SAID THE WORD "CURE."
"I BET IT DIDN'T TAKE YOU VERY LONG, EITHER.

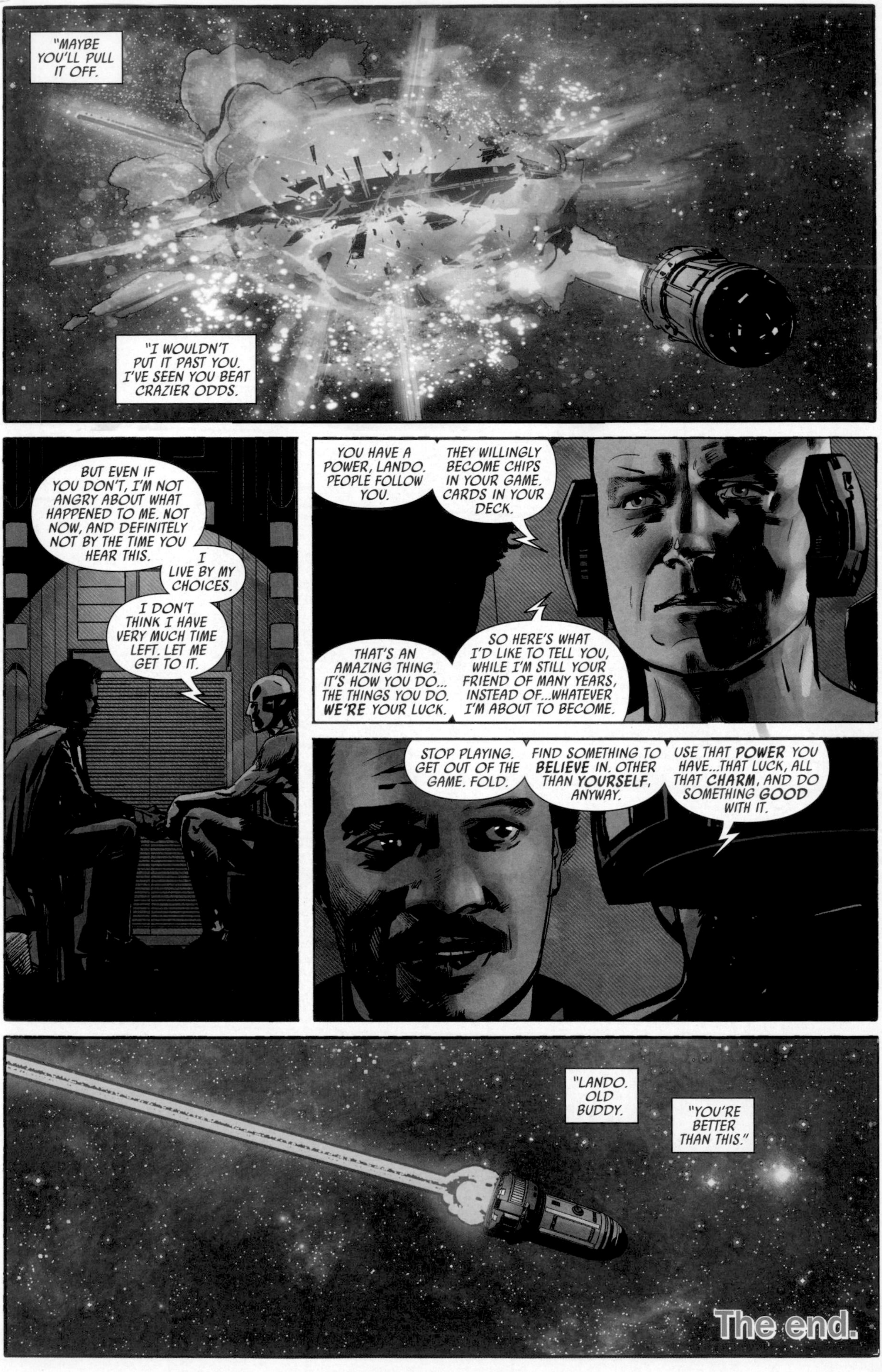
"MAYBE YOU'LL PULL IT OFF.
"I WOULDN'T PUT IT PAST YOU. I'VE SEEN YOU BEAT CRAZIER ODDS.
BUT EVEN IF YOU DON'T, I'M NOT ANGRY ABOUT WHAT HAPPENED TO ME. NOT NOW, AND DEFINITELY NOT BY THE TIME YOU HEAR THIS.
I LIVE BY MY CHOICES.
I DON'T THINK I HAVE VERY MUCH TIME LEFT. LET ME GET TO IT.
YOU HAVE A POWER, LANDO. PEOPLE FOLLOW YOU.
THEY WILLINGLY BECOME CHIPS IN YOUR GAME. CARDS IN YOUR DECK.
THAT'S AN AMAZING THING. IT'S HOW YOU DO... THE THINGS YOU DO. WE'RE YOUR LUCK.
SO HERE'S WHAT I'D LIKE TO TELL YOU, WHILE I'M STILL YOUR FRIEND OF MANY YEARS, INSTEAD OF...WHATEVER I'M ABOUT TO BECOME.
STOP PLAYING. GET OUT OF THE GAME. FOLD.
FIND SOMETHING TO BELIEVE IN. OTHER THAN YOURSELF, ANYWAY.
USE THAT POWER YOU HAVE...THAT LUCK, ALL THAT CHARM, AND DO SOMETHING GOOD WITH IT.
"LANDO. OLD BUDDY.
"YOU'RE BETTER THAN THIS."
The end.

WHAT IS A PRINCESS WITHOUT A WORLD?

STAR WARS: PRINCESS LEIA TPB

978-0-7851-9317-3

ON SALE NOW
WHEREVER BOOKS ARE SOLD

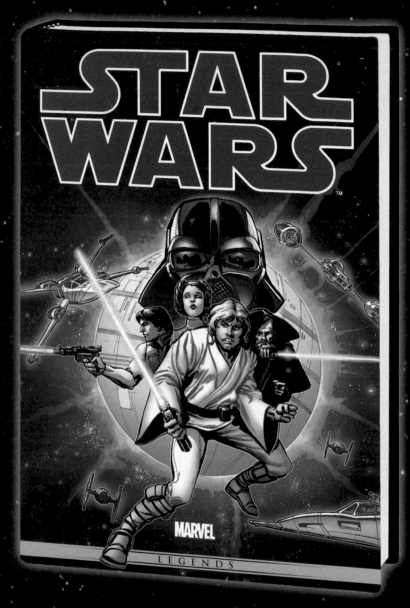
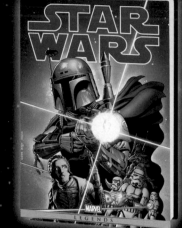